MONARCHIES 1000–2000

<u>Asuka Period</u> – ~~Emperor Kōtoku~~

Taika
Hakuchi

~~Emperor Tenmu~~

Shuchō ~~Emperor Monmu~~

Taihō
Keiun ~~Empress Genmei~~

Wado

<u>Nara Period</u> – ~~Empress Genshō~~

Reiki
Yōrō

~~Emperor Shōmu~~

Jinki
Tenpyō
 Tenpyō-Kanpō

~~Empress Kōken~~

GLOBALITIES

Series editor: Jeremy Black

GLOBALITIES is a series which reinterprets world history in a concise yet thoughtful way, looking at major issues over large time-spans and political spaces; such issues can be political, ecological, scientific, technological or intellectual. Rather than adopting a narrow chronological or geographical approach, books in the series are conceptual in focus yet present an array of historical data to justify their arguments. They often involve a multi-disciplinary approach, juxtaposing different subject-areas such as economics and religion or literature and politics.

In the same series

Why Wars Happen
Jeremy Black

A History of Language
Steven Roger Fischer

The Nemesis of Power: A History of International Relations Theories
Harald Kleinschmidt

Geopolitics and Globalization in the Twentieth Century
Brian W. Blouet

Monarchies
1000–2000

W. M. SPELLMAN

REAKTION BOOKS

In memory of Dorothy Costello

Published by Reaktion Books Ltd
33 Great Sutton Street
London EC1V 0DX, UK

www.reaktionbooks.co.uk

First published 2001
Transferred to digital printing 2012
Copyright © W. M. Spellman 2001

Printed and bound by Chicago Universtiy Press

British Library Cataloguing in Publication Data

Spellman, W. M.
    Monachies 1000–2000. – (Globalities)
    1. Monarchy – History
    I. Title
    909

ISBN 978 1 78023 050 4

Contents

Preface

A book on the subject of monarchy may strike one either as an exercise in the popular, even gossipy history of the privileged and famous or, what is worse in the estimate of some, an unfashionable return to history as high politics and international relations. I hope that what follows avoids both genres, for it is the intention of this brief survey to probe two rather large issues in the human experience over the past millennium while using monarchy as an institutional and intellectual mechanism by which these issues are brought into sharper relief. The first issue involves common assumptions about the ability of humans to shape and control their civil order, their relations with one another in a wider community, a shared environment. The establishment of monarchy as the preferred form of structured temporal authority across a wide band of cultures on every major continent is more than mere coincidence. Rather the adoption or imposition of rule by one speaks to a much deeper human need, a universal desire for permanence and meaning in a world of unpredictability and constant danger. Until very recently kings, queens and emperors have served as an intellectually and emotionally satisfying focus of that great aspiration, legitimizing a variety of social structures and buttressing disparate and unique religious systems over a very long period of time.

The second issue embraces what I would describe as a universal waning of the religious impulse around the world, but particularly in Western societies, over the past 500 years. Because monarchies on every continent were in very large measure originally associated with a particular culture's understanding of the divine, changes in the structure and place of monarchy in a given society often reflected more general shifts in thinking about a transcendent realm of meaning and reality. As humankind's mastery of the natural environment has accelerated over the past three centuries, the viability of divinely commissioned monarchy has been questioned in a number of cultures. This has necessitated the formulation of new explanations for and defences of the institution, interpretations often far removed from traditional religious criteria. In this respect monarchy in many of the states where it still exists has become something very different from its customary incarnation; where for centuries the monarch's moral claim to rule his or her subjects hinged on a supernatural sanction, today the strength of the office rests mainly on its function as national symbol and emblem of cultural identity.

Since I have attempted to investigate monarchy in a fairly wide range of civilizations – and all of this in a very few pages – what follows is by definition merely suggestive and illustrative. I have sought to highlight some of the larger trends in the history of monarchy over the past 1000 years, and in this respect the book represents a starting point for more focused efforts in the comparative history of one of the world's most enduring human creations. Rather than follow a strict chronological approach, this book is organized topically by civilization, thereby allowing for greater thematic unity both within and across a number of global cultures. As will become apparent early on, I have relied very heavily on the detailed labours of historians working in a number of sub-fields, but I have avoided treatment of the historiographical debates in these subject areas in the interest of narrative coherence. What follows is based largely on secondary source material, and my principal audience is intended to include both undergraduate students and generalists. At any rate, no foreknowledge on the part of the reader is assumed. My debts to particular works are cited in the notes, but overall I have limited the references to easily accessible books and journal literature.

It is a pleasure to acknowledge the assistance of a number of individuals and institutions who have helped to facilitate work on this project over the past few years. A 1998 Pew Charitable Trusts Summer Fellowship Program hosted by Calvin College in Michigan enabled me to begin work on the European sections. Participants in Nicholas Wolterstorff's seminar at Calvin, 'Political Theory after Liberalism', offered useful criticism and advice on some early drafts. Anna Mae Bush and the Calvin seminar staff provided timely assistance on a number of occasions. The reference librarians at my home institution, the University of North Carolina at Asheville, worked promptly and cheerfully in securing items through the interlibrary loan system, while my student assistant, Jason Miller, tracked down references and contributed on the word-processing front. Jeremy Black encouraged me to undertake the project, and his support in this as in earlier undertakings is very much appreciated. As with all of my previous typescripts, N. E. Costello assisted with final preparation and proofreading. Margaret Costello and Robert Burke kept the project in perspective by regularly reminding me of worthwhile life claims beyond the computer screen. Finally, a thank you made in quiet remembrance: over twenty years ago, E. G. Hartmann provided much-needed encouragement and direction as I began an unlikely career path. I hope that something of his disciplined manner and commitment to the craft is reflected in what follows.

Introduction: The Idea of Monarchy

But mankind is most a unity when it is drawn together
to form a single entity, and this can only come
about when it is ruled as one whole by one ruler,
as is self-evident. (Dante)[1]

In an increasingly interconnected world where republican
forms of civil organization have secured a near monopoly of
popular approbation, where even the most blatantly anti-democratic regimes make high claims to legitimacy based upon the
mandate of the people, the idea of monarchy as a plausible
model of public authority appears to many as anachronistic at
best, preposterous and irrational at worst. Indeed no other
political institution in the modern period has retreated from the
public scene quite so rapidly as monarchy. With only 27 states
retaining a royal office at the close of the twentieth century, and
with most of these embodying little more than ceremonial significance, the monarchical idea appears today as but a pale
reflection of its former self. And we need not look too far for an
explanation. For the contemporary mind, kings, queens and
emperors are emblematic of a world of ideas and assumptions
long – and thankfully – discarded: human inequality, privilege
associated with the accident of birth, arbitrary social hierarchy,
sacred status, the purity and intelligence of the one against the
depravity and incapacity of the many.[2]

Today we are quick to disparage monarchy because it suggests that the good, the just and the true are best left to the
determination of a specially advantaged individual, an individual whose access to an eternal set of prescriptive rules places
him or her outside the normative parameters of community life.
Rule by one implies dependency, natural differences and human

frailty, and none of these unflattering traits strikes sympathetic responses, particularly in the West, at the start of the twenty-first century. We are all the heirs of Thomas Paine in this respect, silently endorsing his barbed observation that 'apart from the defects of the individual, government by a single person is vicious in itself.'[3]

Every culture in every age is tempted to believe that its values and norms are the only right ones, and our present dim view of monarchy as a model of legitimate government is certainly no small illustration of this principle in action. Our intellectual distance from monarchy, however, does not correspond with the chronological interval. Indeed even if we restrict ourselves solely to the Western European setting, where enlightened notions of human equality presumably run deepest, monarchy was rarely challenged during the two millennia following the collapse of the Roman republic, while it remained in fact the prevalent form of central government up until the conclusion of the First World War in 1918. There were only three republics in Europe at the start of that terrible conflict in August 1914: France, Portugal and Switzerland. But in Britain, Germany, Italy, Spain, Denmark, Norway, Sweden, Belgium, Luxembourg, the Netherlands, Austria-Hungary and the Russian and Ottoman empires, monarchy of one form or another, from constitutional and ceremonial in London to absolutist and theocratic in St Petersburg, continued to command allegiance much as it had a millennium earlier.

Of all the forms of civil organization throughout the entire sweep of human experience, the rule of a single person over a political and territorial unit has been the most widespread and the most enduring. And until recent centuries most political theory was confined largely to discussions of monarchy; alternatives might be feasible in small city-states, but not over larger territories. Even Aristotle, who addressed a range of alternatives to rule by one, believed that the first governments 'were kingships, probably for this reason, because of old, when cities were small, men of eminent excellence were few'.[4]

Writing in the late seventeenth century, the English philosopher John Locke – certainly no yes-man for monarchical rule – claimed that 'if we look back as far as history will direct us, towards the original of commonwealths, we will generally find them under the government and administration of one man.'[5]

One century later, and in a distinctly harsher tone, John Adams wrote to his erstwhile rival Thomas Jefferson that 'the everlasting Envys, Jealousies, Rivalries and quarrels among them [aristocrats], their cruel rapacities upon the poor ignorant People their followers, compel these to set up Caesar, a Demagogue to be Monarch and Master, *pour mettre chacun à sa place*' (to put each one in his place).[6]

The idea of legitimate kingship is almost as old as the experience of humankind, and most certainly predates the rather attenuated span of recorded history. Preserved in the myth and folklore of almost every culture, many ancient kings claimed their elevated place by virtue of charismatic leadership and victory in battle, by popular acclamation, and by maintaining a monopoly over alleged mediational powers between the gods and the people.[7] Indeed the origins of kingship are most likely located in the quest of early peoples for protection against myriad hostile forces – natural, supernatural and human. The successful leader in the hunt or in battle, the forceful orator, the adept at healing or assuaging the disruptive forces within or above nature, the effective arbiter of disputes within the group – these were some of the qualities likely to elevate one individual above his peers in a public leadership capacity.

But most often at the centre of the nascent monarchical principle lay a powerful religious imperative and a long-lived set of social assumptions respecting the 'right ordering' of human institutions. In the end, perhaps, the power to rule rests upon the willingness of the larger community to be led. Superior strength may propel an individual into the role of leader, but if he is to remain there some sort of intellectual justification for his elevated station must be available and widely shared. In *The Social Contract* (1762), Jean-Jacques Rousseau observed that the elite cannot hope to govern by force alone, 'unless they find means of transforming force into right, and obedience into duty'.[8] In virtually every society where monarchy emerged and flourished, this transformation was effected by anchoring the institution of royal authority in a deeply religious culture. From living deities in Ancient Egypt, to direct descendants of the divine in China, Japan and Peru, to human designees of the Jewish, Christian and Muslim God, monarchs found their strongest claim to rule within the larger framework of a religious view of life. For centuries in Europe, monarchy remained the only appropriate model of civil organization because it was thought to be both natural and divinely ordained. The very language of the Christian story affirmed that heaven itself was organized along monarchical lines. The Kingdom of God under the omnipotent and omniscient headship of the greatest of monarchs; an aristocracy of angelic beings in the service of the King of Kings; humanity as wayward subject whose transgressions are forgiven through the sacrifice of the King's only Son – these were the images which formed the core of the Christian story, and if humankind's hoped-for eternal home was governed by an eternal patriarch, then it was only fitting that their temporary abode on earth be fashioned in a manner preparatory to the end of time.[9]

The religious traits associated with kingship in a variety of global cultures are of course common, but none more so than the belief in the monarch as mediator between the social order and a higher cosmic, superhuman reality. In this respect the symbolic or mythical power of earthly monarchs was almost as great as their actual political power. In many early societies the magical or religious power of kings was emphasized. The monarch's adherence to the established requirements of ritual was thought to be essential to the production of a sufficient harvest, the avoidance of natural and man-made disasters, and the overall security of subject peoples in an environment marked by constant danger and uncertainty. These features of kingship dissipated as societies become more complex and as mastery of the natural environment proceeded apace, but even as late as the seventeenth century, the monarchs of England and France were still thought by some to possess the magical power to heal (by simple touch) a skin disease known as scrofula.[10] And while western monarchs, unlike their counterparts in Japan, China and throughout Africa, made no claim to divinity themselves, their practical political power was delegated from God, and prior to the eighteenth century these monarchs were expected to represent God's will on earth. The religious ceremonial of the coronation event, the anointing with holy oil, the presence and endorsement of the institutional Church all made the office of the monarch inseparable from a trans-human agenda. And the continuity of the dynasty, if not the individual monarch, assured the maintenance of the Christian society on earth.

When examining the theory and the office of monarchy during the millennium under consideration in this book, we must be mindful that our modern concept of the state as an abstract set of ideals and a collection of impersonal offices and institutions is of very recent origin. The modern theory of sovereignty inhering in the public 'nation' rather than in a particular individual, and of institutions and officeholders exercising that sovereign authority by delegation, is entirely alien to the historical context in which monarchy emerged and flourished for centuries. Political authority in the name of the people had no place in subsistence economies where the vast majority of wealth and power was concentrated in the hands of one per cent of the population, and where the other 99 per cent could not envisage their world as being otherwise. And in this important respect monarchy as a historical phenomenon must be associated with the confluence of the personal and the public, with the concept of civil society as an expression of the will of an individual who is assumed to enjoy extraordinary intuition into the needs (religious and temporal) of the larger community.

For the first half of our period, monarchy in the world's major civilizations was closely associated with a human purpose or *telos* which transcended mundane concerns in order to affiliate with a divinely ordered universe. In Christian cultures, the monarch was viewed as but one of two leaders (the other being the patriarch of the Church) in a wider religious community whose overriding goal was the eternal salvation of the individual believer.[11] In Islamic society, the caliph or successor to the Prophet Muhammad was not obliged to share his leadership of the religious community with any individual or institution approaching the power of the Catholic Church in the West, but his rulership was salvational in purpose as well. In no single respect could the political culture of Islam be distinguished from the work of guiding the faithful along the path of righteousness. And in China, the emperor was accepted as the central mediator between the territorial 'Middle Kingdom' and the changeless and eternal realm of the divine.

The vast majority of monarchs before 1500 (China is excluded here) led confessional states where religious belief was compulsory and where the primary objective of temporal government was the advancement of an otherworldly ideal of life. In theory all terrestrial concerns were but instrumental to the higher religious end. Kings served in a sacral capacity, holding their power as a divine gift and enforcing heavenly mandates on each and every subject in a hierarchical society. In addition we might add here that monarchy as an institution developed and flourished in societies that were for centuries male-dominated, hierarchical and strongly deferential. Respect for age and authority, while now largely absent in Western societies, stood at the centre of most world cultures until very recently. Regard for precedent and a keen interest in the past were common guideposts for all segments of the social order.[12]

Monarchies, then, have been essential to most civilizations for a very long time. The remarkable staying power of the institution is highlighted by the fact that even the adoption of the hereditary principle as the predominant mechanism for determining legitimacy, a late medieval formation in the West but long the norm in other cultures, did not seriously compromise the institution.[13] It might very well have provided a dangerous solvent, for when considered from a generational perspective hereditary monarchy is an inherently unstable form of political authority, not least due to the fact that any system based upon the vagaries of familial succession can disintegrate in very rapid order. Incompetent offspring and rival claimants place a constant strain on the incumbent (as we shall see most directly in Muslim kingdoms), while the need to delegate power can become more than a little problematic in a structure where personal loyalty is the principal measure of organizational efficiency.

At the start of our study in the year 1000, the institution of monarchy was closely connected in many societies with a deeply rooted culture of aristocratic violence and competing local jurisdictions. These overwhelmingly agrarian societies were already highly stratified in terms of economic, political and social rank. A numerically tiny elite whose wealth was based in the control and exploitation of land, and to a lesser extent in trade, dominated a subject population which in most cases lived at the very margins of material existence. The ongoing support of these ambitious landed elites was indispensable to the success of monarchs everywhere. The rule of hereditary monarchs in Christian Europe, for example, was tempered by provincial magnates who wielded direct authority over their respective territories, while in towns and cities privileged corporations jealously guarded their economic prerogatives and successfully exploited royal grants of local self-governance. The individuals within this governing class were engaged in a near-constant struggle to improve their individual and family wealth and status, and feuding was anything but exceptional. A warlike culture within the ranks of the landed elite had already developed by the eleventh century, and one of the more important challenges facing Europe's monarchs involved harnessing and either ameliorating or redirecting these destructive tendencies for the good of the realm.

Despite these confrontations with rival centres of aristocratic and urban burgher power, the essential 'rightness' of the institution of monarchy was an almost universal conviction amongst peoples everywhere in the year 1000. In Western Europe the word kingship (*regnum*) was most often used for what we would now term country or state, and for men and women living a thousand years ago monarchy meant nothing less than right rule (*recte regere*).[14] King (*rex*) was not only a descriptive word but an evaluative one, and it implied a host of favourable characteristics linked to the fulfilment of God's will on earth.[15] For medieval people in the West it was the Christian king alone who transcended the petty but disruptive disputes between local elites, who placed equity and a sense of impartiality above narrow ambition. The same functions were attributed to the emperor of the Chinese, who stood above regional and provincial differences and governed the enormous Middle Kingdom with the implicit assent of the entire population. And in the Andean empire of the Incas, the monarch reigned as a living descendant of the sun god who by 1500 had unified an empire stretching from Chile to Ecuador and encompassing an area six times the size of France.

Given these widespread and deeply held assumptions, this constant affirmation of the propriety of rule by one, it is hard to accept John Stuart Mill's comprehensive nineteenth-century indictment of the 'old times' when rulers 'were conceived (except in some of the popular governments of Greece) as in a necessarily antagonistic position to the people whom they ruled'.[16] Not only was monarchy envisaged as an antidote to endemic disorder in most societies over the course of the past millennium, it might not be amiss to say that this special form of public authority seems to be one of the few features of formal social interaction and civil order which transcended the boundaries of culture, history and geography. Modern historians of world civilizations are fond of drawing distinctions between the development of relatively autonomous civilizations before Europeans began the process of 'making the world one' after 1500, but irrespective of time and location, the majority of societies around the globe seem to have embraced the monarchical idea as best suited to immediate social needs in the here and now, and – perhaps more importantly – to divine requirements for humanity in an unchanging and infinite order.

This book will investigate some of the key features of this enormously influential form of government, a model whose legitimacy rests not on voluntary consensus or contract but instead almost exclusively on age-old custom, heredity, tradition, and/or religious sanction. We will adopt a global and comparative focus, establishing connections between monarchy as idea and practice in a variety of historical and cultural contexts across a millennium when its worldwide influence was without serious rival. We will examine the intellectual assumptions behind different patterns of monarchy over the past thousand years, and we will trace how each of these assumptions shifted in response to a wide variety of historical factors: expanding literacy, shifts in the social structure, the impact of modern scientific assumptions about nature, the growth of rationalism and the concomitant decline of institutional religion, and the impact of modernization on human aspirations, ideals and political behaviour. In tracing the decline of a religious world view during the course of the last three centuries, the book will address the more recent emergence of conservative ideologies and their role in reaffirming the monarchical ideal on new grounds, examining how monarchy once informed by sacred standards subsequently became monarchy grounded and indeed justified by history, tradition and utility.

Speaking in very general terms, the sacral function began to atrophy and (in the West) face serious trials after 1500. New justifications for the institution of monarchy, new criteria by which legitimacy and success were to be calculated, were put forward as key to preserving the old power arrangements. From Augustine's *City of God* in the early fifth century to Machiavelli's *Prince* in the early sixteenth, the literature on kingship in the West emphasized the need for rulers to exercise the Christian virtues in both their private and public capacities. Personal piety, wisdom, the pursuit of justice, the advancement of charity, and the practice of clemency and mercy all figured prominently in what were taken to be the minimum qualifications of the legitimate monarch. Indeed this is still largely true for monarchs in Islamic nations today. But in the West after 1500, estimates of monarchical competence were increasingly based on experiential assumptions about human nature and the immediate needs of the state. Temporal success in providing security and prosperity gradually overtook the demand for right conduct in the affairs of statecraft.[17] When Machiavelli turned dissimulation into a principle of sober state action, when personal qualities became secondary to effective leadership, when the appearance of virtue – and not the substance -- began to count for more in the affairs of state, it was a signal that a new age in setting the intellectual underpinnings of monarchy had been inaugurated. Kings who once ruled by divine authority on behalf of an eternal kingdom were now expected to devote their chief exertions in the interests of the territorial, and all too mundane state.

Central to this comparative study will be the issue of what we might term 'autonomy and responsibility'. At the core of monarchy as a model of civil authority over the past thousand years is the implicit assumption that one individual is somehow privileged over all other members of the population both to formulate and to enforce a vision of community good, a set of collective values and a concept of social well-being. Often exercising judicial, administrative, legislative, priestly and military command, monarchy implied the existence of an irrevocable chasm between the maturity of the leader and the immaturity and natural incapacity of the subject. At its most basic level, then, monarchy represents the antithesis of the democratic premise; men and women are *not* capable of governing themselves as equals. In the Western Christian tradition, the medieval prince was thought to represent the monarchy of God within a particular fixed territorial dominion; in the Muslim world the caliph carried the mantle of Muhammad's authority and forwarded the will of Allah in a series of remarkable expansion drives; and in the context of the enormous Chinese empire, the successful emperor enjoyed nothing less than the Mandate of Heaven in exercising his autocratic power for the collective well-being of the Middle Kingdom. At a minimum, the remarkable longevity of the monarchical pattern invites each reader to weigh the significance of hierarchy, subordination, and dependence as problematic constants in the human experience. In an era when democracy has become the ideal of politics advanced (at least rhetorically) in increasing numbers of states around the globe, historical consideration of its centuries-old predecessor will help elucidate the scale of the intellectual shift involved in democracy's estimate of human nature and human potential.

Another basic issue at the centre of this survey of monarchy over the past thousand years involves the tension between the institution's absolutist forms and its limited or constitutional alternative. We will discover that only in the West during the first 500 years of our period were substantive constitutional restraints placed upon the prerogative powers exercised by monarchs. These exceptional developments occurred at the very time when Roman Catholic Christianity exercised a substantial influence over the functions of government, when in fact the Church *was* the unitary state, the community of Christians subject to the will of a personal God. Only much later, during the late seventeenth century, and at the very time that the Christian world-view was being challenged from a number of quarters, did more ambitious and absolutist forms of monarchy find a home in parts of Europe. Elsewhere within the global community monarchs faced fewer formal restraints upon their power. In China, the Islamic world and Africa, the prerogatives exercised by individual rulers remained largely unimpaired into the twentieth century. And in other major civilizations at the chronological mid-point of our survey, such as those in pre-Columbian America and in Byzantium, those restraints upon executive authority which did exist were more likely to be informal and loosely associated with notions of consent and service inherent in a particular religious tradition.

Within this larger global framework, it is important for us to distinguish at the outset between the legitimizing principle intrinsic to the type of personal rule described here and the public authority exercised by despots and modern dictators. In one form or another, almost every major non-European civilization has experienced despotic forms of rule over long periods of time. Normally begun in military conquest and marked by the unchecked power and capricious decision-making of one individual, despotism (and in the contemporary world) dictatorship do not allow for the least appearance of political opposition, free expression, a known rule of law and an impartial judiciary, or private property free from the depredations of the ruler. Under the despot or dictator, the subject has no temporal existence independent of the master, no private sphere where one's autonomy is respected.[18]

The ancient Greeks simply refused to equate despotism with legitimate government at all, for in their estimation political authority and civil order required the active participation of free and equal male citizens. According to the citizens of the classical Greek city-states, Asian barbarians like the Persians were slaves by nature and thus willing to submit under the yoke of despotic kings. Aristotle went so far as to argue that oriental despotism was based on the informal consent of the ruled; in his view the entire non-Hellenic world was peopled by slaves who were incapable of mature self-direction. Perhaps the best way to distinguish traditional monarchy from despotism and modern dictatorship, then, is to emphasize that the office of the king was associated in most cultures with an informally agreed (albeit often unwritten) set of duties and informal arrangements. Although the legitimate monarch occupied the summit of the established social and political hierarchy, his power was by no means totally unrestrained. In virtually every setting, while the ruler theoretically 'owned' his kingdom, powerful landed (or in the case of China, intellectual) elites exercised delegated authority in a manner which invariably limited the centralizing proclivities of the royal officeholder. As a result an internal 'balance of forces' was often created whereby monarchical prerogative was in constant tension with aristocratic localism. This dynamic and fluid relationship continued to set practical limits on the power of the king, particularly in the West, well beyond the mid-point of our study.

Over the last 500 years political authority in the name of the people has become widespread throughout the global community. The authority of monarchs has been challenged repeatedly and to striking effect in conjunction with the growth of technology (especially communications) and industry, the spread of popular education, the emergence of nationalism, and the wider dispersal of wealth. Today even the most arbitrary despots boast a popular mandate for their rule, carefully orchestrating the fiction of widespread approbation with mass rallies, street demonstrations, strict control over media and access to foreign news. Their work of translating force into right is a never-ending one. Even in those countries where traditional monarchy remains an effective political force – in the Arab oil states, for instance – the security of the institution rests less with the monarch's role as leader of the community (in the Arab case, of the Islamic community) and more on the ability of the dynasty in question to provide the material comforts and ever-rising expectations associated with a modern welfare state.

After 1500 the subsistence economy that prevailed across the major world civilizations gave way to greater commercialization, the first steps towards industrial production of goods, long-distance travel, and European-led overseas expansion. Increasingly, first in the West and subsequently elsewhere, the rule of kings seemed inadequate to the task of managing the unprecedented and varied interests of a growing commercial elite. New challenges to the institution of monarchy appeared initially in those societies where the strains of economic maturation were most acute – in mid-seventeenth-century England, in eighteenth-century America and France – until by the nineteenth century many of the leading Western powers were redefining the scope of monarchical authority and disassociating it from earlier associations with divine sanction and mandate. Coupled with the fracturing of Christianity in the West during the course of the sixteenth century, new challenges to hierarchical power structures were bound to impact upon popular views of monarchy. As the responsibilities of central government expanded, the need for trained bureaucrats, for increased numbers of educated civil servants in the expanding offices of state, and for greater technical expertise all made the prospect that one person could competently and productively oversee the affairs of state something less than realistic. This together with the growth of democratic ideology made it hard to sustain arguments in favour of monarchs who not only reigned but ruled. The era of ceremonial monarchy bereft of real political power had begun in those states willing to maintain this much-diminished link with the past.

In the twentieth century, the centuries-old chasm between rulers and ruled, where the prerogatives of the latter were based upon the ownership of land and hereditary status, was all but extinguished in the West. But despite the many advances of the democratic principle in the century just concluded, rule by one continued to define the contours of political life around the globe. Whether brutal or benign, unitary rule became during the course of the 1900s something perversely akin to early modern monarchical absolutism, especially in terms of the coercive power exercised over a subject population. Thanks in part to innovations in communication, the power of individual strongmen to compel and constrain was enhanced, while all pretensions to divine sanction were abandoned.

Traditional monarchy, where it survived after the First World War in Europe, was reduced largely to official functions, whereas dictatorship found new opportunities to reaffirm the ancient claim that there were indeed fundamental inequalities within the human race, and that the wisdom and intuitions of the one are inherently superior to the collective will of the majority. In Hitler's Germany, in Stalin's Soviet Union, in Mao's China, and, though on a smaller scale, in Saddam's Iraq, the repudiation of human equality inherent in the monarchical principle has remained with us, at a cost in human suffering and death hardly imaginable by those who ascended their thrones in the year 1000. Ironically and tragically, the collapse of divine sanction for rule by one has been coupled with a dramatic and unprecedented increase in the ability of the modern authoritarian state to degrade humanity at large, and to anchor that degradation in the manipulation of technologies which themselves are the product of a better side of humankind. At the close of the planet's bloodiest century, this fatal misappropriation of the monarchical ideal haunts us still.

As traditional monarchy enters a new era, shorn of its political power in most states and serving instead as an emblem of national tradition, perhaps something of its better side – its older affiliation with a world of value beyond the material and the provincial – might be of some small assistance as humanity struggles to understand the darker moments of the century just concluded.

1 Contemporary portrait of the Chinese Yongle Emperor (r. 1403–24).

ONE

Asian Archetypes:
Chinese Absolutism and
Japanese Symbolism

CONTINUITY IN CHINA

We begin our survey with China for one compelling reason. Unique in so many respects within the family of major world civilizations over the past 2000 years, there is perhaps no more outstanding feature of Chinese culture than the longevity and stability of the imperial office. In the words of one of the leading scholars of China in the twentieth century, 'Never have so few ruled for so long over so many.'[1] Beginning with the Shang dynasty of Northern China (*c.* 1500–1066 BCE) and building upon even earlier patterns of ancestor worship, royal authority in China has always been linked to communication (most often via divination) with higher spiritual forces in the cosmological order. In fact the origins of Chinese civilization have traditionally been associated with great mythical rulers; the so-called Five Rulers of the period *c.* 2852–2205 BCE were thought to be foundational to a unique style of Chinese culture.[2] The commonplace Chinese practice of measuring time by the reigns of emperors and dynasties is but one measure of monarchy's importance to the overall culture.

Nowhere else has the office of emperor been so permanent a feature of the political landscape; in no other state was the position as central to so many people over such a vast territorial expanse. In terms of its symbolic and religious significance, and with respect to the overall stability of this vast land, 'the existence of an emperor, be he heroic leader of his country or puppet dominated by his court, was nothing short of essential'.[3] During the third quarter of the nineteenth century in Europe there were, simultaneously, emperors in France, Germany, Britain, Austria-

Hungary and Russia. In imperial China, where the lands and productive resources under the control of central government exceeded anything owned by Europe's quarrelsome rulers, such imperial fragmentation was unthinkable. At the start of our survey in the year 1000, China under the Song dynasty (960–1279) was the most populous and most urbanized country in the world. With close to 100 million inhabitants and 50 cities with populations approaching 500,000 by the year 1200, monarchy in China was an institution without global rival.

This is not to suggest that China experienced no political upheavals or periods of discord for upwards of two millennia (a long interregnum between 220 and 581 CE is the best case in point), but while dynastic change did occur, while civil wars and periods of anarchy were often brutal and protracted, each new dynasty (including those established by foreign usurpers) adopted a form of monarchical rule that, phoenix-like, was virtually indistinguishable from its predecessors. While never claiming to be divine themselves, emperors from the Zhou dynasty (c. 1066–221 BCE) onward were believed to be divinely appointed, enjoying the 'Mandate of Heaven' (*tianming*) and ruling unhindered by any recognized rule of human law or by an official religious establishment. In theory, and very often in practice, the power of the monarch was unlimited due to the fact that an 'impersonal deity or an abstract moral-spiritual force' had confirmed the right of a particular household to govern in an ethically upright fashion.[4] Above the law, the emperor was also the highest judge in all cases of appeal. The imperial office remained at the heart of the Chinese experience from the establishment of the Qin dynasty in 221 BC, when the first ruler abandoned the title king (*wang*) and adopted the title august emperor (*huangdi*), until the collapse of the Qing in 1912. As early as the second century CE, centralized government under the emperor was integral to Chinese culture and 'its preservation had become the natural and accepted aim of every ambitious statesman'.[5]

Continuity in the idea and practice of monarchy in China is due to a number of important factors, both sacred and profane. Far more than in any other comparable civilization, understanding monarchy in China involves understanding something of the unique place of family in the broader culture. Throughout the course of China's long history, the family rather than the individual has been the key factor in the political life of the local community. The filial piety, ancestor worship and unquestioning obedience that were for so long the hallmarks of domestic life in village China prepared the way for the acceptance of the same qualities of personal conduct in the more formal political realm, and in particular in one's relationship to the emperor and his servants. Chinese monarchs never thought of themselves as mere administrators or bureaucrats; instead, patrimonial values were lodged deep at the core of the institution.[6] Fathers were autocrats, wielding unabridged authority over all members of their immediate family. Paternal wisdom, even after the male parent was no longer able to meet his physical obligations on the land due to old age or sickness, guided the operation of the household at every level. Age over youth, male over female, the training of obedient youngsters, not individual character-formation – these moral guideposts of the domestic kinship system translated easily into the realm of ruler–subject relations.[7]

But while the father was supreme within the family, patterns of land ownership in China tended to prevent the emergence of groups of men whose local interests threatened the state, a landed nobility similar to the one that developed in medieval Europe. Very early on the Chinese abandoned the practice of primogeniture for partible inheritance; thus while headship of the family passed to the eldest son, a monopoly over the father's property did not.[8] Landholding was widely dispersed among the peasantry, with the vast majority living at or near subsistence level and thereby incapable of posing serious challenges to monarchical authority short of organizing with other small and impoverished tillers of the soil. And such coalitions were very rare indeed. When they did form it was normally in the face of overwhelming and prolonged abuse or incompetence at the imperial level, a clear sign that the supernatural mandate to rule had been withdrawn.

Ancient and commonly accepted beliefs regarding the emperor's powers also shaped the institution down into the modern age. The earliest mythical emperors were believed to have given humanity fire, agriculture, hunting, writing, silk, and other key skills and technologies of productive life.⁹ For centuries it was believed that kings could influence ancestral spirits who in turn intervened in nature for the good or ill of a community. For the Chinese, heaven was immanent in nature, not transcendent, and therefore formal rituals and sacrifices were key to the fertility of the soil, the weather, protection from enemies, victory in battle, and a host of other shared concerns. Each year, for example, one of the more important rituals undertaken by the monarch involved the symbolic turning of a furrow of soil, inaugurating yet another growing season and hope for a bountiful harvest. In the Confucian model of government, the emperor was obliged to provide for the material welfare of his subjects; the pursuit of his own ambitions to the neglect of larger public ends was regarded as antithetical to the essence of good government.¹⁰

In the absence of a legitimate Son of Heaven (*tianzi*), the Chinese would be left without divine protection in a universe of unpredictable forces. Kings were vital to social harmony in a cosmological order where human affairs were bonded to a larger divine purpose. The emperor was high priest, warrior and scribe, without rival or peer in the terrestrial realm, and obliged to maintain a correct relationship between heaven and earth.¹¹ Altars and temples designed specifically for state-sponsored rites were built in all of the cities which served as imperial capitals.¹² The first emperor of a truly unified China, Qin Shi Huangdi (221–210 BCE), enhanced this model of royal authority by an aggressive policy of road and canal building, military expansion, authoritarian legal reform, standardization of weights, measures, coinage and even axle lengths. The bulk of these imperial projects proceeded apace thanks to the organization of the empire into 48 administrative units, each under the control of royally appointed military and civilian subordinates. Later dynasties would accept the idea that ministers under the emperor were duty bound to warn the Son of Heaven whenever he governed at odds with the well-being of the community, and this idea was embodied in the development of the office of censor. But in the end the will of the supreme ruler, the omniscience of the one, took precedence over all subordinate counsel. Seemingly capricious acts like the peremptory execution of an imperial official by an unpredictable emperor was, within this framework of understanding, equivalent to a modern-day 'act of God'.[13]

In addition to the strongly felt need for a common ruler, China's geographical isolation from serious competitors in terms of organized neighbouring states allowed its ruling elites to focus attention on internal development and political consolidation over a varied topographical area. It is true that highly mobile nomadic horsemen from the north often threatened and in some instances overturned indigenous dynastic houses, and there was a modicum of caravan contact with central and south Asia beginning as early as the first century CE, but in the main China's emperors did not find themselves faced with sustained challenges from powerful, and hostile, organized kingdoms. And the composition of the Chinese empire was uniquely homogeneous, for the overwhelming majority of the ruler's subjects were ethnic Han who over the centuries successfully assimilated the peoples of South China and expelled most invaders from the north. By the time of the Later Han dynasty (25–220 CE), the lands under the direct authority of the emperor equalled almost the whole of modern China. In terms of population, land and overall wealth, it was certainly every bit as large as the contemporary Roman empire in the West.

But while the later Roman imperial state faced a serious challenge to its hegemony from the nascent Christian Church, with the state ultimately embracing the faith and validating the rival spiritual authority of the bishop of Rome, in China there was no institutional Church or ecclesiastical hierarchy poised to challenge the government of the emperor. Instead, the Confucian ethical system, initially formulated some three centuries before the advent of the Han and fully developed by the first century of the common era, placed the family and the well-being of the state at the core of life's moral priorities. Confucius (c. 551–479 BCE) had not disparaged the conventional religious beliefs and practices of his day, but he had taught that sacrifice and ritual were by no means the exclusive paths to securing a better world. Instead, virtuous action was indispensable to the project of establishing an orderly and contented society. Politics and ethics were treated as one in China, and the state was the patriarchal family writ large.

SERVANTS OF THE EMPEROR

Basic to this monarchical system was the establishment of a highly trained bureaucratic service elite, one recruited on the principle of merit and in the main eschewing the more common notion of political privilege linked to descent through noble birth. Education and aptitude, not blood, provided the criterion for service leadership under the Chinese emperors. This civil service elite, numbering no more than 30,000 scholar-officials in the eighteenth century when the overall population of the empire was over 200 million, and carrying out a wide array of supervisory, administrative, judicial and record-keeping functions, made the Chinese state a durable reality. A numerically tiny service nobility organized the construction of roads and canals, managed public granaries, supervised transport, mining, building, education, and carried on the day-to-day work of coordination and law enforcement essential to any large managerial state.

A competent emperor, by getting to know enough of his senior officials, could reasonably hope to direct such a force. Its recruitment mechanism allowed the emperor to avoid making crucial compromises with kinsmen or military elites over the extent of royal authority. With their rigorous training in the Confucian literary classics, a background steeped in an understanding of the government as an agent of moral supremacy anchored in precedent, these career civil servants made the imperial officeholder a ruler of unparalleled power. And since only a tiny number of successful exam takers were able to secure salaried positions at the provincial level or higher, the bulk of office holders took up unpaid leadership posts in their local communities and villages. This practice facilitated the widespread diffusion of Confucian culture, especially its emphases on obedience and duty, character and virtue, age and precedent, down to the level of the peasant majority. No other major world civilization enjoyed such an all-embracing cultural system whose impact was felt directly at the level of the educated elite, and whose norms were imposed even within the village and family.

Irrespective of locale, the success of all Chinese rulers was associated with the formation and implementation of sound policies, and for the emperors this goal was always contingent upon sensible personnel decisions. The Han founded a school for the training of future administrators, and successive dynasties multiplied the number of formal educational establishments. During the Sui (581–618) and Tang (618–907) periods, for example, examinations covered a variety of subjects, including law, literature, calligraphy, mathematics and classical scholarship. In these schools promising sons of official and even commoner families vied for recognition and state employment. Key to the lasting allegiance of these well-educated officials was the fact that their appointments were, in the end, precarious. 'Even the highest officials were, as individuals, at the mercy of the absolute and despotic state, and were liable to disappear suddenly from view.'[14] Established senior civil servants who sponsored talented underlings for promotion were not immune from punishment themselves should their pupil later prove to be delinquent or venal in his official capacity. In 1020, for example, rules were established whereby sponsors were to be reproved in a manner identical to that befitting the crime committed by the errant protégé.[15]

Scholar-bureaucrats were not allowed to own property in their area of supervision, nor were family members permitted to serve in the same department of government. With the abandonment of primogeniture, the estates of powerful and potentially disloyal families did not remain intact across generations. In Europe a hereditary aristocracy whose wealth was based in the control of land had emerged by the eleventh century, and their potential power to limit absolutism was very much in evidence. No such independent power base was in evidence in China, where primary loyalty was not to locale or to family, but to the emperor as the embodiment of the Confucian world order. As one recent student of Chinese bureaucratic culture has stated, 'Confucian officials took their duties seriously, including their loyalty both to the throne and to the whole system of values in which they had been educated and that gave their careers meaning'.[16]

An element of social mobility was built into the system for those who succeeded at each ascending level of the examination cycle. Higher positions within the official class of government service were open on a competitive basis, not simply to soldiers or to landed magnates, but to all males who exhibited superior intellect. The sense of institutional continuity and dedication to the civil community provided by the highly trained functionaries of the Confucian civil service allowed for monarchical permanence in the face of periodic royal incompetence and dynastic change. Han, Sui, Tang, Song, Yuan, Ming, Qing – each successive dynasty could count on the ethical anchor of the ideologically homogenous Confucian bureaucracy to further the interests of China in a manner consistent with the institution of absolute monarchy. Other than the founders of a new dynasty, emperors rarely attempted to rule without the support of this conservative bureaucracy.

SUBJECTS

We know very little about the millions of peasants whose unremitting labour in a mainly subsistence setting provided the material resources, mostly in the form of taxes, for the Chinese imperial state. While copious records exist for the life of the court and the Confucian bureaucracy, with the exception of official census-records a wall of silence confronts us respecting the everyday life of the peasantry. We do know that over a large part of the past thousand years the Chinese peasant, unlike his counterparts elsewhere, was very likely to be engaged in some cultivation for the market as opposed to immediate consumption. This was especially true in rice-producing areas where specialized cultivation was in demand. Here subsistence level farmers, women and men whose aspirations for life ascended little beyond the hope for survival, nonetheless sold a portion of their produce in a market environment.[17] We also know that government at the sub-county level was left in the hands of local village leaders who were responsible for keeping order, collecting taxes, providing militiamen when requested, and for the maintenance of irrigation and other public works projects. No one at this level was remunerated by the state. In the villages it was the duty of both retired and low-ranking officials to indoctrinate the inhabitants with Confucian values on a regular basis.[18]

Most serious rebellions against the emperors were prompted by natural disasters: floods, drought and attendant famine in the countryside. Population growth, of course, always intensified competition for scarce land, but challenges to authority by desperate people were normally linked to larger forces over which a good emperor was supposed to have some control. Whenever peasant insurrections won the support of local gentry and elements of the official bureaucracy, the end of a dynastic cycle was normally at hand. In the official histories composed by scholars in order to legitimate the incumbent regime, the close of the preceding dynasty is normally marked by natural calamities and heavenly portents, including floods, earthquakes, comets and eclipses.[19]

There were no other viable mechanisms for political opposition. The imperial system did not countenance any sort of national assembly which might represent interests outside the court. In a structure where power was not diffused or shared with landed elites, only successful leadership at the top could both manage the bureaucracy and pursue successful economic and military policies. But if that leadership failed, the consequences could be devastating. When the Mongols overran China in the 1270s as many as 30 million people may have been killed, while the Manchu conquest of the Ming in the mid-seventeenth century resulted in the deaths of upwards of 25 million Chinese.[20] Still, while natural and man-made misfortunes might call into question the emperor's ability to mediate between heaven and earth, to secure the favour of his royal ancestral spirits, so great was the cost of dynastic change that recourse to violent upheaval was very much the exception in Chinese history. The Chinese imperial office survived rebellion, invasion and dynastic alteration due to the conviction that the Mandate of Heaven was made explicit in the work of history. Successful rebellion signalled the withdrawal of divine favour from a particular dynastic bloodline, not divine disapproval of the imperial order of government.

Our millennium spans four major dynasties, two of which were foreign impositions by nomadic warriors from the north. The Song, Yuan (Mongol), Ming and Qing (Manchu) eras, a very long period which Charles Hucker has aptly described as the 'later imperial age', was witness to repeated efforts on the part of the indigenous Han Chinese to rebuff aggressive foreigners, first northern nomads and subsequently Western imperialists.[21] In the end both efforts failed, but not before the emperors became more autocratic and inward looking, until by the nineteenth century the Middle Kingdom had become a vulnerable backwater in comparison with the expansionist and technologically superior West.[22] Such a denouement was perhaps to be expected in a civilization where the official culture viewed itself as the very centre of the universe, a cosmos made up 'of concentric circles becoming more and more barbarous the further they lay from the Chinese core'.[23]

But in another respect the early twentieth-century collapse of imperial China in the face of Western interference can be viewed within the context of a pattern of dynastic change always present in the history of the Chinese monarchy. Normally a new dynasty was begun under the leadership of an aggressive military figure who hoped to pass on his hard-won title to his son. The early emperors were drawn from all ranks of society, and within each dynastic period these early rulers were often the most competent, both administratively and militarily. Only later within a dynastic cycle, after generations of peace and prosperity, did aloof and pampered emperors lose interest in the difficult day-to-day management of the empire. Increasingly influenced by palace insiders, the later monarchs were so much dead wood, incapable of responding in an intelligent manner to China's changing needs. In the event, either domestic rebels claiming a new Mandate of Heaven, or expansionist horsemen and swordsmen from the north, undermined the unity of the state and brought the cycle to a close, usually accompanied by much bloodshed and suffering.[24] The arrival of the Westerners in the nineteenth century merely compounded an existing and long-term problem for Chinese rulers.

After 300 years, the Tang period came to an end with the abdication of the last emperor in 906. Racked by rebellion since 875, the first half of the tenth century saw China under the disruptive, if all-too-familiar control of regional warlords. Nomadic peoples called the Qidan invaded North China, and only in 960 were the Chinese, following the leadership of an army strongman named Zhao Kuangyin, able to begin the work of reconstituting the centralized state under traditional imperial leadership. The 32-year-old emperor pensioned off a number of military commanders and transferred to the palace army the best units of each of the regional commands. This highly mobile and professional army was vastly superior to anything under the control of potential challengers.[25] It was during the era of the Song (960–1279) that the pattern of Chinese monarchical government became more autocratic, and more professionally bureaucratic, than at any previous time in imperial history. Paradoxically, it was also under the Song that China became the world's most economically dynamic and prosperous civilization, a forerunner of what the West would become after 1700.[26]

The vigour of Song absolutism was impressive by any standard. Earlier Chinese emperors were absolutists in theory, but in practice many had to compromise with powerful families, with influential military commanders, and with ambitious relatives.[27] A variety of steps were taken to reverse this deleterious situation starting in the eleventh century. Many aristocratic families had been destroyed during the endemic warfare of the later Tang, while the availability of printed texts enabled lesser gentry families to secure access to the Confucian classics and thus prepare for civil service examinations.[28] No longer faced with a powerful aristocracy, skilled and ambitious emperors began to formalize and consolidate their office. Even after invaders forced the Song emperors to relocate their capital in 1127 from Kaifeng in the north to Linan (modern Hangzhou) in the south, the dynasty continued to enhance its power.

For example, beginning with the Song and continuing through the Mongol, Ming and Qing dynasties, a new and more rigid protocol surrounded the person of the emperor. No longer were imperial counsellors allowed to sit informally with the emperor when discussing policy. Under the Song all officials were required to stand at attention when in the royal presence, and during the Ming dynasty (1368–1644) counsellors were required to kneel before the throne. The Ming emperors also borrowed from their Mongol predecessors the practice of flogging high officials in open court before those who were in attendance. An imperial bodyguard doubled as a spy network for the monarch, and for those accused of offences against the crown there was no recognized rule of law available to protect the defendant. For Ming monarchs, arbitrary behaviour in the treatment of high officialdom was employed as a means to guarantee loyalty.[29]

After the late tenth century, Chinese emperors were much more secretive and physically removed from their subjects than were their European counterparts. The emperor's residential quarters were strictly off-limits to officials and courtiers, while in Europe nobles regularly conducted business with the king in informal and private settings. Chinese emperors were rarely seen outside the palace complex of the Forbidden City (built by the Ming in the later fourteenth century). Even official audiences in the throne halls were elaborate and formal affairs designed to emphasize the insignificance of the supplicant before the great Son of Heaven.[30] And although some emperors took to the field with their armies while others went on the occasional royal progress, normally the ruler was shielded from millions of his subjects by an elaborate bureaucracy and administration.

Under the Song all subordinate offices were for the first time staffed by men who were drawn exclusively from the learned class. No longer was a military background or aristocratic clan allegiance thought to be prerequisite to the management of state affairs; professionalism and efficiency now took priority.[31] Indeed outright disdain for soldiers increased in China in the aftermath of the Mongol and Manchu conquests.[32]

Civil officials bereft of local attachments began to take the place of military governors in the countryside, while relatives of the emperor were excluded from important posts and even in some cases kept away from the capital.

Although there had never been any autonomous sources of government authority in China, the Song emperors concentrated even greater power at the centre than any of their predecessors. They inherited from the Tang a series of administrative departments which would form the main contours of Chinese government down into the early twentieth century. For example, the Song continued the Tang practice of dividing top responsibilities among three large branches: a military general staff, an independent censorate charged with reviewing and investigating government officials, and a council of state which in turn subsumed three branches of its own – Secretariat, Chancellery, and Department of State Affairs. But the Song emperors consolidated many of the duties assigned to these various departments under the authority of the emperor's chief counsellors. And in 1380 the founder of the Ming made himself his own prime minister by abolishing the Secretariat's executive posts. He subsequently fragmented the authority of the military branch, in effect making himself his own chief of staff. Later, less adept emperors allowed some of this authority to devolve to a coordinating agency known as the Grand Secretariat, a very small group of close advisors. The Manchu Qing emperors continued this executive agency, and it was here that regular administrative matters were addressed.

After 1000, fiscal, personnel and military responsibilities were kept out of the hands of the same official, especially at the provincial level. By limiting provincial powers to specific functions, the dynastic monarchs from the Song forward were able to prevent usurpation of royal authority by disgruntled subordinates. But in addition to official office-holders, court eunuchs were employed in key posts within the palace. While posing no threat to royal authority under competent monarchs, under less capable leadership these eunuchs exploited their access to the emperor in order to acquire enormous power at court. Some 10,000 eunuchs were in service when the Ming moved their capital to Beijing, and under the Qing the number rose to over 100,000. In addition, palace intrigue was intensified due to the fact that the emperors kept an enormous number of concubines and produced a surfeit of offspring. By the end of the Ming dynasty there were nearly 9,000 concubines in the Forbidden City, and this number increased under the Qing.[33]

The Song emperors also reformed the examination system. The first exams were now administered at the provincial level on a three-year cycle, a practice which became standard in subsequent dynasties. Successful test-takers at this level then moved on to the metropolitan examination at the capital, and if successful here, on again to the highest level – the palace examination – sometimes administered by the emperor himself. By making these opportunities available to more gentry at the provincial level, the emperors created a large group of landowners who had a vested interest in preserving the political order in general and the office of the monarch in particular.[34] The first Ming emperor, Hongwu, established an extensive network of schools at the county level in order to produce more scholar-bureaucrats and afford more sons of gentry the prospect of advancement.

Political stability under the Song helped to accelerate a process of economic transformation begun during the Tang dynasty, and this in turn facilitated the growth of interdependence across many regions of China.[35] With a population of perhaps 100 million in the year 1000, the Song emperors ruled over the largest subject population in the world. By way of comparison the population of politically divided Europe prior to the agricultural revolution of the eighteenth century was no greater than 80 million. A number of important technological innovations, including the invention of weapons using gunpowder, moveable type, the mariner's compass and the sternpost rudder all made their appearance in the Chinese economy after 1000. By and large most emperors encouraged these innovations, and the results were impressive. Townsmen's and other urban interests, particularly on the south coast and along the Yangtze, helped to transform the economy. The first Song capital had been located on the North China Plain at the modern city of Kaifeng, and with a population in the neighbourhood of half-a-million in the year 1000, it was larger than any European city. After nomadic Jurchen invaders overspread the north in 1127, the capital was relocated to Hangzhou along the Qiantang river estuary. This move to the south represented part of a larger shift in Chinese development whereby the original homeland of the Chinese, the North China Plain, became less important both economically and culturally, while South China and the southeast coast in particular gained in overall significance to the well-being of the empire.

Under the southern Song, large-scale maritime trade began in earnest. Concentrated on southeast Asia and the Indian ocean, the profits from trade facilitated the building of important cities on the south China coast. The Mongols appreciated the potential of long-distance trade as well, and under the Ming a series of famous maritime expeditions took place between 1405 and 1433. Led by the Muslim court eunuch Zheng He, hundreds of ships and thousands of men visited ports in Sri Lanka, the Persian Gulf and East Africa.[36] Imperial supervision of an enormous ocean-going fleet placed the Ming emperors in the enviable position of leading even more distant voyages of trade and exploration a full half century before the first serious Portuguese efforts.

Foreign traders, the majority of whom were Muslim, were permitted to reside in key trading centres subject to the oversight of government inspectors. On the mainland, large-scale iron production using charcoal for fuel resulted in a maximum output of 125,000 tons of iron ore each year (compared with 20–40,000 in seventeenth-century England).[37] Textile manufacture increased thanks to the invention of the spinning wheel and promotion of a system of paper currency, both in the eleventh century. And at the village level, government-appointed agricultural officers introduced farmers to new strains of rice which permitted a doubling of crops per year in well-irrigated lowlands. This last breakthrough led to conditions of unprecedented stability in terms of increased survival. The imperial government also sponsored additional canal and road building projects, and perhaps most importantly established public granaries as a hedge against crop failures. China's surplus agriculture made it possible to support enormous urban populations. For example, 2.5 million people lived in the southern Song capital city of Hangzhou at a time when Europe's largest city, Venice, had only 160,000 inhabitants.[38] It is little wonder that the Venetian Marco Polo was so impressed by China's urban achievements.

But in spite of these many and varied economic advances, Chinese society did not witness the continued growth of a dynamic and multi-talented middle class. The advent of printing, for example, instead of advancing the dissemination of new ideas as would later be the case in Europe, merely broadened the appeal of conservative Confucian values. Similarly, gunpowder weaponry, rather than supporting the growth of regional states, instead gave the imperial centre greater tools by which to eliminate serious rivals to monarchical power.[39] Government monopolies over most consumer goods – salt, iron, tea, wine – may have provided much-needed state revenue, but they also tended to inhibit entrepreneurial development and risk-taking.[40] Although a national market system was in place and production continued for the overseas market, especially in porcelains, silk products and cotton textiles, the government did not encourage the development of an autonomous middle class. Confucianism never acknowledged mercantile activities as anything other than parasitic; imperial control over essential economic activities meant that merchants and overseas traders were at the mercy of official whims and preferences. The Ming emperors ceased to view foreign trade as mutually beneficial and placed it under the category of tribute. Only states which recognized China's suzerainty were permitted the privilege of purchasing Chinese products. Three years after coming to power, the first Ming emperor forbade his subjects travel overseas, and as a result maritime trade suffered inordinately.

The sorts of legal and economic immunities granted by European monarchs to urban dwellers were never forthcoming in imperial China. Unlike his European counterpart, the Chinese merchant and trader won for himself no urban liberties, no autonomous guilds, no self-governing cities, no political access to the centre of imperial power. Nor did he win much respect within the broader culture. His work, after all, was intermediary, non-productive, and in this sense he was of much less value to society than the peasant farmer.[41] In 1436 the Ming emperor unilaterally banned the construction of all seagoing ships, and by the close of the century Japanese pirates had made the seas unsafe. Concerned more with defending the northern frontier than with promoting trading opportunities for south coast merchants, conservative elements within the Confucian bureaucracy managed to halt the emergence of a dynamic bourgeoisie comparable to the one developing in Western Europe.

Outside of imperial or local state service, few educated men were attracted to alternative careers. It is perhaps difficult for the Western mind to appreciate fully a culture where a career in public service, even at the lower levels of administration, is held in highest esteem, and where non-governmental occupations for the educated are associated with failure. There were no independent religious or secular institutions where an intellectual might pursue a scholarly or teaching career outside the control of the state; neither Buddhists nor Daoists enjoyed the sort of social eminence accorded religious leaders in the Christian and Muslim worlds. Trade was certainly not a respectable outlet for a gentleman, while artists and writers normally found success only under official patronage. Those merchants who sought respectability poured their resources into land and education for their offspring, hoping in the end to become assimilated into the dominant culture of the scholar-bureaucrat.[42]

In 1279 the Southern Song empire, after 150 years of remarkable prosperity, succumbed to a protracted Mongol onslaught, and China became, like so much of the civilized world at this juncture in the human experience, part of an unprecedented Eurasian empire which stretched from the China Sea to Central Europe. Under the brutal leadership of Genghis (Chingis) Khan (1162–1227), the Mongol warriors had laid waste to much of North China during the first quarter of the thirteenth century. Governed by his grandson Kublai (r. 1260–94), all of China was for the first time brought under the rule of alien peoples. Locating his capital at Beijing, Kublai Khan and his successors oversaw what was essentially a prolonged military occupation of China. The language of the court was Mongolian and domestic policy never rose above the level of efficient exploitation. Generally despised by the native Chinese, many of whom were reduced to slave status, the emperors welcomed foreigners from as far afield as Europe, and these many adventurers became tax farmers, advisors and collaborators of the Yuan state. In 1315 the foreign rulers reinstated the Confucian examination system, but prescribed quotas for Mongol and non-Chinese test-takers. And all key civil service posts down to the county level were reserved for Mongols. Fortunately, the Mongols' interest in maximizing revenue led them to encourage commerce and agricultural innovation. But in the end, inept Yuan rulers, palace intrigues, and a host of natural disasters prompted a number of peasant rebellions during the 1350s, and these in turn triggered the downfall of the much-loathed regime.[43]

The Mongol occupation was brought to a violent close in 1368 by a soldier of fortune and former monk named Zhu Yuanzhang, who took the imperial name Hongwu. Although the first commoner to become emperor since the founder of the Han dynasty 1500 years earlier, Hongwu had carefully cultivated the support of the Confucian elite and was recognized as having secured the Mandate of Heaven through victory over the foreign Mongols. As first emperor of the Ming dynasty, he immediately set about the restoration of traditional governmental practices, and more than any other individual 'he was responsible for the style and tone of life that characterized China into modern times'.[44] With the advent of the Ming, political power was further concentrated in the hands of the emperor. During a 31-year reign, Hongwu took direct control of the administrative bureaucracy and instituted a programme designed to benefit men of common origin like himself. The emperor took personal charge of the army, encouraged elementary schooling at the village level, and scrutinized the work of important civil servants. Slavery was abolished and large estates were confiscated and redistributed to the poor by the government. The emperor also ordered a survey of the land and several censuses of the population. The information gathered proved invaluable in terms of assessing taxes. Under the second Ming emperor, Yongle (1403–24), the capital was moved from

Nanjing in central China to Beijing in the north, where the Mongols had established their base of operations, and it was under successive Ming emperors that the walls, temples and palaces of the great imperial capital were built.[45] Yongle's palaces and temples in Beijing easily rivalled the grandeur of Louis XIV's later efforts at Versailles.

Despite these accomplishments, the first Ming emperor was a man haunted by fear of conspiracy, and over the course of his long reign royal paranoia resulted in the deaths of tens of thousands of subordinates.[46] Thus the despotic and arbitrary nature of the office was brought home to all observers during the second half of the fourteenth century. Also in evidence by the early fifteenth century was a new insularity and distrust of all foreigners. For while the emperor sponsored the seven overseas expeditions of Zheng He, he also denied his subjects the opportunity to establish contact with foreigners outside officially sanctioned trade links. The emperors commissioned a massive rebuilding of the great northern wall as a barrier against the perennially troublesome northern nomads, and in general a defensive posture was adopted with respect to the wider world. A Mongol raider captured and killed the emperor Zhengtong during a clash in 1449, and Mongol raiding expeditions continued to pose a threat well into the sixteenth century. Along the coast, the Mongol decision to abandon large-scale naval defences led to an increase in Japanese piracy and interruption of trade with the West. Personal factors also created problems. While the first Ming emperor was an able manager of men, later rulers were dominated by factions at court and by intriguing eunuchs in the palace.[47] Enormous defensive projects like the 3000-mile Great Wall undermined the fiscal stability of the regime, and while relatively low tax demands were welcomed by the peasantry, the central government rarely had enough funds to carry out its responsibilities.

Several of the Ming emperors were excessively cruel and arbitrary men. In a famous account of one sixteenth-century imperial official, Hai Rui (1514–87), who dared to rebuke the emperor Jiajing (r. 1521–67), it was reported that the brave man arrived at the palace with his own coffin, fully expecting the emperor to order his immediate execution. In the event the emperor, informed of the minister's actions, forgave the bureaucrat for his insubordination.[48] Still, there was little opportunity to influence errant monarchs. Jiajing was not alone in his preference for inordinate periods of seclusion from his chief ministers. In the worst example of executive indolence and neglect, the emperor Tianqi (r. 1620–27) handed over power to the palace eunuch Wei Zhongxian (1568–1627). The royal favourite proceeded to carry out brutal purges of reform-minded officials and filled top posts with his own sycophants.[49] The continued abuse of the civil service by eunuchs and palace insiders, together with the failure of the censorate to remedy the problem, led to a situation at the start of the seventeenth century where many qualified men refused to enter official office.[50]

A fateful combination of peasant rebellions in the northwest and a new aggressive neighbour to the north brought the Ming period to a close in 1644. When domestic rebels captured the capital city in that year, the last Ming emperor hanged himself in the palace grounds. A frontier general loyal to the Ming invited the northern Manchus to join him in suppressing the rebels, but the outsiders, who had won the support of many Chinese fighters disillusioned by Ming military incompetence, took the opportunity to claim the imperial throne for themselves.[51] Like the Mongols, the Manchu Qing were foreigners from the north who never constituted more than a tiny minority of the total Chinese population. The new emperors kept special garrisons of Manchu troops posted outside the major cities, but unlike their much-loathed Mongol predecessors, the Manchu respected and encouraged Chinese scholar-bureaucrats to continue their monopoly of the administrative apparatus. Governing for over 250 years, the Manchu supported traditional Chinese institutions and allowed local government to remain in Chinese hands. Despite their status as outsiders, the Qing emperors were able to secure for themselves Son of Heaven status thanks to their skilful cultivation of the Confucian ethic, their achievement in handling military threats from the northwest, and their success in expanding the boundaries of the empire through the annexation of Tibet, Xinjiang, Mongolia and Manchuria.

True to the pattern established by most imperial dynasties, for the first 150 years of the Qing period the usurpers provided China with good government under the leadership of dedicated and competent emperors. The new rulers assumed the historic title of Son of Heaven and its attendant responsibilities, but in addition the Manchu claimed for themselves universal power thanks to two highly militant and non-Chinese conceptions of rulership. The first involved the idea of Inner Asian khanship, associated with military activity, slave ownership and lineage-based support. The second was the Buddhist notion of a wheel-turning king, a religious leader who by action in this life moves the wheel of time and advances the created order towards salvation. Both of these concepts gave to the Qing monarchy a deeper association with the right order of despotic government.[52]

Two of the early monarchs enjoyed exceptionally long reigns: Kangxi (1662–1722) and Qianlong (1736–95). Population continued to grow under the new dynasty, especially after the introduction of the American sweet potato which allowed the Chinese to cultivate hilly areas outside of the traditional rice growing lowlands. Domestic peace was secured, and the appeal of Chinese culture and Chinese products in the West remained insatiable. Doubtless the most remarkable of the Qing emperors was Kangxi, whose 61-year reign was contemporary with Louis XIV's tenure in France and whose physical and mental abilities were unique in any age. Military leader, patron of the arts and poet, student of Latin under Jesuit tutors, familiar with the latest thinking in mathematics, science and western technology, the emperor also corresponded with European monarchs, including the pope.[53] Kangxi's reign was clearly exceptional in terms of careful executive rule, and his many campaigns of military expansion were, unlike Louis XIV's, largely successful. The emperor defeated rebels in the south and brought Taiwan under imperial control by 1683. After defeating the Russians in a conflict over the Amur River valley in 1689, China signed its first treaty with a European nation, one that acknowledged the emperor's claims to the lands in question.

Just as Versailles provided the grand setting for Louis' court, so too the Forbidden City in Beijing was a striking reminder of the emperor's unrivalled position in Chinese society. Walled, moated and heavily guarded, beyond the sight and sound of ordinary subjects, the emperor carried out his charge in an environment where symbolism and protocol were of the utmost importance. The emperor wore red while his officials wore black; he alone faced south while subordinates faced north. The characters of the royal personal name were never written, while all references to the Son of Heaven in official documents were carefully placed above the rest of the lines on each page. Temples were built in honour of the emperor, and all subjects performed the traditional kowtow in the imperial presence. The term *sheng* (sacred) was often applied to everything about the ruler, while his physical separation from his subjects reinforced the aura of superiority inherent in the imperial person.[54]

In the end, however, Manchu fidelity to Confucian precedent and tradition would prove a liability in the face of Europe's dynamic expansion. Stability became a synonym for opposition to innovation and economic progress; change was eschewed despite the many signals of Western imperial designs on China. And successful government needed the constant attention of skilled monarchs. On a typical day, the ritual duties of the emperor were combined with an enormous round of civil and military business. Towards the end of his long life, the emperor Kangxi reflected on the burdens of executive power in the world's most populous monarchy.

> A minister can enter or retire from government service as he pleases, but the emperor has no end to his work ... Some hold the theory that the emperor should attend to only very important affairs and leave the routine to the officials. I do not agree with this theory. For a tiny mistake in a little thing may give troubles to the whole country and a moment's carelessness may bring unhappiness to people of hundreds of generations.[55]

In the early nineteenth century, population pressures and rising peculation in the civil service led to a gradual breakdown of fiscal administration. By mid-century the combined impact of foreign imperialists, domestic rebels and crises over the succession sapped the regime of much of its strength.

In 1514, the first Europeans to establish oceanic trade contact with China landed at the southern city of Guangzhou (Canton). These Portuguese merchants were eager to carry on a regularized relationship with the empire, but before any formal trade links could be secured, the westerners were first required to disabuse themselves of any notions of equality with their celebrated hosts. The Chinese imperial understanding of proper relations with other countries was based solidly within the Confucian hierarchical paradigm. According to the six-teenth-century Jesuit missionary Matteo Ricci (1552–1610), 'the extent of their kingdom is so vast, its borders so distant, and their utter lack of knowledge of a trans-maritime world is so complete that the Chinese imagine the whole world as included in their kingdom.'[56]

Just as the Chinese social order was firmly tiered, so too the community of global kingdoms was ordered vertically. China was the centre of the world, the Middle Kingdom, and anyone outside this privileged culture was *ipso facto* a barbar-ian. Hence the origins of the imperial tribute system, whereby those seeking trade relations with China had first to present gifts to the emperor in a highly formalized ritual. While presenting their offerings, foreigners were required to perform the kowtow, prostrating themselves before the Son of Heaven while acknowledging the superiority of the Middle Kingdom. If trading rights were then granted, the imperial government alone set the terms. Most often these included the restriction of westerners to specific areas (what were called factories) in the city of Guangzhou, and the con-duct of all business with the government-approved guild known as the Cohong.[57]

The three rulers who reigned between 1662 and 1796 were each able and conscientious monarchs who consistently placed public affairs ahead of personal pleasure. The Qing continued the Ming indifference to naval affairs, but due to the fact that the Japanese shoguns, for reasons of their own, forbade their subjects from sailing or supporting a navy after 1636, the Chinese enjoyed a respite from the piratical attacks of the previous two centuries. The eighteenth century was an era of great commercial expansion in China, as revenues from the export of tea, porcelains and silk to Europe allowed the Qing to moderate taxes on land and dedicate funds to internal improvements. Efforts were undertaken to alleviate some of the rural distress experienced by a burgeoning population during the late Ming, including the repair of dykes, canals, irrigation systems and roads. Visitors were enormously impressed by the grandeur and cultural sophistication of the Qing state, while from afar Europe's enlightened *philosophes* marvelled at a successful polity which lacked the twin 'oppressions' of revealed religion and a hereditary aristocracy. 'Although the emperor's subjects always prostrate themselves before him as if he were a God', wrote Voltaire, 'still this does not prove his government to be despotic and arbitrary.' For Voltaire, 'if ever there was a state in which the life, honour, and fortune of the subject was under the protection of the laws, it is that of China'.[58] Even the priests of the Society of Jesus (Jesuits), admitted to the Qing court as scientific and technical advisors, were careful to adapt themselves to indigenous customs and ritual traditions.

However the enormous pressure of population growth, booming from 100 to 200 million in the century after 1650, and more than doubling again by 1850, made even the best efforts of the imperial government to improve the quality of life for its subjects very difficult indeed. Whereas industrial England at mid-century had a population of some 7 million, agrarian China embraced 410 million. The Qing dynasty was totally unprepared to deal with the problem of maintaining such numbers without substantial increases in productivity at every level of the economy, increases now beginning to take place in Western Europe thanks largely to the advent of large-scale industrial manufacture. As pressure on available lands intensified during the course of the eighteenth century, family plots were reduced in size until reaching the point where a single poor growing season spelled famine. Under such conditions, the bargaining power of tenant farmers decreased. Ambitious landlords were able to call in loans or impose a harsh sharecropping scheme, with one result being the acceleration of an ever-widening gap between rural landlords and peasant labourers. Ominously, many of the oppressed – and the dispossessed – in the countryside turned to the secret societies and cults which had kept alive early resentment against a foreign dynasty. Peasant revolts became more commonplace in the 1790s, ending over a century of domestic peace and signalling a deep crisis in the social fabric.

In addition to these challenges on the economic front, problems within the imperial civil service made the work of the emperor more complicated. At the start of the dynasty the Qing emperors had paired Manchus with Chinese officials in the same office in an effort to neutralize potential power blocks. And until the middle of the nineteenth century, hardworking monarchs had effectively curbed the influence of court eunuchs and empresses. But by the close of the eighteenth century, just as Europe's power was expanding in Asia, the Qing government was beset by increasing levels of internal corruption. Imperial funds dedicated for state projects and essential public works were diverted into the pockets of powerful local families. Military preparedness declined and armaments were not updated. The examination system was increasingly beset by cheating, favouritism and bribe-taking on the part of examiners. The overall effectiveness of the imperial system, now confronted by ill-mannered Western 'barbarians' who were unwilling to acknowledge their tributary status before the Son of Heaven, declined precipitately in the 50 years after 1800.

Something of this unhappy transformation in power relations between the Qing and the Western monarchs can be deduced from two imperial dispatches to the British monarch, the first addressed to King George III in 1793 and the second to Queen Victoria in 1839. In 1793 the monarch's representative, Lord Macartney, had requested equality of diplomatic representation with the Qing and free trade privileges for British merchants. The Qianlong emperor consoled George III for 'the lonely remoteness of your island, cut off from the world by intervening wastes of sea' but there would be no recognition of equality or any broadening of trade rights for barbarian intruders. The king of England was, however, applauded for his 'respectful spirit of submission', a clear indication of the emperor's traditional approach to foreign relations.[59] The letter is undergirded by a tone of moral and material superiority which had for centuries been at the heart of the Chinese imperial world-view. The Middle Kingdom was self-sufficient and self-contained, and it was only the generous indulgence of the Son of Heaven which allowed limited trade at Canton. The westerners had nothing to teach China, nothing to trade except silver bullion and perhaps mechanical clocks for the elite.

Fifty years later, in the midst of another heated trade controversy, the message to Victoria was conciliatory and respectful. This new struggle involved the one commodity for which a Chinese market was at last receptive: opium. By 1838 an estimated 1 per cent of China's 400 million population were addicted to the powerful drug, and the Middle Kingdom's balance of trade was reversed, with silver now leaving the empire in payment for this one nefarious commodity. When the Qing emperor proscribed the import of opium (a product of British India) and in 1839 ordered his representative at Guangzhou, Lin Zexu, to destroy the existing stocks held by foreign traders, the British government responded with a military expedition complemented by naval gunboats. Overmatched in large part by the technological superiority of British forces, in 1842 the imperial government was obliged to accept the first in what was to become a series of humiliating 'unequal treaties'.

Ironically, just as the Qing emperors had finally broken the military power of the nomadic steppe peoples to the north (for centuries the principal source of danger to Chinese regimes), they were faced with an even more vehement challenge from the ocean-going westerners. With the lopsided conclusion of the first 'Opium War' (1839–42), the tributary status of the foreign barbarians was at an end, and from this point onward the Chinese emperor entered the community of monarchs, not even as an equal, but instead as a lesser luminary in a constellation of bright and ambitious European rulers. The Western success in opening imperial China to the merchants and missionaries of Europe greatly assisted in the eventual collapse of the 2000-year-old system of monarchical rule in less than half a century. The 'unequal treaties' (which were not abrogated until 1943) allowed foreign powers the right to build self-governing settlements for merchants, opened the coastline and inland waterways to foreign ships, allowed Christian missionaries to travel unhindered, and limited the customs duties that the imperial government could impose.[60] While foreign merchants extolled the merits of consumption and development, missionaries carried the message of individual equality before a personal God. The entire turn of events was nothing less than a crash course in a set of values directly antithetical to the ancient Confucian ideal, a model of the human condition and of the purpose of the state directed against the practice of two millennia, and the full force of this message is still at work in China at the start of the twenty-first century.

The dangerous combination of peasant unrest, brought about by the scarcity of land, increased levels of banditry, exploitation by landowners, taxation, official corruption and military defeat at the hands of the barbarian westerners, provided the backdrop to China's most costly civil war in its long history: the Taiping rebellion. Beginning in 1850 and raging for sixteen years, the rebellion took a greater toll in human life (20 million) than the combined deaths experienced around the globe during the First World War.[61] Originating in the south and led by a millenarian convert to Protestant Christianity, Hong Xiuquan, millions of desperate peasant rebels rejected their Confucian heritage and called for the establishment of the kingdom of God on earth. For the rebels, such a goal would entail the end of the gentry landholding class and the subsequent redistribution of property along communal lines. The rebels also called for educational and social equality for women. Not for the last time in modern Chinese history would a foreign ideology find itself coupled with traditional peasant grievances to spur revolutionary action. Taking Nanjing as their capital in 1853 and on the offensive until 1856, the Taiping rebels were in the end defeated by imperial forces, but not without help from Western governments in the form of loans, modern weapons, and even the employment of some European and American commanders by the imperial army.

In the aftermath of the rebellion, new and greater concessions were made to the westerners, including complete freedom of movement for missionaries throughout China, foreign supervision of imperial customs, grants to foreign governments of legal jurisdiction over their nationals living in China (extraterritoriality), the opening of additional ports to trade, and the legalization of the sale of opium. Subsequent tensions between the dynasty and European powers led in 1860 to a joint British and French expeditionary force which seized the imperial capital and burned the emperor's summer palace. By the final decade of the nineteenth century, 90 ports had been opened to some 300,000 European and American traders and missionaries, while foreign diplomatic missions, long rejected by the Chinese emperor, were now imposed on the Manchu court. Urban centres at Hong Kong and Shanghai were completely under the direction of foreign governments, and steam-powered European gunboats along the great Yangtze river protected the commercial interests of the non-Chinese merchants.

At a time when Europe and America's industrialization was well underway and when Asian powers like Japan were fast embracing the model of Western modernization, China's leaders had become more myopic and conservative. In the judgement of one scholar, the Qing dynasty was too weak militarily to protect itself against foreign aggression, but simultaneously 'too strong culturally to surrender political initiative to Western-oriented modernizers' within the bureaucracy.[62] The Middle Kingdom was rapidly orbiting out towards the periphery of great-nation status, its monarchical establishment failing to demonstrate the historic claim to govern in the name of all Chinese. Further military defeats at the hands of Russian, French and Japanese opponents resulted in the evaporation of influence in Southeast Asia, loss of control over the island of Formosa, and the recognition of Korean 'independence' under Japanese auspices. For the first time since the seventeenth century, the Koreans were freed from the obligation of paying tribute as a satellite of the Middle Kingdom.

The military losses to the despised Japanese represented a

particularly painful blow to Chinese imperial pride. For in 1853 Japan, like China, had been humbled and bullied by the military might of the West. Now only 40 years later, the Japanese had somehow managed to appropriate the secrets of Western military technology in a successful effort to acquire great power status. Only China remained immobilized, seemingly incapable of expelling the foreigners or understanding the nature and challenges of a modern economy. To many Chinese, reformers and traditionalists alike, the emperor's concessions to the barbarians were strong evidence that the Mandate of Heaven had been withdrawn. Secret societies were once again active in the effort to overthrow the foreign Manchu. A reform movement, receptive to westernization but hoping to link new ideas and techniques with the traditional monarchical order, had a brief moment of success in 1898 when the young emperor Guangxu lent a sympathetic ear. During the summer of 1898 Guangxu issued 40 reform decrees covering such matters as education, technology, police administration and the economy.[63] But conservative elements within the imperial household, led in particular by the empress dowager Cixi, successfully undermined the whole effort, banishing or executing reform-minded officials and returning to the path of intransigence. With the connivance of senior military leaders, Cixi had the emperor placed under house arrest and declared herself regent.

So thorough was the reaction that by the opening of the new century, Western-educated Chinese students and other exiles were obliged to work for fundamental social, political and economic change from their temporary homes in Japan and America. When another Western coalition crushed the anti-foreign Boxer rebels and occupied Beijing in 1900, the instability and intellectual bankruptcy of the monarchy, a monarchy now seen to be in subordination to the forces of Western imperialism, was brought into sharp relief. The empress dowager now desperately reversed course and attempted to rapidly modernize the government and centralize power in Beijing. Ministers now donned business suits and the military adopted Western-style uniforms. Professional associations were encouraged in the cities and calls for greater self-government at the local level were heard. In 1905, shortly before her death, the empress dowager promised the adoption of constitutional monarchy and sent a series of missions overseas to study arrangements in Germany, Japan and England. Perhaps most significantly, modern schools were established, and in 1905 the Manchus abolished the 2500-year-old imperial examination system. With one stroke the enormously influential tradition of scholar-bureaucrats was brought to an inglorious close in the face of domestic disillusionment and Western encroachment. What replaced it, an amalgam of Chinese and Western thought, only served to further destabilize the old regime.

A number of local revolts against the Manchu, fomented largely by secret societies, had taken place after 1900, and in 1911 these disturbances culminated with the defection of the regime's top military commanders. On 12 February 1912 the last of the Manchu emperors, a six-year-old boy named Puyi, abdicated. Replaced by a Western-style republic initially under the presidency of the westernized civilian Sun Yat-sen (1866–1925), the world's longest monarchical system came to an end. The civilian leader of the newly declared republic was unable to hold power for long, however. Disgruntled military commanders and regional landlords were the real force behind the collapse of the Manchu in 1911, and by March 1912 Sun Yat-sen had resigned the presidency to a former imperial army official, Yuan Shikai.

Yuan favoured Western-style science, military technology and administrative reform, but he was less than enthusiastic about Western-style representative government, democracy and egalitarianism. By the following year, Sun Yat-sen was in exile in Japan. Yuan's subsequent attempt to make himself the new emperor of China was met by revolts in the countryside. Yuan died in 1916 and his military subordinates divided the country into regional power bases. The turbulent era of regional warlord government was underway, with all sides ignoring the authorities in Beijing. In just under one century, imperial China had ceased to be the centre of the known universe. In abjuring the heritage of Confucianism with the abolition of imperial examinations, republican China was left without indigenous intellectual resources upon which to build a new society; in failing to respond to the incursions of the Western imperialists, the emperors had failed to uphold their principal charge. Sun Yat-sen's attempt to graft Western political institutions on a political culture with no experience in self government found few supporters among the landholding elite. Their day of reckoning would come in another 30 years.

In the end, both the demographic problem and the lopsided encounter with the West secured the termination of the imperial order. The peace imposed by the Manchu after their successful conquest in 1644 had facilitated rapid economic growth throughout the Middle Kingdom. This in turn was the main engine of an unprecedented growth in population, from an estimated 200 million in the mid-eighteenth century to over 400 million a century later. Migration to marginal lands, more intensive cultivation, the introduction of new crops like potatoes, sweet potatoes and peanuts: none of these measures was able to lift an expanding subject people out of the grinding cycle of poverty as the nineteenth century progressed. Repeated humiliation at the hands of Western powers, together with an unwillingness to adjust traditional cultural forms in favour of Western economic and industrial models, placed the Manchu emperors in an untenable position. The failure of imperial leadership had for centuries been the signal for a change in dynasty, the establishment of a new Mandate of Heaven under rulers who would revitalize China's claim to global primacy. In the twentieth century, this time-tested pattern was no longer sufficient; having been denied the luxury of insularity, China would struggle to regain its autonomy without the aid of its emperors.

SACRED SYMBOLS IN JAPAN

As the seventh largest country in the world in terms of population (123 million) and boasting one of the most dynamic economies in the global community, the fact that modern democratic Japan maintains the world's longest-surviving monarchical dynasty is a point of some significance. Located just 120 miles from the southern tip of Korea, early Japan was insulated from larger political difficulties on the Asian mainland for centuries, and this fact of geography facilitated the development of an indigenous political culture where the monarch, while never challenged by a rival dynasty, nonetheless rarely exercised direct political power. Japan consisted of four main islands and over a thousand small volcanic islands whose total land area roughly equals the state of California in the United States; the institution of monarchy first emerged on the largest of the four main islands, Honshu, some time during the sixth century CE.

Prior to this time, early Japanese society was dominated by warlike clans or *uji*, groups of families related by blood and venerating a common ancestral deity. Each of these hundreds of clans was dominated by a small warrior aristocracy. In the eighth century, when the first Japanese written records emerge, one-third of the nobility claimed Korean or Chinese descent, indicating a strong level of cultural contact with the mainland over a number of centuries. By this time Buddhism had also made its imprint on Japanese society, providing an other-worldly perspective missing from the indigenous Shinto animistic worship of gods and spirits in nature. Still, the people of early Japan retained much that was unique within their own island culture, and nowhere was this more evident than in the political realm.[64]

The leadership of each clan unit was vested in one family on a hereditary basis, and the leader was both a military chieftain and a priest. In a mountainous land where only 7 per cent of the countryside was under regular cultivation, centralized political authority was absent. Building upon widespread Shinto beliefs, the clan which first claimed religious and political hegemony over all others dominated the broad plain of Yamato in the southeast corner of Honshu and traced its ancestry to the sun goddess Amaterasu. According to Japanese legend, the current emperor is a direct descendant of Jinmu, the 'first emperor', who in turn was descended from the sun goddess. Ancient Shinto religious thought holds that the sun goddess first created the Japanese islands and then brought the rest of the material world into existence. Tradition dates this reign, and the beginning of empire, to 660 BCE, but in fact it was centuries later, most likely in the fifth century CE that the Yamato ruling elite first asserted its hegemony over its neighbours, and it was only through victory in battle that the Yamato won recognition from other chieftains.[65]

During the course of the seventh and eighth centuries, the government sent a number of embassies to the sophisticated Tang court in China. The Yamato had already borrowed heavily from China, embracing the Chinese script in the fifth century, employing Chinese scribes in a nascent bureaucracy, and adopting Buddhism as the official religion of the Yamato domains in the late sixth century. One result of these extended contacts was the espousal of a governmental reform programme designed to reshape the Japanese monarchy according to the Tang imperial model. In a decree known as the Taika Reform Edict (645), the Yamato ruler undertook to found an autocratic monarchical system. The emperor was now to be acknowledged as the divinely appointed ruler of Japan, exercising absolute power and claiming ownership of all land in the kingdom. He also reaffirmed his status as Shinto high priest, thereby combining supreme religious authority with newfound political primacy.[66]

It is worth noting in this context that Japanese monarchs, like their Chinese counterparts, faced no independent – and potentially rival – religious authorities. Both pope and sovereign, sultan and caliph, these eastern monarchs embodied the highest religious and secular authority in their kingdoms.[67] The Japanese monarch was the supreme priest of Shintoism in the worship of the sun god and other important deities. Indeed in one official letter to their Chinese counterparts, the Yamato styled themselves 'emperors of the rising sun'. A Confucian-oriented bureaucracy – complete with civil service examinations – was envisioned, plans for a peasant conscript army were drawn up, and Buddhist monks spread the message of obedience to strong monarchy and a unified state. A permanent capital was established at Nara in 710 and over the next a hundred years Chinese-inspired practices, including currency and coinage modelled after the Chinese system, emphasized the elevated status of the Japanese emperor. Throughout this period, Confucian ideals informed most of the governing priorities of the ruling elite.

In reality, however, the Taika Reform Edict did little to alter the status of powerful and semi-autonomous aristocrats in the countryside. Lacking both China's material resource base and the tradition of strong centralized government, Japanese monarchical rule was ill-suited to the clan-based regional leadership style of the past.[68] While Chinese cultural and political forms dominated life in the capital until the ninth century, a hierarchy of provincial clan heads continued to enjoy great autonomy under the emperors, and Japan remained largely a rural land where the overwhelming majority of the peasant population knew little of the priorities of the court. The emperor continued to be respected in a ritual fashion as a divine figure by most Japanese, but his sacred status paradoxically placed him well above the everyday management of temporal affairs. During the seventh and eighth centuries, eight females occupied the imperial throne, but otherwise the office has been dominated by males, and the emperor was viewed as the father of the Japanese.[69] Fatherhood did not entail authority, however, for by 830 political and military leadership had been appropriated by one of the leading families of the court, the Fujiwara.

The Fujiwara successfully married into the royal family, managed the extensive royal estates, served as regents for many child emperors, and controlled the chief offices of state. Other powerful court families like the Fujiwara used their influence to buy up enormous tracts of land near the capital, now situated 30 miles north of Nara at Heian (modern Kyoto). In the northern and eastern parts of Japan, meanwhile, warriors continued to struggle against earlier inhabitants known as Ainu, and the fighting discipline associated with the warrior or samurai class set these groups outside the formal control of the emperor in Kyoto. Lands under the direction of distant military bands were effectively tax exempt, and while the emperor's theoretical supremacy was never successfully called into question, in fact a full-blown feudal system not unlike that which had emerged earlier in Europe became the norm throughout Japan. Increasing emphasis was placed on the lord–vassal relationship at the local and provincial levels while lands and tax powers were gradually denied the imperial family at Kyoto.

During the Kamakura period (1192–1333) when the Minamoto clan dominated the scene from their military base on the Kanto plain, the Japanese emperor was no more than a symbolic figurehead performing ceremonial and religious functions while banditry and general lawlessness became the norm throughout the islands; even Buddhist monasteries employed armed bands for protection in a strife-torn society. By the eleventh century, private rights had clearly superseded public obligations and localism usurped the prerogatives of central authority. For the next 800 years, Japanese monarchs reigned but did not rule. The fact that outright usurpation of the throne did not occur, however, is testimony to the strength of the royal claim to hereditary priestly leadership within the island kingdom.[70] Indeed unlike the Chinese model, where usurpation was interpreted as the legitimate transfer of the Mandate of Heaven to a more worthy leader, in Japan belief in the divine descent of the emperor and the importance of unbroken succession guaranteed the survival of the monarchy throughout the difficult medieval centuries.[71]

In a politically fragmented warrior culture where family honour and the military tradition constituted the benchmarks of personal value, and where failure or retreat merited ritual suicide, efforts to substantiate the hegemonic claims of the monarchy were futile. The peasantry was reduced to servile status, bound to the land which they worked and treated as little more than personal property by the military elite. Ever shifting court factions, each attempting to gain influence over the emperor, engaged in chronic civil wars whose only result was to inflict enormous suffering on the peasantry. In the early fourteenth century, one of the branches of the ruling family revolted against the Minamoto and succeeded in establishing the Ashikaga shogunate (1338–1573). The emperor at the time of the successful revolt refused to recognize the Ashikaga and was subsequently driven from his capital in Kyoto. The power of regional warlords grew without check during this period, while their samurai retainers were offered land in return for military service. The nadir of central authority occurred during the period of the Onin War (1467–77), when rival heirs to the Ashikaga shogunate reduced the imperial capital of Kyoto to rubble. Soon after this debacle, Japan was divided into almost 300 tiny states, each one governed and misgoverned by provincial warlords known as *daimyos*.[72]

Only with the advent of Portuguese penetration into Japan beginning in 1543 were steps taken to reverse the centuries-old pattern of local dominion and endemic samurai warfare. The foreigners, with their innovative gunpowder technology, enjoyed an enormous weapons advantage over the Japanese feudal cavalry. Muskets and cannons, quickly adopted by the Japanese, brought an abrupt close to the samurai warfare long associated with a feudal system. The process of centralization began under a successful general named Toyotomi Hideyoshi and continued under the preponderant power of the Tokugawa Shogunate (1603–1867). The militaristic values which had dominated elite culture did not disappear at the opening of the seventeenth century, but the Tokugawa were able to enforce a broad peace while also banishing European Christian missionaries and restricting trade with the West to Dutch merchants in the tightly controlled port of Nagasaki. Native Japanese were forbidden to travel overseas, the construction of ocean-going vessels was prohibited, and shipping was restricted to the coastal trade. The Tokugawa inaugurated a period of Japanese isolation that would last until the middle of the nineteenth century, when once again Western penetration would spur a radical reform of governing institutions.

Tokugawa military rule, referred to as the *bakafu* (tent government), brought about the pacification of the country and laid the groundwork for 250 years of population growth, modest domestic economic expansion, and the introduction of a money economy. Between 1700 and 1850 Japan 'was more peaceful, more equitably fed, and more secure than any other society in the world'.[73] The social values stressed by this military rule included discipline, loyalty, endurance and respect for one's natural superiors. Hideyoshi claimed to be of Fujiwara descent and sought legitimation from the powerless emperor Ogimachi (1516–93). The imperial court had fallen into its worst condition during the era of civil war, but the Tokugawa were careful to revive imperial finances and buttress imperial prestige. Although the emperor remained secluded in Kyoto during the centuries of Tokugawa rule, the shogun recognized the ultimate source of his legitimacy in the person of the monarch. By seeking imperial approval for political power won on the battlefield, Hideyoshi reaffirmed the centrality of the emperor to Japan's political order and prepared the way for the restoration of royal power which occurred three centuries later.[74]

With peace restored throughout the country, the traditional military services of the samurai elite were no longer needed, and the Tokugawa shoguns insisted that all important feudal lords spend a portion of the year in Edo, where they and their families would be under the watchful eye of the rulers. The Japanese did not abandon the belief that the emperor, now living in seclusion in Kyoto, was in theory the supreme political and religious authority, but the Tokugawa family successfully portrayed itself as the viceregal administrative and military instrument of the god-emperor. No feudal lords were permitted to approach the imperial court or the person of the emperor without the permission of the shogun.[75] By the opening of the nineteenth century, class lines in Japan were beginning to blur as prosperous merchants vied with the increasingly idle warrior class for prestige and influence. Social tensions, brought about by fundamental economic change and fuelled by resentment at Tokugawa unwillingness to engage the outside world, prepared the way for a remarkable transformation in the role of the monarch during the second half of the nineteenth century.

In 1853 the American naval commander Matthew Perry arrived with a powerful fleet near Tokyo and threatened to bombard the city unless the Japanese opened up trade with America. American penetration of the Japanese main islands, begun the following year, was quickly followed by Dutch, Russian and British encroachment. Anti-Tokugawa clan leaders, awakened to the fact of their technological, and especially naval, inferiority and finding the only solution to be in the creation of a strong central government, turned to the traditional monarchy as the rallying point for modernization, an alternative and ancient source of political legitimacy.[76] Between 1858 and 1865 attacks on foreigners escalated. Ironically the emperor Komei counselled the shogunate to strengthen defences in an effort to maintain Japan's isolation; at this moment the monarchy took the side of defending the status quo against the corrupting influence of the outside barbarians.

Against the considerable opposition of the Tokugawa shogun and the emperor, then, economic, military and political modernization became the rallying cry of those samurai elites and urban commercial leaders who were determined not to allow Western domination of the country to proceed unchecked. Turning from the shogunate to the imperial office for support, a new monarchical regime called 'Meiji' or 'Enlightened Rule' was inaugurated after the death of the emperor Komei in January 1867.[77] Leaders of the four most important feudal families turned over their estates to the new 15-year-old emperor Mutsuhito (1852–1912) in a gesture of insurgent nationalism. In a memorial addressed to the emperor, the clan leaders maintained that they were returning to the Son of Heaven what had originally been his 'so that a uniform rule may prevail throughout the empire. Thus the country will be able to rank equally with the other nations of the world.'[78] In July 1869 an imperial decree ordered all other landed elites to make the same submission. In return these aristocrats would become provincial governors under the crown; private political authority in the countryside, the norm for over a millennium, was now defined as usurpation and effectively brought to a close.

Under Mutsuhito, the 122nd monarch in a line from Jinmu, calls for the overthrow of the Tokugawa shogunate intensified. Seeing the scale of the opposition to his family's rule and unwilling to plunge the country into civil war, Tokugawa Yoshinobu abolished the family office – and eight centuries of military government – in November 1867. Establishing a new capital in Tokyo (formerly Edo), the emperor enjoyed enough support from disgruntled samurai warriors, clan leaders and urban commercial interests to defeat the hold-out troops of the now defunct shogunate. There ensued three decades of unprecedented reform, catapulting feudal Japan into the industrial age. Feudalism was officially abolished in 1871, a national conscript army based on the German model was created, and Western military advisors were recruited in order to assist with the building of a modern navy. State-sponsored and mandatory elementary education was adopted, the Gregorian calendar was introduced, a representative system of local government was created, and a robust commercial and industrial revolution began, the first of its kind in the non-western world. No other non-European nation responded as quickly and as effectively as Japan to the threat of Western imperialism.

The ideological components of the revolution which occurred in Japan in 1868 centred on two key elements: nationalism and *tenno*-ism.[79] The historic uniqueness of Japanese civilization was stressed while the monarchy was held up as the embodiment of the nation's highest ideals, its closest bond with earlier times. There was no establishment of direct imperial rule in 1868, but instead the emperor's authority was gradually enhanced as anti-Tokugawa reformers claimed a mandate from the divine ruler. By linking the ancient institution of monarchy with the innovative programme of economic modernization and social change, reformers hoped to make change more palatable in traditionalist circles. Not the least of these changes involved the new national political institutions. After a series of delegations sent to Europe and the United States during the 1870s and 1880s returned with their suggestions for constitutional reform, in 1889 a new framework of government, reflecting the German imperial model, established a bicameral parliamentary structure with cabinet responsibility for national policy. The lower house or diet, elected on a restricted franchise which excluded 95 per cent of the adult male population, served as an advisory body to the government, but the emperor retained control over the military and named his chief ministers, all of whom served at the pleasure of the monarch. An upper house composed of former nobles and Meiji leaders rounded out the parliamentary system.

The first article of the new German-style constitution emphasized the centrality of the sacred monarch's role in the new government. Here it was stated plainly that 'The empire of Japan shall be reigned over and governed by a line of emperors unbroken for ages eternal.'[80] Ito Hirobumi, one of the principal authors of the new constitution, provided a commentary on the document which encapsulates the thinking of the Meiji reformers. The emperor, according to Hirobumi, 'is Heaven-descended, divine and sacred; he is pre-eminent above all his subjects. He must be reverenced and is inviolable. He is indeed to pay due respect to the law, but the law has no power to hold Him accountable to it.'[81] Unlike his predecessors, the Meiji emperor undertook a new public role designed to link the monarchy with the actions of the state. Reviewing troops, giving audiences to foreign envoys, presiding at various public awards ceremonies, placing his name on a large list of policy decrees, the emperor became the exclusive focus of national loyalty. At court, traditional dress was abandoned in favour of mandatory Western styles, and young Japanese eagerly embraced the idea of modernization in the service of the monarchy.

It is in this last idea – service to the tenno (lord of heaven) – that the uniqueness of Japan's drive towards modernization must be assessed. The revolution of 1868 was not a middle-class, bourgeois-inspired call for an individualistic and capitalist state along Western lines. Instead the reforming oligarchs who were responsible for the end of the shogunate continued to emphasize the virtues of obedience, loyalty and acquiescence in the service of one's superiors. In an imperial rescript on education issued by the emperor in 1890 – a document destined to be memorized by generations of schoolchildren down to 1948 – young Japanese were exhorted to 'offer yourselves courageously to the State; and thus guard and maintain the prosperity of Our Imperial Throne coeval with heaven and earth. So shall ye not only be Our good and faithful subjects, but render illustrious the best traditions of your forefathers.'[82] These values, it was hoped, would combine to shape a nationalist ideology unique in its association with the institution of monarchy.

The Meiji Restoration represented a unique combination of revolutionary economic and social change tied to a conservative view of political authority. And while the emperor at no time after 1867 personally directed the government on a day-by-day basis, he continued to legitimize and influence government by appointing key ministers and cabinet officers in the name of the crown. Increasingly the Meiji emperor conducted himself like a European monarch, 'appearing resplendent in

Western-style uniform, acting the part of both head of state and commander in chief'.[83] The long-standing sacerdotal role of the emperor was now complemented by an enhanced administrative and political one. Officially, the restored monarch and his three successors down to the present day have reigned as constitutional figureheads, but at key junctures before the Second World War they exercised considerable personal influence in affairs of state. Always respectful of the decisions made in accordance with constitutional procedure, the restored Japanese monarchs were also symbols of a social and moral tradition anchored in Shintoism, particularly those aspects of the faith connected with emperor worship.

Elevated to new heights during the final decades of the nineteenth century, the emperor fostered the development of a brand of nationalistic and patriotic sentiment that was unique in its Asian setting. The unqualified victory of centripetal over centrifugal tendencies clearly assisted the Japanese leadership in its efforts to avoid the imposition of semi-colonial status at the hands of the West. By 1900 the emperor, the tenno, was poised to lead a modern industrialized nation into the arena of global imperial competition. Interestingly, and very unlike the West, no great charismatic political leader rose to the forefront of Japanese politics during the frenetic period of industrialization and political reform. Instead, attention was directed towards the tenno as the key to Japan's emergence as a great power. And with a system of universal education which stressed loyalty to the emperor and duty to nation before individual freedom and personal accomplishment, popular commitment to the new expansionist agenda was exceptional.

Japan's defeat of China on the Korean peninsula in 1894, followed by an even more remarkable victory over Russia in 1905, placed the emperor's dominions at the forefront of global power at the beginning of the new century. In 1902 the government signed a military alliance with Britain, and when Japan annexed Korea outright in 1910 no Western power attempted to interfere. Two years later the Meiji emperor died and a year-long period of national mourning began. His successor, Crown Prince Yoshimoto, named his era Taisho, 'Great

Righteousness', but the new ruler was a serious disappointment as a national leader. Meiji's grandson Hirohito served as teenage regent for the ailing emperor, and during the First World War Japan successfully honoured its alliance with Britain by attacking and seizing German territories in China.[84] In the aftermath of this global conflict Japan sat as one of the victorious powers at the peace conference at Versailles. Assigned Germany's Pacific colonies as part of the overall settlement, the post-war Japanese government joined the League of Nations and focused its attention on economic opportunities throughout Asia.

In 1925 the government extended the franchise to include all males over the age of 25, but real power still lay with an oligarchic elite who linked economic progress with state power. Emperor Taisho died in 1926, and Hirohito began his reign with a keen interest in affairs of state. Growing wealth and rapid industrialization transformed the resource-poor islands into a unique society, one where the military continued to wield enormous authority under the emperor. In the Western capitalist democracies the armed forces had been placed under civilian authority, but in Japan the ministers of war and of the navy were required by the 1889 constitution to be active generals or admirals. These ministers reported not to the elected diet but to the emperor alone. Hirohito continued to hold ultimate political power in theory, and ministers who acted in his name exercised enormous influence on public policy despite the emergence of universal manhood suffrage. State-supported Shintoism emphasized the importance of obedience to those who acted on the emperor's behalf.

During the course of the 1930s the power and influence of the military over the national government increased dramatically. At the time of the Meiji Restoration, the population of the country numbered around 30 million; by 1940 there were 70 million Japanese, and the Great Depression of the 1930s made this growing population supportive of a government building programme focused on military priorities. In the autumn of 1931 Japanese troops took direct control over most of Manchuria, proclaiming an independent nation in 1932 and placing the last emperor of China, 'Henry' Pu-yi, on a new

Manchurian throne. In May 1932 a group of army officers murdered prime minister Inukai Tsuyoshi for his outspoken criticism of the Manchurian adventure, and while the military did not take direct control over the civilian government in Tokyo, officers like general Tojo Hideki repeatedly interfered with elected officials. Fearful lest Japan be excluded from sources of raw materials in an economic climate where global depression fuelled protectionism, in 1931 Japan's military had inaugurated a programme of brutal military expansion against China.

For the next decade, Emperor Hirohito passively acquiesced as the armed forces followed a deliberate policy of aggression and Pacific domination, what the Japanese leadership later referred to as the 'Greater East Asia Co-Prosperity Sphere'. The tenno became the symbol of Japanese fascism, of imperialist expansion and national destiny. When, in 1934–35, a professor of constitutional law at Tokyo's Imperial University named Minoke Tatsukichi spoke of the emperor as a mere 'organ' of the state, traditionalists forced him to resign his post in the upper house of peers. Minobe's books were banned and he narrowly escaped assassination in 1936. Such was the power of the military establishment which used the imperial office as the focus of nationalist and expansionist ideals.[85]

With the attack on Pearl Harbor, the militarists led by Tojo, now prime minister, gambled that by crippling the United States Navy in the Pacific, Americans would lack the resolve to fight a protracted war in the East while simultaneously engaged against Germany. The emperor supported the military's war plans, and during the course of the conflict he often appeared in public dressed in uniform. 'By reviewing troops, attending ceremonies, and seeing off departing servicemen, he not only symbolized the legitimacy of Japan's war but also lent imperial sanction to the conflict.'[86] In the end the decision to attack the US failed disastrously, and by August 1945 some 3 million Japanese had died in the war, one quarter of the nation's capital assets had been destroyed, and industrial production was at 10 per cent of the pre-war level. The bombing of Hiroshima and Nagasaki brought the emperor out of his passive political role. On 14 August Hirohito announced Japan's acceptance of all Allied terms for ending the war. Soldiers who had fought fanatically against all opponents, refusing to surrender irrespective of the odds, immediately obeyed the Son of Heaven's command. Given the ferocity of the resistance to allied approaches to the Japanese main islands, this cessation on order from Hirohito was a welcome conclusion to a brutal conflict which had, globally speaking, cost over 50 million lives.

By the terms of the surrender agreement, the Japanese empire was dissolved, the military was completely demobilized, state-supported Shintoism was abolished, and a new Western-style constitution was adopted, complete with an independent judiciary, bicameral legislature, security for individual rights, and voting rights for women. Seven of the top military leaders were tried, convicted of war crimes, and hanged, while most of the other top leaders were sentenced to long jail terms. Both the Soviets and the British wished to go one step further and try the emperor as a war criminal, but the American commander in Japan, General Douglas MacArthur, vigorously opposed this course of action. Writing to General Dwight D. Eisenhower, then chief of staff to President Harry Truman, in January 1946, MacArthur claimed that Hirohito's 'connection with affairs of state up to the time of the end of the war was largely ministerial and automatically responsive to the advice of his councilors'. Even more importantly, advised MacArthur, the emperor remained an important symbol uniting all of Japan, and the work of reconstruction would be made much more difficult should he be indicted. 'Destroy him and the nation will disintegrate' and the ensuing resentment 'will unquestionably last for all measurable time. A vendetta for revenge will thereby be initiated whose cycle may well not be complete for centuries if ever.'[87] The emperor, in announcing Japan's capitulation to the allies, could be portrayed as having saved Japan from ultimate destruction and not as the focus of ultimate responsibility for the conflict.[88]

In December 1946 eleven of the fourteen imperial princes and their families lost their status and their wealth, but Hirohito remained in office.[89] Earlier, in January 1946, he had formally renounced his divine status. No longer to be regarded as a sacred figure, his role was reduced to one of constitutional fig-urehead. New school textbooks were introduced which por-trayed the emperor as a ceremonial head of state. But while the retention of the monarchical office, and of Hirohito in particu-lar, may have helped facilitate widespread acceptance of the terms of the peace in Japan, the emperor was not without his critics. Some blamed him for Japan's disastrous wartime expe-rience and called for an end to imperial institutions. To retain the emperor solely on the grounds of political expediency did not square with the call for genuine democratic reform. By the 1950s, however, most of the harshest criticism had abated as economic prosperity and political stability overshadowed the memories of war. Emperor Hirohito adjusted to his new status as symbol of a democratic people, successfully shedding him-self of traditional linkages with sacred status.

Under the new post-war constitution, the emperor became 'symbol of the State and of the unity of the people, deriving his position from the will of the people with whom resides sover-eign power'. When the Showa era finally came to a close with the death of Hirohito in January 1989, his son and heir Akihito acceded to the throne of one of the world's greatest economic powerhouses. The new reign era name Heisei, or 'Achieving Peace' reflected the exceptional status of the Japanese democ-ratic system in the global community. Unlike its Chinese coun-terpart, then, monarchy in Japan successfully weathered the upheavals of the twentieth century and entered the democratic age with the hereditary principle intact.

- Early Japan (until 710)
- Nara and Heian Periods (710 - 1192)
- Kamakura Period (1192 - 1333)
- Muromachi Period (1338 - 1573)
- Azuchi - Momoyama Period (1573 - 1603)
- Edo Period (1603 - 1868)
- Meiji Period (1868 - 1912)
- Taisho and Early Showa Period (1912 - 1945)
- Postwar Period (since 1945)

2 Benin (Nigerian) bronze plaque showing an *oba* (chief) with his retinue, *c.* 1600.

TWO

Monarchy without Manuscripts:
Sub-Saharan Africa and the Americas

THE ANCESTRAL FUNCTION IN AFRICA

It cannot be said that the enormous African continent, three and a half times the size of the United States, followed the more typical pattern of territorial, kingdom-based development that was so familiar to Asian and European peoples. At least one cannot speak of such a model of development south of the Sahara prior to the advent of expansive kingdoms in the savanna grassland region known as the Sudan (from the Arabic *Bilad al-Sudan* or 'the land of the black man') during the late ninth century. Given the diversity of Africa's topography and climate, languages and cultures, uniformity of political organization is not to be expected. Hampered by a wide range of parasitic diseases in the tropics and low-lying coastal areas, thin soils in the savanna or grasslands, and extensive mountains in the east, the peoples of Black Africa evolved varied lifestyles, languages, religious beliefs and forms of social control in a manner difficult to associate with any larger single pattern of civilization. Instead, political organization in sub-Saharan Africa was very often limited to the self-sufficient village level, and in parts of West Africa this model remained the norm well into the nineteenth century. Although there were a few important kingdoms and states a century ago, 'the greater part of the continent was occupied by a very large number of small independent communities ranging from the hunting bands of the Bushmen and the Pygmies to the tribal chieftaincies and the minor kingdoms to be found in almost every region'.[1]

Without serious threat from distant enemies or regular opportunities for overland trade, and living in conditions where the soil did not lend itself to high population densities, many Black Africans found no need to establish larger political units or what have come to be known as coercive states or kingdoms.[2] Central authority, definable frontiers, formal bureaucracy, a subject population – these attributes of typical state formation were unnecessary to the successful organization of hunting and gathering peoples, or to those who practised simple agriculture without the advantages of ploughs and draught animals. We must turn to political anthropologists for information at this point, for the peoples of sub-Saharan Africa did not develop systems of writing or formulate broadly based structures of law prior to the spread of Islam south of the great desert during the eighth century.[3] In general, for over two millennia authority was exercised most effectively at the village level, where the elders of extended family units (lineages) ruled in the name of a common ancestor.

These stateless or non-centralized societies were based on ideas of custom, kinship and cooperation where decision-making involved large networks of related persons. The concept of private property was unknown in such communities, and notions of individualism were subsumed under the larger needs of the lineage community. On occasion these stateless societies lived alongside formal territorial units throughout the sub-Saharan region. Indeed from the equatorial jungles southward, in lands dominated by Bantu-speaking peoples, a hunting and gathering existence remained the norm well after 1000. By way of contrast, today in post-colonial Africa, less than 1 per cent of the indigenous population continues to live in small hunting and gathering bands.

The incipient 'political' kingdoms in Africa after 900 most likely developed out of these family or kinship associations to include ever-wider circles of clan membership. Family in Africa included not only living members, but dead ancestors and unborn children as well. Groups of lineage lines, possibly in possession of iron weapons, would associate into larger clan units (what Western colonial powers referred to as tribes) for mutual protection and production. The king would normally be selected by a group of inner councillors from among the most adept military leaders. Primogeniture was rare in Africa, and succession often involved military struggle.[4] In most African kingdoms, the rulers did not seek to foster loyalties stronger than clan allegiances, but these clans were used successfully to build the great coalitions supporting the institution of ritual-based monarchy. The growth of trade led to new political economies where an unequal sharing of resources for the first time had a profound impact on Black African life. The first monarchies emerged in Africa – as in so many civilizations – as mechanisms for the management of human inequality.[5]

The role of polygyny in the solidification of royal power in Africa was paramount. While ordinary men might have several wives, monarchs normally sought to marry into most of the lineage groups under their direct authority. Sometimes these royal marriages would involve a single monarch with hundreds and even thousands of women. Obviously kings could never hope to engage in normal married relations with their brides, but royal harems produced vast numbers of future military and political leaders who symbolized the bond established between royalty and a particular lineage group.[6] As additional peoples were absorbed into a kingdom, royal marriage alliances provided one of the key factors in diffusing the resentment of the defeated party. In smaller kingdoms the royal court might consist of a couple of hundred individuals – wives, children, members of the military – who would provide for the basic needs of the monarch without becoming a burden to the wider community. At the end of the eighteenth century, perhaps half of the total population of the continent lived in kingdoms of a few thousand people.[7]

Not surprisingly, the majority of kings in sub-Saharan Africa were associated with divine power in the sense that they were ritual specialists who preserved ancestral practices.[8] While not gods in the traditional sense, African monarchs were first and foremost spiritual leaders who wielded the ancestral powers previously inherent in early lineage-group leaders. Performing the daily rites associated with his own people and directing the activities of other cults, the king was expected to preserve the spiritual well-being of his subjects while also defending them against outside aggressors. His conduct was always sanctioned by ancestors who served as intermediaries between the living and the life force which, emanating from God, permeated the natural world.[9] While individual leaders might be unexceptional, their office was an essential link between human rule and the spiritual governance of the universe. This was one reason why many African monarchs did not appear in public. It also explains why elderly or infirm monarchs were sometimes dismissed or even killed. Since the chief responsibility of the king was to intervene with the ancestors for the benefit of the community or kingdom, his inability to carry out this essential function disqualified him from continuing in such an exalted post. In the small kingdom of Ankole in East Africa, for example, the ailing monarch was expected to take poison prepared by his own spiritual advisors. The successful performance of ritual, therefore, has long been linked to the maintenance of political loyalty in African kingdoms.[10]

In addition to the archaeological record and the study of oral traditions, our knowledge of sub-Saharan Black Africa comes to us largely in the form of Muslim written accounts. Thanks to the trade routes established between North Africa and the Sudan beginning in the eighth century, Arab travellers and geographers recorded their impressions of Sudanic peoples in great detail.[11] The growth of African trade centres stimulated the formation of social and economic distinctions which cut across kinship lines and furthered the need for more formal models of political organization. It appears most likely that dominant groups within major clans forged the earliest states in the Sudan. The kingdom of Ghana was the first to emerge, serving as a crossroads between North Africa and the gold and ivory-producing regions in the grasslands to the south.[12]

The significance of African gold production to the monetarization of the medieval Mediterranean economy cannot be overestimated. After the mid-thirteenth century, African gold began to replace silver as Europe's main currency, and this accelerated the trend towards the organization of larger African kingdoms south of the Sahara.[13] Gold from Africa, for example, provided about one-quarter of the revenue of the Portuguese king at the start of the sixteenth century, and gold remained West Africa's most valuable export commodity until it was eclipsed by the trade in slaves around the year 1700.[14]

The first reference to Ghana in Arab sources is from the ninth-century writer al-Fazari. Subsequent writers spoke of a powerful monarchy organized around the collection of gold from peoples to the south and its exchange for salt and North African manufactured products.[15] Extending over 500,000 square kilometres between the Senegal and Niger rivers, the kingdom was the largest recorded empire in Africa. In the mid-eleventh century, the Spanish Muslim geographer al-Bakri gave an account of the monarchy in Ghana which portrayed the ruler as an autocrat of almost divine status. As supreme judge and head of an army of 200,000 men, some of whom may have been cavalry units, the king of Ghana (who was always from the Soninke people) enjoyed supremacy over a large number of lesser regional heads. He was a semi-divine figure who appointed and dismissed his chief officers at will.[16]

The Sudanic kingdom of Ghana reached the height of its power in the ninth and tenth centuries, and its kings appear to have maintained traditional religious structures despite contacts with the Arabs. In 1076, however, a Muslim conqueror overran the lands of Ghana and the leaders of all subsequent kingdoms in Sudan – Kanem (near Lake Chad), Takrur in the Senegal valley, Mali and Songhai – eagerly embraced the new faith. The net effect of the expansion of Islam into Sudanic Africa was to affirm the state's value and capacity to create the good society on earth. The Muslim world since the time of Muhammad had eagerly embraced the notion that the leader of the state, the caliph, must seek to create the conditions under which each Muslim can do God's will pursuant to salvation. This dynamic religious-political ideology helped to shape the course of political development in Africa for centuries.[17]

Like Ghana, each of these Sudanic monarchies based their coercive authority on the control of trade, whereas most non-African kings before 1500 anchored their power in the regulation of land and agriculture. Gold, ivory, ebony, pepper, kola (a stimulant) moved north across the desert while in exchange salt, dates, copper, glassware and clothing were transferred south. The kingdom of Mali traced its origins to the thirteenth-century warrior Sundiata, but the greatest of the kings of Mali, Mansa Musa (r. 1312–37), ruled over an empire of 40 million people and 400 towns. Known throughout the western world for his prodigious wealth, in 1324 Mansa Musa astonished fellow Muslims in Cairo with the extent of his wealth as the monarch passed through the city en route to the pilgrimage at Mecca. According to the fourteenth-century chronicler al-Omari, the king of Mali was 'the most important of the Muslim Negro kings; his land is the largest, his army the most numerous; he is the king who is the most powerful, the richest, the most fortunate, the most feared by his enemies and the most able to do good to those around him'.[18] Employing Spanish and Middle Eastern scholars, Mali's cities developed into centres of Islamic learning, with new mosques and Islamic schools to further literacy.[19]

Ghana, Mali (c. 1250–1400) and Songhai (c. 1460–1590) are often referred to as great empires by historians, but in truth these monarchies were no more consolidated than Charlemagne's late eighth-century Germanic dominions. In other words, the principal African Sudanic kingdoms are better described as loosely organized overlordships where local governing regions, led by lineage chiefs and village headmen, agreed to pay tribute and cooperate under the general direction of one monarch. Royal administrators were constantly pressed to maintain the allegiance of lineage chiefs, and success was normally contingent upon the personal dynamism of the individual monarch. As we have noted, with the one exception of Ghana the ruling elite in these kingdoms adopted Islam, but the vast majority of the subject population maintained their loyalty to traditional religious forms. Still this veneer of Islam at the top of the political structure served to lessen the cultural divide between clan groups within the respective empires. Monarchs who embraced Islam were of course eager to secure the obedience of their people, thus they 'generally patronized all their subjects' religious activities in an eclectic manner'.[20]

The Islamization of Sudan thus facilitated the sharing of values among a previously divided elite, while Muslim schools like the University of Sankore at Timbuktu provided educated administrators for the imperial households. At the height of Songhai power in the early sixteenth century, the Islamic state contained a majority of people who were non-Songhai in an empire stretching almost 1500 miles from east to west, yet government functioned effectively.[21] For 200 years the monarchs of Songhai descended from the general Alhaj Mohammed I, but their Islamicized state ruled over a myriad of clans and peoples. By and large commoners were little affected by the rise of empires within their midst, and court culture rarely imposed itself on the non-Muslim population. In addition, there was no single rule of law, no monopoly on the use of force, no clear administrative structure or formal bureaucracy in these African kingdoms. Perhaps most importantly, none of the Sudanic states established a clear rule of succession. Not unlike later Muslim (Mughal) rulers in India, repeated conflict among royal family members and members of the military nobility left these African states vulnerable to the forces of decay. When fellow Muslims from Morocco invaded Songhai in 1590 with an army of 4,000 men, the advantage of muskets and cannon proved decisive over some 10–20,000 Songhai cavalry troops and archers. By the mid-seventeenth century, the era of the great Sudanic kingdoms was at an end. The important cities were in decline and political disorder returned to the lands south of the Sahara. Between 1651 and 1750, for example, Timbuktu had 128 military rulers, but none of these men was able to re-establish the boundaries of the old empire.[22]

Bantu-speaking African kingdoms also emerged in central, eastern and southern Africa, although these were usually smaller in scale than their Sudanic counterparts in Ghana, Mali and Songhai. Arab traders undertook to establish commercial links along the east coast of Africa beginning in the late seventh century, using their coastal sailing vessels or dhows. These contacts led to the development of African city-states and small kingdoms whose success was based upon the export of slaves, ivory, gold and iron ore to a Middle East and South Asian market. East African peoples then began trading with Persia and India as early as the tenth century. The eastern monarchies were powerfully influenced by contact with Muslim traders along the coast. By 1500 there were over 30 small city-states along the east coast, and many of these were situated on islands just off shore. Here a new lingua franca, Swahili, emerged combining African, Persian and Arab elements in order to facilitate communication, and contacts as far east as China were ultimately established. At the opening of the fifteenth century the Chinese explorer Zheng He reached Africa's eastern coastline, and while trade links were temporary, contact with Asia's major civilization enhanced the trade potential of the African kingdoms.

We know considerably less about the origins of formal kingdoms in the southern savanna region, south of the equatorial forests. Archaeologists have investigated an empire in the southern highlands known as Great Zimbabwe which apparently reached the peak of its power between 1250 and 1450. Gold and copper were being mined in the Zimbabwean highlands by the year 1000, and it is likely that trade with the east coast was carried on by organized political societies centred in these mining areas. In the absence of written records, the physical remains of stone-built ruins, some 200 in total, indicate the existence of a significant indigenous civilization based on Bantu stock.[23] A large capital complex near the Zambezi river, probably dating from the fourteenth and fifteenth centuries, suggests that the kingdom commanded the allegiance of many Bantu peoples. In the estimation of one scholar, by the fourteenth century 'virtually all of the gold-bearing highlands may have been under the rule of one great priest-king at Great Zimbabwe, or of kinglets who gave allegiance to him'.[24] A successor kingdom, called Monomotapa by the Portuguese in the sixteenth century, controlled over 700 miles of the upper Zambizi, while in the seventeenth century the Butwa kingdom was able to expel the Portuguese from interior trade fairs. Each of these Bantu kingdoms of the Zimbabwean plateau enjoyed extensive and lucrative commercial links with the east coast of Africa and beyond.

Thanks in part to Portuguese contacts which began in the mid-fifteenth century, information about Bantu kingdoms in West Africa is more detailed. The kingdom of Kongo, located on the Atlantic coast just south of the mouth of the great Congo river in present-day Angola, was made up of a series of smaller Bantu kingdoms which had been conquered by a single ruler from the Mwissikongo clan. Captives taken during the conquest were enslaved and worked as agricultural labourers, and a centralized army and tribute system was established. The king of Kongo was not an absolute ruler, however. Instead he headed a series of provincial chiefs who in turn directed the traditional village heads in a kingdom which reached inland from the coast some 250 miles. Kongolese monarchs were obliged to govern in consultation with a series of councils and lineage groups. In fact a council of lords elected the king from among qualified members of the reigning family. Unfortunately, there was no clear rule of succession, and internecine warfare was the norm at the death of each reigning king.[25] North of Kongo in what is today southern Nigeria, the kingdom of Benin emerged as a prosperous monarchy two centuries before the arrival of the Portuguese. The kings or *obas* of Benin derived their wealth from the proceeds of overland trade with the Sudan. Living in large palaces surrounded by courtyards, the obas were advised by hereditary officials who were also related to the royal family. Like Kongo, government outside of the capital of Benin city was conducted by village chiefs who owed allegiance to the oba.

There were a number of lesser Bantu kingdoms in central Africa at the time of Europe's first contact in the fifteenth century, but most of these monarchies were unstable and short-lived. Bantu states suffered from a failure to respect a clear right of succession to the throne, and from the difficulty of maintaining the loyalty of subordinate kinship groups far removed from the centre of power.[26] Starting at the close of the fifteenth century, contact with the European maritime community changed the relationship between West African monarchs and the outside world. Whereas Africa had been at the margins of the Eurasian civilized world prior to this time, mobile and well-armed European traders began to circumvent the overland Muslim trade with West Africa and in the process established direct contact with African kingdoms. The arrival of the Portuguese in the mid-fifteenth century slowly undermined the economic monopoly over the gold trade enjoyed by the Songhai monarchy in the Sudan, and, as we have seen, in the 1590s a Moroccan army crossed the desert and defeated the once-powerful Songhai.

Sustained European contact with West Africa began in the mid-fifteenth century, and while the terrible Atlantic slave trade brought Black Africa into the web of global commercial exchange, the institution of slavery in Africa was well established prior to the arrival of the Europeans thanks in large part to centuries of contact with the Muslim world. Islam prohibited the enslavement of converts to the faith, but the majority of sub-Saharan Black Africans who embraced traditional belief systems were potential targets for enslavement. Between 1300 and 1500 the slave trade became a basic feature of society in North Africa, Ethiopia and along the east and west African coastlines. Beginning as early as the mid-seventh century and extending to the start of the sixteenth century, over seven million Black slaves, mostly women, were transported across the Sahara to serve in harems and as household servants, while another two million were sold into Arabian and Indian markets. 'African rulers often enslaved war prisoners, and the prisoners were sold into the slave trade – often for shipment to distant places where escape was less likely.'[27] After 1075 the Saifawa dynasty of Kanem, a pastoral state located north of Lake Chad, specialized in the northward export of slaves.[28] There was also a considerable agricultural slave system south of the Sahara, one driven by chronic under-population and thus the absence of a sufficient labour force. In the kingdom of Songhai, for example, the Muslim king Askiya Dawud (1549–83) established large plantations worked by non-Muslim slaves.[29] Most of these slaves came from stateless societies to the south. Indeed annual cavalry raids into the south became a common practice long before first contact.[30]

Europeans were unable to penetrate Africa's interior until the second half of the nineteenth century, and despite the negative impact on indigenous population growth caused by the transatlantic slave trade, Africans managed to maintain their political independence from Europe until the 1870s. Prior to this point, only the Atlantic coastal regions of the vast continent were known to White Europeans, a fact which speaks to the continuing political strength of West African kingdoms. As late as 1900 a quarter of the interior of the continent remained unexplored by outsiders. Still, the commencement of the Atlantic slave trade, ultimately involving upwards of 11 million women and men between 1450 and 1870, transformed the political order of many African societies. Its impact on the institution of monarchy was both dramatic and enduring.

In 1532 the first slaves to be shipped directly to the Americas left their West African homelands. European diseases had already ravaged the Amerindian peoples of the Americas, while Black Africans enjoyed a degree of immunity to northern disease systems which made the cost of transport economically advantageous to colonial planters. By the close of the sixteenth century almost 80 per cent of all West African slaves in the Americas were living and labouring in Portuguese-controlled Brazil, where a plantation sugar economy flourished. From an African perspective, the slave trade benefited those monarchical states whose leaders embraced commercial relations with the Western Europeans, but in general the expansion of the trade during the seventeenth century undermined the long-term stability of existing African kingdoms. In the kingdom of Kongo, for example, the Christian king Afonso I (r. 1506–43) restricted the export of slaves to convicts and foreigners. In a letter to the king of Portugal in 1526, Afonso laments the fact that his own subjects, 'keenly desirous as they are of the wares and things of your Kingdoms', resort to slaving as a means of securing European manufactures. These traders 'kidnap even noblemen and the sons of noblemen, and our relatives, and take them to be sold to the white men who are in our kingdoms'.[31]

By the end of the century the crown had a standing army of 5000 at its disposal, but Portuguese support for independent rulers north and south of Kongo led to increasing challenges to the monarchy. In 1665 at the Battle of Mbwila, King Garcia II was defeated by a coalition armed by Portuguese allies eager to exploit Kongo's human and copper resources. The Kongo slave trade now amounted to almost 15,000 captives per year, and the monarchy disintegrated under pressure from well-armed neighbours.[32] Along a large portion of the West African coast, old land-based empires collapsed and new commercially oriented slave-exporting states emerged. Despite the British Parliament's decision to abolish the slave trade in 1807 and subsequent naval efforts to enforce this political decision, the export of Black Africans continued into the mid-nineteenth century.

Many African monarchs, including the kings of Asante, Dahomey and Lunda on the west coast, resisted the abolition of the slave trade out of fear that it would undermine their immediate authority at home.[33] The Asante kingdom, for example, emerged as a West African power closely associated with European trading networks during the early eighteenth century. The monarch or *Asantehene* lived in exceptional luxury, holding court from his capital at Kumasi, and overseeing an annual 'yam ceremony' where all subordinate chiefs paid him homage. It is estimated that the population of the capital swelled from 15,000 to almost 100,000 during this event, with a well-armed standing army protecting the royal family from all potential challengers.[34] Occupying most of present-day Ghana, in 1701 the Dutch appointed an ambassador to the court of the first king, hoping thereby to expand the exchange of guns for slaves captured by the Asante. The monarchy derived most of its material strength from the collection of tribute and the sale of slaves and gold. Hoping to build a strong centralized state, in reality the bonds of loyalty remained closely tied to traditional kinship practices. Each lineage line within the kingdom had its own headman who represented it at the clan level, and a district chief was selected by the assembled lineage headmen. The king in turn was installed by the clan leaders to maintain good relations between the community and the ancestors. He did not attain anything approaching despotic powers, serving instead mainly as a unifying figure, a king of clans, who represented peoples across many religious boundaries.[35] In this respect the king was expected to practise that element of reciprocity which was at the heart of historic royalty in Africa. 'The ruler protected his people and brought them prosperity through good harvests and his healing touch.'[36]

With the advent of the slave trade, however, prosperity had come to be associated with something more than crops and health. Continued involvement in the slave trade, a decision which engaged a wider circle of political elites, came to define effective governance. When that trade was abolished by the Europeans, the entire economic infrastructure of kingdoms like the Asante collapsed, and the government was no longer able to purchase the guns, hardware and textile goods which were key to the state. And once these had evaporated, the tenuous loyalty of tributary peoples was broken.

Unlike their European and Asian counterparts, then, the central feature of monarchy in pre-colonial Africa was the clan loyalty of dominant peoples within specific geographical areas. Clans united by common consent and sometimes by force, and in the latter case 'it becomes ever plainer that the largest states of precolonial Africa tended to have the fragility of card-houses; one unexpected challenge, and they would disintegrate into their component particles'.[37] The kings who led these coalitions were constantly obliged to prove their credentials as preservers of unity among the various clans. None of the non-Muslim African kingdoms developed a system of writing or a nascent bureaucratic structure whereby continuity of governmental forms was possible irrespective of the political skills of the individual monarch, and in this one important respect the integrity of the system was deeply compromised. Lacking these institutional and structural features, African monarchs found themselves increasingly disadvantaged in all of their relations with the Europeans, a sobering portent of things to come in the late nineteenth century.

MONARCHICAL RULE IN THE AMERICAS

The story of monarchy in the Americas can be divided sharply into two periods, the first involving major indigenous civilizations from 1000 to 1500, and the second coinciding with the period of Spanish, Portuguese, and later English and French colonial domination from 1500 until the 1820s. The transition to European control over the Americas occurred at a time when the indigenous Indian population may have been as high as 50 million (compared to Europe's 60 million and

China's 100 million), but the important monarchical systems encountered by the newcomers were limited to parts of Central and South America.[38] The failure of American Indians to rebuff the Europeans was due to a variety of political, technological and epidemiological factors which, taken together, precipitated a rapid collapse of native institutions and practices. For 300 years following the conquest, Spanish, Portuguese, English and French monarchs claimed large portions of the Americas as their personal possessions, administered in the name of the crown by appointed military and civilian subordinates. Finally, by the second decade of the nineteenth century, a series of anti-colonial revolts took place across Central and South America, and the success of these movements for independence, coming soon after the victory of republicanism in the United States against the British monarchy, set the stage for the creation of lasting, if unstable, republics throughout the southern continent.

Human development in the Americas was unique (with the exception of Australasia) by virtue of the fact that the two continents remained completely isolated from the other great centres of civilization in Africa and Eurasia until just over 500 years ago. Arriving from Siberia during the last Ice Age around 20,000 BCE across a land bridge protruding from what is now the Bering Strait, the Mongoloid peoples who fanned out across the new continents developed their own models of social and political organization in response to varied environmental conditions. In sparsely populated North America at the time of the European incursion, most native peoples pursued a hunting, gathering and fishing lifestyle, while in Central and parts of South America an advanced farming culture was in place. In the latter setting, agricultural surpluses and the establishment of formal structures of political authority allowed for a level of material culture that was in 1500 roughly comparable to that achieved in ancient Mesopotamia, Egypt and the Indus Valley 4000 years earlier.[39] But lacking metal tools, wheel technology or many domesticated animals, the inhabitants of the Americas had not effected a transformation of the natural environment comparable to that witnessed in Eurasian civilizations, where cultural borrowing and the exchange of new ideas had been at the core of economic development for centuries. This is one reason why the polytheistic religious beliefs of Mesoamericans were so central to their overall culture; in conditions where survival on the land was always precarious, placating the savage gods who controlled nature became an all-consuming project.

Historical records before the arrival of the Europeans are scanty. However solid archaeological evidence for the presence of sophisticated civilizations in America comes to us in the form of enormous religious centres located in a belt between the central plain of present-day Mexico and the Andes mountains in Peru. Indeed as the archaeological record continues to unfold, it is clear that these great pre-Columbian kingdoms were directed by priest-rulers whose pre-eminent functions were always associated with propitiating a wide variety of influential deities. The monumental stone-built ceremonial and temple complexes of the Olmecs (c. 800–400 BCE), Maya (c. 100–1200), Inca (c. 1200–1530) and Aztecs (c. 1350–1520) all testify to the existence of an overarching religious impulse and a capacity for the efficient organization of human labour over extended periods of time. Priestly control over the political life of these civilizations seems to have been the norm, for even innovations in calendar development, the use of numbers and in hieroglyphic writing systems all have reference to issues involving ritual and the cycle of religious observance. And one of the main features of pre-Columbian patterns of settlement in Mesoamerica, the urban centre, was most often associated with temples and palaces, while the majority of the population lived in villages of mud and straw on the outskirts of these stone-built religious complexes.

Unfortunately, we do not at present know a great deal about the administrative side of life in these societies, how labour was organized by elites in a manner consistent with the ability to provide the military resources necessary for expansion and survival. Yet it is fair to say that, with the exception of the Incan empire, none of the great Mesoamerican civilizations was organized as a tightly controlled territorial state. Instead, most Indian societies were based on the principle (familiar to Africans) of extended kinship groups – tribes, clans, confederations – all of whom accepted the leadership of one family in a religio-political capacity.

In Mayan civilization, for example, central political organization was entirely absent. Instead, a broad range of competing and often hostile city states, each ruled by priests and nobles, and constantly in need of victims for purposes of religious sacrifice, formed the core of an always unstable political culture. At the height of Mayan influence between 300 and 700, there were a few dozen of these cities in the lowland rain forests of eastern Mexico. And while a number of attempts at greater consolidation took place over the centuries, each of them failed to achieve any lasting results other than to perpetuate the cycle of debilitating warfare. At the start of our period, Mayan civilization was already in decline, perhaps from factors related to soil exhaustion, peasant rebellion or invasion. Archaeologists and historians continue to investigate the possible causes, but it is doubtful that any definitive answers will ever be established.

Unlike this divided city-state model, the Aztec empire was in 1500 a very large confederation of about 25 kinship-based tribes whose main capital was located at Tenochtitlan, on the shores of Lake Texcoco. The Aztecs were not the first to settle here, and there was much intellectual, religious and material borrowing from their predecessors. Around 1100 a warlike people known as the Toltec had occupied the central valley of Mexico and established their capital at Tula, 50 miles north of present-day Mexico City. Their dominance was perpetuated by the enslavement of neighbouring peoples and the use of forced labour to carry out large-scale building projects.[40] The Toltec were succeeded in the mid-fourteenth century by the Aztecs (or Mexica), who had migrated from the north and who by 1500 dominated the entire region of central Mexico. Around the year 1430 the Aztec ruler Itzcoatle encouraged the formation of a new image of the past in which the Aztec elite were descended from the Toltec nobility and the Toltec god Quetzalcoatl.

Following the example set by the Toltecs, the Aztecs under Axayacatle (1469–81), Tizoc (1481–85), Ahuitzotl (1486–1502) and Montezuma II (1502–20) ran a harsh tributary empire, exercising direct control over lands around their capital at Tenochtitlan and receiving grain, slave labour, prisoners to be used as sacrificial victims, and military service from conquered peoples elsewhere.[41] At its height, the empire contained an estimated 20 million subjects, 100,000 of whom lived in the capital.[42] The ruler was elected by a select group drawn from the nobility, and he served as commander of the army, supreme lawgiver and religious head. Normally the electors would choose the eldest son of the deceased ruler, but all legitimate sons as well as brothers and nephews were potential candidates for the highest office. As ruler the monarch was principal mediator between the gods and his subjects, and while not worshipped as a deity himself he was thought to be a sacred being in close relationship with the principal gods. The last ruler, Montezuma, sought to depict himself as a god-king, and Cortes observed that the customs of the royal court were more elaborate than those of a comparable Asian emperor. Writing to Emperor Charles V, Cortes confided that 'the palace inside the city in which he [Montezuma] lived was so marvellous that it seems to me impossible to describe its excellence and grandeur. Therefore, I shall not attempt to describe it at all, save to say that in Spain there is nothing to compare with it.'[43]

Within the capital city, twenty clans or groups of families each managed their own affairs with a large degree of autonomy. From the twenty clans a council of state was chosen, and out of this body four members were selected to serve as executive officers in the service of the absolute ruler. Aspirant political leaders received intensive training in religious lore and ritual at centres of formal instruction, but the institution of monarchy was sustained in the end by superior force alone. Although claiming divine authority, the high level of violence involved in securing human victims for sacrifice ensured that the Aztec monarch would never enjoy the voluntary and unqualified support of his widely dispersed tributary subjects. All Aztec men were obliged to serve as warriors, and the choicest place in heaven was reserved for those who died in battle in the service of securing prisoners and tribute for the gods.[44]

Unlike most other world religions where animal sacrifice was thought to be the appropriate form of thanksgiving to and propitiation of the gods, most Mesoamerican religious systems followed the practice of human sacrifice. The theory was that the gods had offered their own blood sacrifices in the act of creation, and a continuation of this practice at the human level helped to maintain the divine energy of the deities. The Aztecs were particularly aggressive about the need for constant oblations of this nature, believing that the world was in constant danger of destruction lest the gods be appeased through the ritual taking of human life. Driven by this cosmological belief system, Aztec priests effectively defined the parameters of state military action. Twenty thousand people were said to have been sacrificed at the dedication of the great pyramid of Tenochtitlan in 1487, while Montezuma II insisted that almost double that number were put to death at the time of his installation in 1502. During the final years of Aztec rule, at least 15,000 persons were sacrificed to the gods each year. This brutal practice, often accompanied in Aztec culture by the custom of decapitation, flayings and the ripping out of hearts while the victim was still alive, meant that the Aztec empire was essentially a war state, constantly in conflict with its neighbours. The insatiable need for more and more victims guaranteed that when the Europeans arrived in 1519 they would find ready allies among the non-Aztec populations who had for so long suffered at the hands of their predatory neighbours.

The Incan empire, in a manner very much distinct from its Aztec contemporary, was organized in a more centralized fashion. First emerging in the Andes mountains of contemporary Peru and Bolivia during the twelfth century, by 1400 Aztec rulers had forged a single political unit stretching from Ecuador to central Chile. The military campaigns of the ruler Pachacuti (1438–71) were decisive in this burst of expansion. Imperial forces, numbering at the height of their power over 200,000 men, were constantly on the march against other ethnic groups. Pachacuti's son, Topac Yupanqui (1471–93), continued military operations both north and south, and during the long reign of Huayna (1493–1527) a series of rebellions were suppressed along the frontiers. By the start of the sixteenth century, the Incan empire ruled over an estimated 9–13 million people, and this was accomplished without benefit of a written language to facilitate communication and administration.[45]

Under a supreme ruler or 'Sapa Inca' who was thought to descend from the highest deity, Inti or the sun god, each monarch was viewed as the sun god's immediate representative on earth. Thus all important religious rituals, and especially the cult of the sun, converged on the person of the ruler. So important was the association of the Inca with the principal god that the queen was normally the ruler's sister. This relationship, it was thought, would ensure the purity of the succession within the same divine bloodline. Despite this practice, however, concubinage was common in the imperial household, and the numerous offspring of these unions were immediately accepted into the royal family. The queen held an elevated position at court as sister of the Inca, but at the death of the ruler, the widow, together with concubines and servants, were killed and buried along with their master. The centre of the state religion was the Temple of the Sun in the capital city of Cuzco, and it was here that the mummified remains of earlier Incas were worshipped and preserved. Human sacrifice was not as widespread as in Aztec society, but it did take place on occasions such as the coronation of a new Inca or at the start of key military campaigns. In large measure the worship of local deities by subject peoples was permitted by the authorities, but throughout the empire the cult of the sun, and by implication the worship of the Inca, who was no less than a god himself, was mandatory for all subjects.

The Incan monarchs attempted to impose a centralized regime upon the whole of their extensive empire through the development of a road system totalling 20,000 kilometres and a corps of officials to administer in the name of the Great Inca.[46] In an effort to ensure loyalty, provincial governors were drawn from the hereditary Incan nobility. Quechus was promoted as the official language of state service, and defeated local rulers were in many cases permitted to maintain their positions under the direction of Incan 'federal' administrators. The male children of these local elites were often taken from their families and educated in the Incan capital, thereby improving the chances for conformity with imperial orders once they returned to their home provinces. For millions of commoners, obligatory labour on the roads or in the mines, together with a prohibition against travel without official permission, was enforced by a large military establishment. The European concept of private property and the culture of the market were unknown in the Incan empire as the state controlled the production and distribution of goods without regard for the individual will. Forced resettlement was the normal lot of troublemakers.

Despite many successes, the logistics of control in a mountainous environment extending over 3000 miles were very difficult, and discontent among subject peoples was exploited by the Europeans straightaway. In addition, the Inca's penchant for multiple marriages created conditions by the early sixteenth century where rival claimants for power had emerged. This was the situation in January 1521 when the Spanish conquistador Francisco Pizarro set out to conquer the empire with 180 men, 27 horses and two cannon. The death of Emperor Huayna Capac in 1527 had led to a bitter succession struggle between his two sons, Huáscar and Atahualpa. Atahualpa emerged the victor, but before he could consolidate his power the Spanish under Pizarro captured the Inca, collected an enormous sum in gold and silver as ransom for his release, and then proceeded to violate their agreement by executing Atahualpa. After taking Cuzco, Pizarro appointed Atahualpa's half-brother, Manco Inca, as a puppet emperor.[47]

EUROPEAN ARRIVAL

The rapid and dramatic collapse of the Aztec and Incan monarchies, the two most sophisticated of the Mesoamerican empires, was due to many factors. Technological superiority in the form of steel swords and guns, together with the employment of the horse in battle and the practice of fighting in disciplined ranks, all gave the outmanned Europeans a distinct advantage over their hosts. Aztec belief that the Spanish might be agents of the man-god Quetzalcoatl were strengthened by the coincidence that the Europeans had arrived at Veracruz on what was by some Indian accounts the appointed date for Quetzalcoatl's return from exile. When Montezuma sent the

Spaniards an array of gifts upon their arrival, the dual purpose of the action was to impress the newcomers with the wealth and power of Aztec society and possibly to appease the advance guard of the returning god. The Spanish, for their part, took this as a signal of the riches waiting to be plundered. And in battle the Europeans broke all of the commonly accepted conventions of Indian warfare. Aztecs and Incas fought to gain tribute and submission; the Spanish conquistadors fought to destroy and to extract wealth. Thus when the Europeans attacked, they immediately focused on the centre of the empire, seeking to usurp the power and nullify the religious authority of the Indian leaders.[48]

It is with this last variable that the rapidity of the collapse can best be understood. The fall of the Aztec and Incan empires can in large measure be attributed to the very fact that they were centrally organized, militaristic societies under the leadership of a single priest-ruler. The rigid form of consolidated control established by the Aztec and Incan ruling elite proved to be a major liability once that elite was successfully removed. After capture and murder by the Spanish, the entire political and military establishment became paralysed. Combined with the fact that both empires consisted of an assemblage of peoples who lived in a subordinate and restive relationship with their dominant overlords, the rapidity of the European conquest between 1520 and 1540 is more comprehensible.[49] Like the Japanese, the later Aztec and Incan emperors demanded extreme forms of deference from their subjects, including the requirement that subjects avert their eyes when the godlike ruler passed in public. Projecting the image of absolute authority, subject peoples within each empire were quick to renounce their allegiance once the Europeans offered a credible opposition to the imperialist ambitions and sacrificial depredations of the indigenous empire.

What initial military action secured in terms of a transfer of authority, European disease confirmed in a tragic and spectacular manner. Smallpox, typhus, influenza, measles and mumps took the lives of almost 80 per cent of the native population of Mesoamerica during the course of the sixteenth century. In Mexico alone, a population estimated at 25 million in 1492 had been reduced to a mere one million by 1600. And the inadvertent annihilation was similar throughout the Americas wherever native people came into sustained contact with Europeans.[50] Isolated from the other major centres of civilization, Americans were vulnerable to the shared disease pool of Eurasian peoples. The civilizations which arose after this demographic disaster owed little of their basic social, economic or political structures to older Indian patterns or traditions. In particular, the governing institutions of Mesoamerica were dramatically altered with the coming of the European. For the next 300 years, imperial monarchy would define the political culture of the 'New World'.

And that new form of monarchy would be deeply laden with Catholic symbol and substance. In fact the intervention of the papal monarch in the affairs of Spanish and Portuguese oceanic exploration occurred only one year after Columbus returned from his first voyage to the Americas. The newly elected pope, Alexander VI, was a Spanish Borgia and his 1493 bull assigning Spain 'all islands and mainlands whatsoever found and to be found ... in sailing or travelling toward the west or south' understandably upset the Portuguese king John II. Appealing directly to King Ferdinand and Queen Isabella of Spain, the Portuguese monarch was able to negotiate the following year for a new line of demarcation. In the Treaty of Tordesillas a north–south coordinate was established at a meridian 370 leagues west of the Cape Verde Islands, giving Portugal complete access to West Africa – King John's main concern – but inadvertently also providing the Portuguese with a large portion of new world territory in soon-to-be-discovered Brazil. Later, the eastern focus of Portuguese exploration was confirmed when the king immodestly assumed the title (confirmed by the pope) 'Lord of the Conquest, Navigation and Commerce of India, Ethiopia, Arabia and Persia'.[51]

The arrival of state-sponsored Spanish adventurers in the Americas at the close of the fifteenth century, combined with the advance of crown-supported Portuguese seafarers down the west coast of Africa, represents one of the major turning points in global civilization. Focusing here on the American experience, the rapid incorporation of two new continents into the cultural orbit of the Europeans and the destruction of the political and religious structures of the indigenous peoples permitted the institution of European monarchy to extend its influence in an exceptional fashion. The Italian-born Columbus claimed the lands which he happened upon during four voyages (1492–1504) for his employers Ferdinand and Isabella, and one century later monarchical proprietorship was reaffirmed in Virginia by employees of a crown-chartered joint-stock company – this time on behalf of the Scottish-born king of England, James I. In the interim the personal possessions of the Spanish and Portuguese monarchs in Central and South America took on the attributes of a colossal royal patrimony, with all governing authority centred ultimately in the person of the monarch. The Castillian gentry who made up the European population spoke regularly in terms of promoting the interests of cross and crown, and although their actions often belied both, their conduct was in a real sense animated by the same crusading spirit which had guided their fathers and grandfathers in the struggle to put an end to 700 years of Muslim civilization in the Iberian peninsula. And that protracted war against the infidel was only successfully concluded, ironically, in the same year that Columbus set out to reach the Indies by sailing west.

The Spanish conquest of the Americas opened up the possibility of a truly global empire for Charles V of Spain when he succeeded to the throne in 1501 at the age of 16. In 1519 this same Charles followed his grandfather Maximilian I as ruler of the Austrian Habsburg lands and, more importantly, as Holy Roman emperor. The election to the last post occurred in June 1519, two months after Cortes landed in Mexico. The sheer sweep of the emperor's European inheritance, which also included Burgundy and the Netherlands, dwarfed all territorial possessions since the time of Charlemagne, and with the addition of the American empire Charles became the focus of enmity and opposition at both the French and English royal courts. Hernan Cortes grasped something of the significance of the Americas in terms of the Spanish monarchy's potential when he wrote to Charles that the riches of Mexico were such that 'one might call oneself the emperor of this kingdom with no less glory than of Germany, which, by the Grace of God, Your Sacred Majesty already possesses'.[52] By the time the English established their first permanent colony in North America in 1607, the Spanish crown's American possessions extended nearly 8000 miles, from southern California to the Straits of Magellan. During the course of the sixteenth and throughout the first half of the seventeenth century, the silver bullion extracted from this new empire in the Americas proved to be essential in the Catholic monarchy's prosecution of religious wars on the continent and in the ongoing struggle against the Ottoman Turks.

The kings of Spain insisted that the whole of America constituted a separate kingdom from the crown of Castile, and that all of the native inhabitants of the colonies were the direct subjects of the king. King Philip II (1527–98, r. 1555–98) gave testimony to this division by adopting the official title 'King of Spain and the Indies'. And the highest moral authority in the Spanish colonies, the international papal monarchy, supported these claims, declaring in various bulls and encyclicals the crown's personal responsibility for the conversion and welfare of the natives. In 1493 Pope Alexander VI granted the Spanish monarchs full and perpetual dominion in America in return for the crown's commitment to bring all native peoples into the faith.[53] But obviously neither Charles, who stepped down from power in 1556, nor his son and heir to the Spanish Habsburg dominions, Philip II, could hope to govern personally what amounted to the largest territorial empire in the Western world since the fall of Rome in the fifth century. The king's rule in America may have been defined in personal terms, but over the course of the sixteenth century an elaborate set of bureaucratic mechanisms and offices were evolved which gave fairly effective meaning to the notion of patrimonial empire. Together with the personnel sent out to the New World by the Roman Catholic Church, crown control was immediate and lasting.

The chief government agency with overall responsibility for the empire was the Council of the Indies, created in 1524. This body functioned as a branch of the royal court in Spain and it issued all colonial laws, both religious and civil, in the name of the king. The council also served as the highest court in judicial matters involving the colonies, and it played a key role in financial affairs by auditing the accounts of colonial treasurers. An additional regulatory body, based in Seville and known as the *Casa de Contratación*, supervised and licensed all trade with America, and collected customs revenues for the crown. Beginning in 1535 the empire itself was divided into the viceroyalties of New Spain (with the capital in Mexico City) and Peru (Lima). The crown-appointed viceroys in the colonies were the personal representatives of the Spanish monarch and carried with them 'something of the ceremonial aura of kingship'.[54] They superintended the work of nine *audiencias* and a wide array of lesser officials down to the level of municipal corporations or *cabildos*, and their power and discretion was so large that the crown tended to appoint only nobles of middling rank, fearful lest the major noble houses of Castile might seek to use the office as a base of independent authority. During the eighteenth century under the Bourbon kings of Spain, two additional viceroyalties were created to handle the growing administrative workload.

Many of the Iberian bureaucrats who took up civilian administrative posts in the new world were *letrados*, university graduates trained in the law, and their attachment to the monarchical principle was in certain respects akin to the allegiance of Chinese bureaucrats to the emperor. They were full-time salaried officials of the crown, and promotion within the bureaucratic hierarchy was tightly regulated by a monarchy wary of independent loci of authority. This explains why officials were often rotated (not unlike the Chinese practice) to a variety of posts during their stay in the colonies. In America, royally appointed magistrates enforced laws made in Spain, collected taxes and organized the public labour which was required of all natives. While their personal discretion was a function of their distance from the imperial centre, firm allegiance to crown priorities was the essential prerequisite to advancement.

This highly bureaucratic and hierarchical system had its measure of inefficiency, corruption and jurisdictional squabbles, but over the course of 300 years it continued to function in a relatively efficient manner. Part of its uniqueness lay in the fact that 'a continent-wide governing structure came into being where nothing comparable had ever existed before'.[55] Most importantly, there never emerged in Spain's Latin American empire a well-organized core of opposition to the legal and legislative authority of these crown officers. According to one scholar, this 'high degree of quiescence is in part a reflection of the sense of deference to the crown inculcated from one generation to the next'.[56] Institutions of self-government never evolved in a manner comparable to developments in British North America, and virtually all of the top government officials in Spain's colonies were *peninsulares*, born and educated in Spain. Most of these men hoped to return to the seat of empire once their 'tour of duty' in America was complete. Throughout the entire colonial period, for instance, only four viceroys were American-born; of the 706 bishops, 601 were peninsular Spaniards.[57] American-born offspring of Spanish landowners and government officials, known as *creoles*, while able to inherit or acquire considerable landed wealth, were not permitted the same opportunities for political advancement as their parents, and the children of mixed Spanish and Indian marriages, known as *mestizos*, could count on even fewer opportunities. The high incidence of intermarriage between male *peninsulares* and Indian women was due to the fact that fewer than 100,000 Spanish (and these mostly men) migrated to the New World during the course of the sixteenth century, less than the total number of English and Scots who settled in Ireland during the same period.

The Spanish monarchy originally allowed the conquistadors broad powers of authority over the native populations through grants of *encomienda*, which legitimized forced labour on the land. Cortes envisioned a settled society of Spanish landowners and conquered Indians working together for the advancement of crown interests and the Christian religion.[58] Under *encomienda*, native peoples were bound to work the land which they occupied for upwards of 4000 individual Spanish grantees, while an elite ruling caste of European settlers dominated the economic life of the colonies. But the grantees never became European-style fiefholders with rights to jurisdiction or the prospect of hereditary noble status. The crown consistently resisted the perpetuation of *encomiendas* through inheritance, an essential requirement for the formation of a landed aristocracy, and this decision contributed to the failure of grant-holders to achieve political power commensurate with their control over land and labour.[59] The crown, eager to avoid the creation of a powerful hereditary nobility in Latin America, began to abridge grants of *encomienda* as early as the 1550s. The right to inheritance of these estates and their Indian labourers was ended, and by the 1620s the system was defunct.

The omnipresent Roman Catholic Church was the other essential bulwark of royal authority in the colonies. The early stages of Spanish colonization witnessed the conversion of hundreds of thousands of Indians, and representatives of the Franciscan, Dominican, Augustinian and Jesuit orders took it as their special charge to protect the natives from the worst excesses of the *encomienda* system. In 1508 Pope Julius II granted the king virtual authority over all high Church officers in the Indies and a share in the monies collected from the tithe. Later concessions from Rome included the power of veto over all papal dispatches to America and control over the building and endowment of churches. Church and state were effectively fused in America, and one result was that strongly royalist clergy were committed to inculcating obedience to the crown as essential to the life of authentic Christians.[60] Schools and universities were staffed by religious teachers, and the tribunal of the Inquisition was introduced in order to root out nonconformity among the settler population. And when religious orders posed a challenge to the monarchy, as occurred in the mid-eighteenth century when the Jesuit order resisted the new centralizing campaign of King Charles III, they were brusquely expelled from the colonies.

Beginning with the conquest, Latin America was almost immediately drawn into the world economy thanks to the extraction and export of silver bullion. Throughout the long colonial period, the crown set the agenda in terms of economic priorities, and at the core of imperial policy was the mercantilist restriction of all trade to certain key ports. Mining provided important revenues for the monarchy, and during the sixteenth and seventeenth centuries the overwhelming majority of trade involved the export of bullion. Central Mexico proved to be the richest source for mining operations, and it was here that a great capital city, one rivalling European urban centres in terms of population and public architecture, rose to prominence during the 1700s. Imported American foodstuffs such as maize, potatoes, sweet potatoes and tomatoes played a large role in Europe's ability to sustain unprecedented population growth, and agriculture as a whole began to assume a larger role in the colonial economies by the eighteenth century.

During the 1700s the Bourbon monarchs of Spain attempted to expand imperial tax revenues in the Americas by tightening controls over the native creole elite and by better enforcing the mercantilist trade system whereby all transport was limited to Spanish carriers within the empire. But in the long run the exclusion of the creoles from positions of administrative power led to a growing sense of disenchantment with the monarchy in Spain. Colonial leaders took umbrage at the efforts of the crown to increase royal control just as the economies of Latin America were experiencing significant prosperity (thanks largely to the widespread use of slaves in mining and plantation agriculture).

In the meantime, the English and French monarchies had taken advantage of the relative decline of Spain and Portugal to make inroads into the trading monopoly with Latin America, and within the colonies this exacerbated creole resentment at the restrictive trade policies mandated by Madrid and by the continuing domination of high offices by peninsular Spaniards. Wealth generated through mining, herding and cash-crop plantation agriculture led increasing numbers of creoles to call for greater political power for American-born descendants of Spanish settlers. These sentiments were dramatically enhanced by the late eighteenth-century examples of the American and French Revolutions.[61] When Napoleon Bonaparte overthrew the Spanish Bourbon king Ferdinand VII in 1808, a wave of colonial revolts against the puppet monarchy of Napoleon's brother Joseph ensued. The initial revolts (with the exception of those led by the Venezuelan Simon Bolivar) were undertaken on behalf of the exiled Bourbons.

After the restoration of King Ferdinand in 1815, however, creole sentiment turned sharply against a monarch who blindly attempted to re-establish the old mercantile system. In 1816 the Argentines refused to admit crown officials and declared their independence. A decade of military conflict between Bourbon royalists and proponents of independence ensued, with the result that by the year 1824 a number of new – and fragile – republics were in place across Latin America. In Argentina, Uruguay and Chile, independence had come thanks to the efforts of the Spanish-educated creole army officer Jose de San Martin (1778–1850). Martin preferred the establishment of constitutional monarchy instead of the republican model, but he and the republican Bolivar were unable to forge an effective alliance during the years of struggle against Spain. 'The independence movements in both Spanish South America and Brazil lacked the coherence of ideology and leadership present in the American Revolution', and the continued economic dependence of the new nations on European capital and commerce presaged a difficult future.[62]

In just over one decade a 300-year-old empire, headed by European monarchs who administered the Americas as a personal possession, had been lost to the restive forces of creole republicanism. When the Mexican rebel leader Agustin de Iturbide (1783–1824) had himself crowned Agustin I, Emperor of Mexico in May 1822, neither the army nor the civilian population supported his arbitrary rule, this despite the residual monarchism of many creoles who thought that some form of continued connection with European royalty was essential for establishing the legitimacy of new governments in America. Unfortunately for Iturbide, his Mexican birth disqualified him from any genuine association with royalty. Within one year he had abdicated and fled to Italy. Upon returning to Mexico the following year, he was captured and executed.[63] Indigenous monarchy would have no place in Central America after the defeat of Spain. And by mid-century even bone fide European royalty could no longer win the support of Mexico's landed elites. During the second quarter of the nineteenth century, the brutal regime of a military leader named Antonio Lopez de Santa Anna had brought economic ruin to the entire country.

When a successor republic defaulted on its debt payment to France, the French emperor Napoleon III imposed a puppet regime, under the rule of Maximilian (1832–67), younger brother of Austrian emperor Francis Joseph. Maximilian arrived in Mexico City in 1864, and while attempting to work with liberal reformers, his presence only fuelled the ongoing civil conflict. Captured in June 1867 by resistance forces under the leadership of Benito Juarez, Maximilian was executed by firing squad.

Monarchy would have no future in Mexico, but republicanism under creole leadership remained a deeply flawed alternative. Having no substantive experience with self-government, the wealthy leaders of the new republics, military men and conservative landowners alike, would enter the republican era ill prepared for the responsibilities of self-rule. There was certainly little thought given to the political wishes of the majority population, largely impoverished, landless and illiterate. Instead of developing a pattern of political inclusiveness for all white males parallel to that witnessed in North America, a minority of European-descended elites opted for oligarchy, authoritarianism and economic exploitation. Very soon after independence, infant republics descended into military dictatorships, while economic development was stunted by the continuing reliance upon cash-crop exports to Europe and the United States. From the point of independence from European monarchy onward, political instability became the norm throughout most of Latin America.

Only Portuguese Brazil embraced the monarchical principle advocated by San Martin, and only here was protracted conflict and widespread destruction avoided. After fleeing Lisbon and the forces of Napoleon in 1807, Prince Regent John of Portugal (John VI after 1816), together with the entire royal family and court, took up residence in Rio de Janeiro for fourteen years. In deference to the British who had escorted the royal family to the Americas, Brazilian ports were opened to all nations, thus dramatically increasing the level of trade with Europe. And the presence of a European court in the Americas temporarily buoyed the pride of Brazilians of Portuguese descent. For one ebullient subject, Ignacio de Macedo, 'the unexpected transference of the monarchy brought a brilliant dawn to these dark horizons, as spectacular as that on the day of its discovery. The new day of regeneration, an omen of brighter destinies, will bring long centuries of prosperity and glory.'[64]

In certain respects, this sort of optimism was not misplaced. Independence, when it came to Brazil, was achieved with a minimum of bloodshed, while the large-scale physical and environmental destruction which characterized the liberation struggles throughout the rest of Latin America was absent in a country whose boundaries embraced nearly one half of the South American continent. Unlike Spain's colonial possessions in Central and South America, Portugal's colony in the New World was 'far more populous and prosperous than the tiny mother country'.[65] With a population of four million in 1822 (one half of whom were slaves), British merchants quickly established lucrative trade links. By mid-century Brazil was Latin America's largest exporter of primary goods.[66] Rio de Janeiro emerged as a bustling capital during the early nineteenth century, and the presence of the Braganza royal family contributed to the successful transition to independence under unified rule. The monarch promoted agricultural improvements by supporting the introduction of new strains of sugar cane, coffee and tea, while also advancing cultural life by establishing a national library, a museum and a botanical garden in Rio. During these early years plans for an extensive public building programme were undertaken. Twenty thousand Portuguese and other Europeans immigrated to Rio between 1808 and 1822, bringing the total city population to almost 100,000.[67]

On 16 December 1816, the king elevated Brazil to the status of a kingdom. And when the monarch reluctantly returned to Portugal at the insistence of the Cortes in 1821, his son Pedro was appointed regent with full control over internal Brazilian affairs. Personally declaring Brazilian independence the following year, the new monarch enjoyed the qualified backing of the majority of the Brazilian elite who quite naturally resisted the efforts of Portugal to re-enforce mercantilist regulations. Most of these landowners 'saw in the monarch a guarantee of national unity' missing in the Spanish-speaking countries of Latin America, and for his part the liberal constitutionalist Dom Pedro was in favour of convoking a Constituent Assembly where the voice of the landed elite could be expressed.[68] After considerable wrangling over the text of the new fundamental law, the king issued a constitution in 1824 which reserved extensive powers to the crown, including the right to appoint ministers and to dissolve the Chamber of Deputies, but the document did provide for the protection of personal and property rights, together with toleration for non-Catholics. The constitutional commitment to human rights, while issued unilaterally by the monarch, would become a centrepiece of Brazilian political debate for the next century, providing a yardstick against which all reform efforts would be measured.[69] The king seems to have been personally opposed to the continued enslavement of almost one-half of his subjects, but given the country's overwhelming dependence on this labour source for its major export products, he never attempted to force the issue in the Assembly.

Dom Pedro I (r. 1822–31) abdicated the throne after a protracted struggle with leaders of the Assembly who opposed the king's desire to put an end to the slave trade, a failed military effort to prevent Uruguay from securing independence, and a wave of street protests against the king's involvement in a Portuguese succession struggle. He left the throne to his five-year-old heir Dom Pedro II, and a regency was established under a shifting array of ministers. The new king declared his majority in 1840 at the age of 14 and over the next two decades he worked fairly effectively with the legislature, the lone dynastic ruler in an otherwise republican and increasingly authoritarian continent. A two-party political system emerged and, more ominously, the size of the professional army expanded during the course of a protracted conflict with Paraguay.

During this conflict, both the institutions of slavery and monarchy came under increased scrutiny.[70] The abolitionist movement gained momentum during the 1870s as acute labour shortages developed in the countryside. These were explained in part as stemming from the reluctance of European immigrants to enter a slave-dominated culture. When Pedro II signed legislation abolishing slavery without compensation for owners in 1888, however, a rebellion supported by sugar plantation magnates and disaffected military officers forced the emperor to abdicate. Growing from a nation of four million at independence in 1822, Brazil's 14 million inhabitants in 1888 took no concerted action in defence of the monarchy. A strong republican movement had begun in the 1870s, and while they never controlled the Chamber of Deputies before 1888, their constant demand for an elected presidency and a bicameral legislature had great appeal for Brazil's younger generation. For them the crown had come to be associated with economic backwardness and political intransigence, and on a continent where republics like Argentina had apparently discovered the key to sustained economic growth, royalty in its American setting was no longer tolerable. Like his father before him, Dom Pedro assembled his family and departed for Portugal in November 1889.[71] Two years later he died in Paris, an exile in a nation which, like his own, had repudiated the monarchical principle.

3 Contemporary portrait of the Mughal Emperor Jahangir (r. 1605–27) holding an orb.

THREE

Theocratic Monarchy:
Byzantium and the Islamic Lands

ROME RELOCATED

At the beginning of our period, one of the world's great imperial powers was facing a military and economic crisis of unprecedented proportions. The Byzantine empire, the 'New Rome' on the Bosporus which had been founded by the emperor Constantine in 330, lost control of almost all of its Asiatic provinces to the Muslim Seljuk Turks at the Battle of Manzikert in 1071. In addition, Byzantium was facing increasing military pressure from Bulgarian rebels to the north and from an expansive Norman presence in southern Italy and in Greece. The loss of so much territory to the Turks placed severe financial strain on the emperors in Constantinople, and on their armies in the field, but a new dynasty, the Comneni, was able to restore control over what was now a much-circumscribed state, and Byzantium survived to face yet another threat at the start of the thirteenth century, this time in the unseemly form of fellow Christians from the West.

The Republic of Venice in northern Italy had become the major Western trading partner with Byzantium, and by the middle of the twelfth century this wealthy Italian city-state had secured for itself a dominant position in the commercial activities of the empire, enjoying special tariff concessions and even securing important rights to territory within the imperial domains. These erstwhile allies turned against their hosts in 1204, however, when crusading armies from Europe, instead of liberating Jerusalem from the Arabs, attacked the beleaguered Christian capital in the East. The great city of Constantinople was sacked by the crusaders, and the 'Franks', as the Byzantines contemptuously called the mixture of French, Flemish, German and Venetian freebooters who slaughtered indiscriminately en route to their wholesale looting of the city, occupied the great capital until they were finally expelled in 1261. A battered and diminished empire continued to function under much straitened circumstances for another two centuries, but the belligerence and greed of its Christian neighbours to the West had prepared the way for an eventual Ottoman Turkish takeover.

These crises, however dramatic and transformative they were for the empire, often obscure the remarkable successes of a monarchical system which survived for over a thousand years at the crossroads of Europe and Asia. In a number of respects Byzantium's political and military experience paralleled that of its Chinese counterpart. Over the course of its long history, for example, Byzantium was confronted with repeated barbarian attacks from across the Danube to the north, Sassanian Persian strikes from the east, and Arab and later Turkish invasions from the south and east. Indeed imperial defences constituted a major portion of the expenses of the empire throughout the millennium of its existence. No other major civilization successfully faced such a wide variety of opponents for so long, often shielding a less developed Western Europe from the depredations of more powerful enemies. The very fact that Muslim armies were at the gates of Vienna within a century after the fall of Constantinople in 1453 is compelling testimony to the power and (at the time unacknowledged) strategic importance of Byzantium to the independent emergence of the Western European monarchies.

Thus, while we tend to focus on the end of Byzantine rule with the surrender of Constantinople to the Ottoman Turks in May 1453, it is perhaps more instructive to consider the remarkable economic vitality and political staying power of the Byzantine monarchical order for upwards of 1000 years. Despite being besieged for most of its existence, in the end this heavily populated, highly developed and wealthy portion of the old Roman empire both protected underdeveloped Western Europe and remade the civilizational map of Slavic Eastern Europe, spreading its version of the Christian faith northwards and contributing directly to the cultural and political formation of the Russian monarchy. Byzantium's many contributions to the preservation and wider dissemination of classical and Christian learning, to the systematization of the Roman imperial law, and to the definition of theocratic monarchy on the western reaches of the Eurasian land mass, cannot be overestimated.

The Eastern Roman empire reached its high point of power and influence just at the close of the tenth century, as the wealth, cultural and artistic achievements, military power and religious authority of the emperor (*Basileus*) were unrivalled anywhere outside of China. Surviving for almost 500 years into the period covered by our survey, the Byzantine state became 'the longest-lived single government structure the Mediterranean world has ever known'.[1] That this government was monarchical in design should not surprise us, for monarchy had been a staple of the political culture of the region for almost a thousand years.

In one respect, it is an unfortunate modern scholarly convention to use the adjective 'Byzantine' in describing the Roman empire from the fourth to the fifteenth century.[2] For in the eastern reaches of the original empire, the rulers and their subjects continued to view themselves as the direct heirs of the Romans despite the political collapse of effective jurisdiction in the West during the fifth century. The inhabitants of Constantinople were the descendants of a long and proud political tradition whose emperors were *augusti*; only in the ninth century did an illiterate Western ruler by the name of Charlemagne, with the rash backing of the papacy, arrogantly declare himself emperor in the West and thus question the universality of the Roman state centred in Constantinople. Not surprisingly, the Byzantines continued to refer to these Germanic upstarts as mere kings under the universal emperor.[3] In the East, imperial authority remained unimpaired despite the movement of Germanic tribesman into Western Europe, and in Byzantium the assertions of the Roman popes to spiritual and jurisdictional hegemony over the universal Church were dismissed as arrogant pretence.

Church and state were coterminous in Byzantium for

upwards of a thousand years, from the time of Constantine's relocation to the imperial capital on the Bosporus in 330 until the Ottoman conquest of Constantinople in 1453. And the true ruler of this dominant and durable empire, the only *kyrios*, was thought to be Christ himself. Coins bore the head of Jesus crowned with the imperial diadem, monuments were inscribed 'Christos Basileus' – Christ, Emperor of the Romans – and laws were promulgated in the name of 'The Lord Jesus Christ, Our Master'. The mortal emperor, who was equal to the apostles, served as God's first deputy, endowed with full executive, legislative, military, judicial and religious power over all Christians, not simply those under direct Byzantine control.[4] In a very strong sense, the interpretation of imperial power set forward by Eusebius, bishop of Caesarea, chronicler, historian, and apologist for the first Christian emperor Constantine, tightly encapsulated the picture of royal power shared by Byzantine theorists until the collapse of the empire in the mid-fifteenth century. For Eusebius the Roman empire was nothing short of an earthly reflection of the divine kingdom. As there is but one God in the eternal kingdom, so there can be only one all-powerful ruler in the probationary sphere; monarchy was thus the only form of legitimate government. The emperor was divinely charged to be the interpreter of God's word and to see to it that all of his subjects prepare themselves for their heavenly home. Indeed the great Church dedicated to St Sophia, the Holy Wisdom of God, was symbolic of that same wisdom which guided the head of state. In a manner not entirely dissimilar from the Chinese concept of the Mandate of Heaven, the monarchy centred in Constantinople was nothing less than a mirror of the only permanent monarchy in heaven, and as long as there was an emperor on the throne, as long as innovation was avoided, the divine order of the world would remain intact.[5]

In theory the office of the Byzantine Roman emperor was elective. The senate, the army and the people were thought to exercise choice by acclamation, with this popular endorsement interpreted as implementing the will of the Almighty.[6] Of course the reality was quite different. The senate rarely functioned as a credible check on the emperor and the approval of the people was little more than a ritual which followed a succession. For only 30 of the 843 years between 610 and 1453 was the empire ruled by men who were not the heirs by blood of their predecessors.[7] Once elected – or acclaimed – the emperor was freed from all earthly restraint. Shielded from the population by eunuchs and soldiers, the elaborate ceremony surrounding court life magnified the ruler's special relationship with the King of Kings. His images were accorded the same honour as his person, and a rich iconography developed to celebrate each reign.[8] The Christian calendar set the rhythm of court life, with the rituals of both Church and state dedicated to the glory of God and His lieutenant in the earthly realm. The emperor was the one indispensable figure in this elaborate mirroring of the sublime.

As a theocratic ruler, the monarch served as the supreme authority in both temporal and religious matters. Religion and politics were so intimately bound together in Byzantium that the failure to pay taxes was regarded as a sin, while by the tenth century the Virgin Mary – represented in innumerable icons – was referred to as the assistant commander to the emperor.[9] It was he who selected the Church's spiritual head or patriarch from a list of names presented to him by religious leaders. And it was the emperor who determined their fate as Church leaders. Of the 122 patriarchs of Constantinople elected between 379 and 1451, for example, the emperors forced 36 to resign.[10] The monarch also called and presided over Church councils and signed all of the decrees agreed by the delegates. He created, promoted and dismissed bishops, approved appointments to all high offices in the Church, arbitrated disputes between theologians, and remained above the power of excommunication wielded by the patriarch in Constantinople. Although never an ordained clergyman and thus prohibited from administering the holy sacraments, the emperor's unique relationship with God placed him at the apex of power within the orthodox communion, making and revising the laws of Church and state without effective restraint.

When the Ottoman Turks finally captured Constantinople in 1453, the most common intellectual response was to attribute the disaster to the general sinfulness of the people and not to any inadequacies on the part the of imperial leadership. When, some 60 years before the fall of the capital, Patriarch Antony IV reminded the Grand Duke of Moscow, Basil I, that the beleaguered emperor was not to be compared with other rulers and local princes, the enduring model of Byzantine monarchism over a thousand years was made explicit. Despite being encircled by the Turks, the emperor

> still presently receives the same investiture from the Church, the same rank, the same prayers, through holy unction he is ordained Basileus and autokrator of the Romans, that is, of all Christians ... Indeed, it is not because the barbarian peoples have encircled the territory of the Basileus that the Christians should scorn him; for, on the contrary, that should be a source of instruction and wisdom for them: if the great Basileus, master and lord of the earth, he who holds such power, has come to such distress, what might be the suffering of the rulers of small territories or of notables of small populations ... [11]

To conceive of the Church without the emperor seemed an impossibility in the late fourteenth century.

The autocratic ruler stood at the head of a governmental system, highly centralized and bureaucratized, unique in medieval Europe. This administrative system reached far and wide into distant provinces, successfully extracting tax revenues from diverse peoples and regulating the economy, both in terms of production and distribution, in a manner not unlike that witnessed in China. From the standpoints of both efficiency and accountability, there was nothing to compare with the Byzantine model anywhere in Western Europe before the seventeenth century. Above the peasants whose taxes sustained the system and the soldiers who fought in the imperial armies, each official within the state was directly responsible to his superior, with the highest officials, normally generals who administered *themes* or provinces, answerable to the emperor directly. All bureaucrats, heads of departments, military officials and Church leaders were similarly responsible to the emperor alone. Comparable to the much older Chinese bureaucratic tradition, government positions were theoretically open to all on the basis of merit and recruitment came from a range social classes, but in reality (again like China) only the wealthy elite could realistically aspire to such heights.

The exceptional prosperity of the empire over the centuries was due in large measure to its geographical location at the crossroads of East–West trade. Finished products from India, Ceylon, the Arab kingdoms and China, en route to Western European markets, invariably made their way through the empire and provided import and export revenue. In addition, domestic production of high quality silk goods, tapestries, gold embroidery, leather products and decorated religious objects all served as important sources of income. Only imperial China produced more luxury goods of comparable quality to those coming out of Constantinople. Domestic agricultural products included grain, olive oil, wine and cheese, and production levels remained high despite the absence of technological innovation. Independent farmers long remained the backbone of the economy in terms of taxable wealth.[12]

Every aspect of economic life was regulated by the imperial state, from wages and production targets to prices for basic foodstuffs and commercial items. Food prices were kept artificially low in order to support urban labourers, while pay for the professional military was often in the form of grants of land. Provincial bureaucrats oversaw these commercial rules and regulations and monitored the quality of manufactured items, while a network of spies kept the central government informed of misdoings and corruption. Again like China, the merchant class in Constantinople never secured the sort of political power that their counterparts in Western Europe were to realize after 1000. Service to the state, or more particularly to the emperor as the embodiment of the state, was inculcated as a value far superior to one of individual aggrandizement.

THE MUSLIM CALIPHATE

After almost 800 years of conflict with the forces of Islam to its south and east, the Christian Roman empire centred in Constantinople succumbed to the superior military force of its opponents. But the example of Byzantine theocracy was not lost on the empire's Muslim successors. The faith which guided the Ottoman sultans who now occupied the great capital on the Bosporus had originated some eight centuries earlier in the inhospitable lands to the south, the arid home of Bedouin nomads and pastoralists. To these peoples of the pre-Islamic Arabian peninsula, the most important social units were the tribe and its various clans. The tribal division or *umma*, and the early emergence of alliances or federations of tribes, was enlarged and then transformed by Muhammad and his successors during the course of Islam's first century.[13]

The Prophet Muhammad was a member of the Benu Hashim clan, part of the larger Quraysh tribe centred in the trading city of Mecca. Employed as a merchant in his mid-twenties, Muhammad had many opportunities to travel and learn about the monotheistic ideas current in Jewish and Christian communities. Around the year 610 he embraced and began preaching a monotheistic faith based on a series of revelations transmitted to him by the angel Gabriel. Almost immediately Muhammad and his band of close followers were opposed by the polytheistic majority who ultimately obliged the reformers to flee Mecca and travel north to the city of Yathrib (later named Medina or 'city of the Prophet'). Here the new faith spread amongst a mixed Jewish-Arab population, with Muhammad claiming to be the true Messenger of God or Seal of the Prophets. Clan feuding in Medina had been threatening to destroy the town, and as a last resort Muhammad was invited in to arbitrate the many disagreements. His success in this political capacity enhanced his overall standing in the community, and after 622 he took upon himself the combined roles of political leader, teacher, prophet and judge, setting a powerful precedent which with one exception would be adopted by his immediate successors.[14] Muslims mark the year 1 from the point at which Muhammad assumed political authority in Medina, and the Prophet's experiences during the years 622–29 helped to define the subsequent role of political leadership in the Islamic community.

Finally returning to Mecca at the head of a military force in 629, adherents of the new faith quickly triumphed over the polytheistic inhabitants of the city. And in the wake of this military success a common faith, not kinship or clan allegiance, became the defining characteristic of a now much-extended *umma* or community, where a new fellowship of equals before the one true God bore witness to non-believers while upholding and even extending the faith through force. Within the incipient Islamic community itself, the Qur'an and the words of the Prophet regarding war, charity, food, drink, marriage and wider social relations, came to represent the basic constitution which would shape and inform the brotherhood of believers. Perhaps most importantly, Islam would become the mechanism for ending the incessant feuding, vendettas and war between clans and Bedouin tribesmen which had for so long divided the inhabitants of Arabia. The new faith sanctioned a powerful and dynamic form of political and religious authority, capable of directing one of the most remarkable feats of conquest in human history. Within a century of his death, the brotherhood inspired by Muhammad, the Islamic world, would embrace peoples as distinct and culturally diverse as Africans, Persians and South Asians, creating the most cosmopolitan world civilization of its age. For the first time in the global experience, one politico-religious movement would bind together previously separate civilizations in common allegiance to the same God. The implications for the institution of monarchy were unprecedented.

With Muhammad's death in 632 the union of Prophet and sovereign came to an end, but successive members of the Quraysh tribe, all in-laws of the Prophet and companions in his battles, stepped forward to assume the role of caliph or *khalifa* (meaning companion, viceregent or lieutenant). While claiming no special prophetic powers, the early caliphate refused, like Muhammad, to draw any distinction between issues of Church and state, *regnum* and *sacerdotium*, instead confirming a theocratic structure of governance where the ruler served as head of the Islamic community, commander of the armies, principal judge and leader in public worship.[15] The office of caliph would survive for the next 1300 years, until officially abolished in 1924 by the Grand National Assembly of the newly established Republic of Turkey. In an accession speech, the first caliph,

Abu Bakr, outlined the close connection between religious and civil leadership, together with his own responsibility as leader. 'I have been appointed to rule over you, though I am not the best among you ... Obey me as long as I obey God and His Prophet. And if I disobey God and His Prophet, you do not owe me obedience.'[16] The caliph was charged with enforcing the God-given sacred law (*shari'a*), and in theory his position was contingent upon the his dutiful fulfilment of this role.

These early successions, where leaders of the Muslim community elected the caliph on a non-hereditary basis, were not effected without struggle and violence, however. Muhammad had secured for himself individual oaths of allegiance, an unwritten pact or *bay'ah*, in 628 while engaged in a pilgrimage to Mecca. After the Prophet's death, this oath was given on behalf of all subjects by the leading members of the brotherhood. Muhammad's closest friend and father-in-law, Abu Bakr, served successfully as leader for two years, but the next three caliphs, Umar (634–44), Uthman (644–56) and Ali (656–61) each died while engaged in public prayer at the hands of assassins who were not prepared to accept the *bay'ah*. From this point forward Muslim politics would display serious signs of instability, and the quest for a single Muslim brotherhood organized within one overarching polity never withstood the pressures of distance, ethnic diversity and dissent.

Especially divisive was the struggle between Uthman, a member of the Umayyad clan, and Ali, the prophet's cousin and husband of his daughter Fatima. Muhammad had died without indicating how a new leader should be chosen and the split which developed between the warrior elite who emphasized succession based upon the acclamation of the companions of the Prophet (Sunni Muslims) and a minority group which stressed legitimacy anchored in descent within the same clan (Shi'ite Muslims), continues to this day. For the latter group, only those from the Hashim clan were entitled to inherit the mantle of the Prophet's leadership, blood right and inheritance counting for more than mere personal association. In the words of one recent authority, 'no stronger or more provocative thread runs through Islamic development than this question of succession that emerged immediately following the Prophet's death'.[17]

After a series of bloody exchanges between the supporters of rival claimants and the murder of Ali in 661, the governor of Syria was recognized as caliph, and a new Umayyad dynasty (661–749) transferred the seat of government to Damascus. From this important trading city the Arab leaders, who now for the first time followed the strict hereditary principle in succession matters, claimed suzerainty over the political and religious affairs of peoples as far away as Gibraltar to the west and the Indus river valley to the east. The Umayyads abandoned the old model of Arab rule over non-Arabs and instead began a process of integrating all conquered peoples into the fabric of Islamic government. Strongly influenced by the imperial traditions of Byzantium and Sassanid Persia, a total of fourteen Umayyad caliphs established a revenue and administrative system which greatly enhanced the temporal authority of the ruler, who now referred to himself as 'deputy of God'. Critics of the Umayyads sometimes argue that the genuine caliphate ended with the emergence of the Damascus regime, pointing to the increasing worldliness of these *mulk* or kings, their lack of piety and penchant for high living. But in general most Sunni Muslims accepted the new leaders in what remained an ever-expanding empire.

During the course of Islam's dynamic and expansive first century, men known as *ulema* or specialists in the interpretation of sacred law, began to dominate the study and explication of the Qu'ran, and to claim for themselves religious authority equal to that previously reserved to the caliph. Their work continued after the fall of the Umayyad caliphate in 750, when a new dynasty, led by direct descendants of the Prophet's uncle and based in Baghdad, claimed central authority over the now vastly expanded and increasingly unwieldy Islamic community. The Abbasid caliphs (750–1258) were deeply influenced by the Persian autocratic tradition, leading them to change their official title from 'Successor of the Prophet' to the more exalted appellation 'Shadow of God on Earth'.[18] Islamic scholarship – especially the translation of Greek, Latin and Persian texts into Arabic – architecture, law, science and trade flourished under the patronage of the Abbasid caliphs, and the wealth of the empire was for the first time anchored in peaceful commercial activities instead of military conquest. Baghdad developed into an intellectual, artistic and commercial centre where a lavish court life stood in stark contrast to the simplicity of the early Arabian caliphate.

Despite these achievements and the rulers' strong claims to absolute power, succession struggles and breakaway movements continued to damage the institutional integrity of the imperial office. Even at the height of Abbasid power, under the caliph Harun al-Rashid (r. 786–809), the ruler's two sons quarrelled and plunged the empire into a ten-year civil war after the death of their father. In Muslim Spain an Umayyad prince refused to recognize Abbasid authority and subsequent defections occurred in Morocco, Tunisia and Egypt. After 1000 a process of political fragmentation afflicted even the centre of the empire. As early as the year 946 the Abbasid caliphate was forced to concede real political power to a succession of regional warlords or emirs who governed various portions of the empire, ostensibly in the name of the caliph. In 945 a Shi'ite dynasty from northern Persia invaded the capital on the Tigris and seized power. The usurpers left the caliph on the throne as an imperial figurehead, but effective Abbasid leadership ceased at this point.

By the start of the eleventh century, the Seljuk Turks began annexing lands in Persia and Mesopotamia, clashing with both the Abbasids and the rival Fatimids of Egypt. In the early thirteenth century, a Muslim general conquered Delhi and declared himself an independent sultan over all of north India. This 'sultanate of Delhi' spanned three centuries (1211–1526) and involved five different dynasties. The political unity of the Near East was thus at an end at the beginning of our period, and five centuries of general instability ensued, punctuated first by the assaults of Western crusaders and later by the much more significant Mongol onslaughts: the grandson of Genghis Khan, Hulegu (brother of Kublai Khan), executed the last Abbasid caliph in 1258. Islamic society and culture withstood these politically troubled centuries of civil disorder, but for the period 1000–1500 the territorial ambitions of Muslim caliphs were largely frustrated.

The period 1500–1650 witnessed the emergence of three highly efficient absolutist monarchies in the Muslim world. Indeed while the Western monarchies were to predominate over their global neighbours in the long run, from 1500–1650 one might argue that the extensive Muslim land-based empires posed a serious challenge to the continued viability of the Western Christian states. Having long abandoned the ideal of a universal Muslim caliphate, the separate Islamic sultanates of the early modern era dominated an enormous arc of land between the eastern Mediterranean and the Ganges river basin in India. In the west the Ottoman Turks ruled over all of Asia Minor, North Africa, the Balkan lands, and Arabia; the centre of this cultural-religious block was controlled by a Persian Safavid state whose lands included present-day Iran; and the bulk of the Indian subcontinent, long divided into petty principalities, was united and subjected by the Mughals.

All three of these Muslim empires shared certain distinct features. Each traced its origins to the nomadic Turkic peoples of the Central Asian steppes; each was committed to aggressive territorial expansion based upon a strong military tradition and the use of the latest firearms technology; each was ruled by an absolute monarch; and each economy was based on the efficient taxing of an agrarian social order. The wealth, military readiness and administrative efficiency of these empires during the 150 years subsequent to Columbus's 'discoveries' represented the pinnacle of Muslim authority in the global community; indeed during the first half of the sixteenth century it appeared very unlikely that Christian Europe, torn by religious and dynastic wars, would ever pose a credible challenge to the military and economic pre-eminence of the Islamic world. As far west as Iceland the Lutheran Book of Common Prayer asked God for protection from 'the cunning of the Pope and the terror of the Turk'.[19]

At the opening of the sixteenth century the absolutist Ottoman caliphate seemed much the better model of effective government when set in relief against Europe's limited monarchies. Founded by the nomadic Turkish warrior Osman (1299–1326), the Ottoman dynasty (Ottoman is an Italian corruption of Osman)[20] was enormously successful in a series of military engagements against the Christian Byzantines in the Anatolian peninsula. The Turks were originally a Central Asian people who had first come into contact with Islam as Arab forces moved eastward across Persia during the eighth century.[21] Beginning in the ninth century, Turkish fighters began to appear in the armies of the Abbasid caliphs, first as slave warriors and later as commanders and even provincial governors. And after 1000 these fierce warriors began to establish themselves as leaders in the world of Islam, a role which they would not relinquish until the late nineteenth century. In 1055 the Seljuk Turks conquered the city of Baghdad, displacing the Abbasid caliphate, and in 1077 a Seljuk force entered Anatolia and defeated a Byzantine force at Manzikert. In the aftermath of this battle the borders of Christian Byzantium were pushed well back into western Anatolia. During the course of the thirteenth century, however, Mongol invaders swept into Anatolia and effectively destroyed the centralized monarchy created by the Seljuk Turks. After 1243 additional Mongol raiders penetrated into central Anatolia, and by the early fourteenth century a number of small territorial principalities, some Mongol and others Turkish, fought amongst each other and against the Byzantines. Osman was the leader of one of these groups located in western Anatolia.

Ottoman armies were led by *ghazis* or Islamic warriors who viewed their struggle as a supreme religious duty to bring new peoples under *Dar al-Islam*, the rule of an Islamic state. After seizing virtually all Byzantine lands in Asia Minor, the Ottomans crossed into Europe and overcame Serb, Bulgar and Macedonian opponents, sometimes with devastating impact. Following the victory over the Serbs at the Battle of Kosovo in 1389, for example, where both the Ottoman sultan Murad I and the Serbian king Lazar died in battle, thousands of Serbs were sold into slavery, inaugurating a legacy of mutual distrust which remained at the heart of Serb–Muslim relations into the contemporary period.[22] By 1400 all of Anatolia and large portions of the Balkan lands were under the direct control of the militant Turks.

The climax of this remarkable expansionist agenda occurred in 1453 when the thousand-year-old capital of Eastern Christendom fell to the sultan Mehmed II, 'the Conqueror' (r. 1451–81). After a 54-day siege the formidable city walls were breached and three days of looting and slaughter ensued. In the wake of this victory the ruined city was renamed Istanbul and the population swelled from 10,000 inhabitants immediately after the Turkish conquest to some 700,000 in the year 1600, making it larger than any contemporary urban centre in Western Europe.[23] Mehmed II instantly became the most important sultan in the Muslim world and according to one contemporary 'the Conqueror believed that thanks to this city he could extend his rule over the whole Christian world'.[24] Thus the frontier state built around a warrior elite had become a great Muslim empire. An enormous building programme was undertaken in Istanbul, and Jewish, Christian and Muslim merchants gradually returned the city to its status as one of the key trading centres of the Mediterranean. These non-Muslim communities, known as *Millets* and led by the Greek Orthodox patriarch, the Armenian patriarch and the Jewish chief rabbi, were not only tolerated but were in fact protected by the sultans.[25]

Surprisingly, all of this occurred under the arbitrary rule of an imperious, warlike leader who embodied many of the worst aspects of absolute rule. Traditionally the monarch in Turkish society served as a leader in battle, a lawgiver and an ecclesiastical official.[26] Mehmed II, while a cultivated man who took an active interest in the life of the mind, was in addition firmly committed to a realization of his own notions of Ottoman supremacy. And supremacy involved an uninterrupted programme of conquest. To feed the population of Istanbul Mehmed imported thousands of Balkan peasants and enslaved them in villages near the capital. Although generally tolerant of non-Muslims, the sultan's great fear of assassination led him to order the deaths of thousands of his subjects during his 30-year reign.

Mehmed II also introduced the so-called 'law of fratricide'

in a crude and brutal attempt to simplify the succession question. Turks generally located legitimacy in a single ruling family, but they did not follow the principle of primogeniture where the eldest son succeeded. When combined with the polygynous marriage practices of Islam, the result was a series of contending claims to the sultanate put forward by male offspring and siblings. Under the 'law', each new sultan executed all but one of his brothers and half-brothers after identifying the one male relative who was deemed best fit to govern a vast empire. One of Mehmed's successors, Selim the Grim (r. 1512–20), killed his brothers, nephews and sons with the exception of one child, Suleiman.[27] In his turn Suleiman killed two of his three sons, Mustapha in 1553 and Bayazid in 1561, leaving the fortunate survivor (Selim) to succeed to power without contest. The last-recorded practitioner was Sultan Mehmed III, who upon succeeding to the throne in 1595, ordered the execution of his nineteen brothers and almost as many pregnant women.[28]

Despite his brutality, Mehmed was an adept and efficient administrator as well as a skilful military strategist. Effectively employing forged metal siege cannons against the walls of Constantinople in 1453, Mehmed ushered in the age of the 'gunpowder empires' whose drive to dominate weaker states was in its Muslim setting allied with a parallel desire to expand the faith. The sultan was also careful to maintain trade links with the Italian city-states, first granting tariff concessions to the Venetians and later, after declaring war on Venice in 1463, encouraging Florence to step in as principal Western trade partner.[29]

During the 1520s, as Henry VIII of England dissipated his father's legacy against his fellow Christian prince Francis I of France, Ottoman forces had already routed the Mamluk rulers of Egypt, raided Italian port cities, and captured Belgrade and Budapest. When Francis I was captured by the emperor Charles V at Pavia in 1525, the French ambassador in Istanbul asked the sultan to launch an attack against the Holy Roman Empire. In 1529 the Turks laid siege to the Habsburg capital at Vienna, and but for the substantial rainfall which made the transport of heavy cannon difficult, Suleiman's armies might have taken the city. Despite this setback, the Ottomans placed the Holy Roman Empire in a precarious defensive posture. Europe's mutually distrustful Christian monarchs were incapable of united action against this threat, preferring instead to ally themselves with the 'infidel' Turk when it served their strategic interests. Under Suleiman I (r. 1520–66) the territorial sweep of the empire reached its height, and the sultan now assumed the more exalted title of caliph. Northwest Africa, Arabia, Egypt, Palestine (the historic heartlands of Islam), Syria, Anatolia and the Balkans north to Belgrade all fell under his dominion. The population of Christians, Jews and Muslims under the direct rule of the caliph grew to almost 12 million, at a time when Henry VIII of England governed and misgoverned a mere 2.5 million subjects. Ottoman annual revenues dwarfed those enjoyed by European monarchs. And by 1600 the subject population in the Ottoman lands had increased to almost 30 million.[30] Not until 1683, when another great siege of Vienna was repulsed by the Habsburgs, was the Ottoman threat to Western Europe finally checked.

Early Ottoman rulers, little removed from marcher lord status, were content to style themselves chiefs (*uj begi*) of the *gazis*. Bayezid (1347–1403, r. 1389–1403) was probably the first to adopt the title of sultan and thought of himself as the legitimate successor to the Seljuk Turks.[31] Subsequent sultans who led expansionist efforts enjoyed enormous military, civil and religious powers, and their courts took on all the trappings of Byzantine and Persian imperial rule. In theory Islamic holy law precluded the notion of the sovereign as creative lawmaker; under this tradition law emanated from God alone and the sovereign himself was bound by it. But since the sultan, and subsequently caliph, was the guardian of Muslim sacred law, and because this law conceded to the ruler absolute powers, his understanding of its nature and requirements permitted enormous discretion.[32] During the fifteenth century the sultans established a close relationship with the *ulema*, experts in the interpretation of the *shari'a*. This development blurred the distinction between the ruler's law-giving powers and his functions as the head of the Islamic community; in effect obedience to law was a religious obligation as well as a civil one. When in

1538 Suleiman added the title of caliph to his office, the theocratic nature of the ruler's position was confirmed. The claim to the caliphate was based on Ottoman status as the foremost protectors of Islam, and the sultans commonly attributed Ottoman power to the will of God.[33]

There were few key officers of state during the height of Ottoman power in the mid-fifteenth century. All were appointed by the ruler and served at his pleasure. The Grand Vizier acted as the chief secretary or chancellor for the sultan, supervising meetings of an imperial advisory council known as the *divan*, directing the day-to-day affairs of a large bureaucracy, and even on occasion leading armies in the field.[34] Additional advisors supervised the treasury, served as judges, and organized military and foreign policy matters. In the provinces officials with the title *pasha* oversaw both civil and military affairs and also attended the *divan* on those few occasions when it met in formal session. The *pashas* were transferred to different locales on a regular basis in order to prevent the creation of independent power bases. The essentially military side of provincial administration was always stressed, especially in occupied lands which were predominantly non-Muslim.

By the mid-sixteenth century the sultan maintained between 20–25,000 civil servants and troops as part of his personal household. Centred at the Topkapi palace built under Mehmed II in Istanbul, this large bureaucracy was reminiscent of its Byzantine predecessor and was filled with elites whose power was based on the violent acquisition of land and plunder. Ultimately the army was key to the success of the Ottoman state. Originally composed of volunteer *ghazis* who fought in the name of Islam while amassing booty and slaves, a more formal system of recruitment and organization was instituted by the sultans in an effort to guarantee the regime's security against a sometimes recalcitrant *ghazi* military elite. As we have already noted in Africa, Islamic law prohibited the enslavement of fellow Muslims, but the Ottomans were active participants in the North African slave trade, while in the Balkans young boys from Christian families became part of a non-voluntary levy known as the *devshirme* (collecting). Brought to Istanbul and forcibly converted to Islam, the most promising of these men were received into the janissary corps, elite units of the Ottoman army whose only loyalty was to the person of the sultan.[35]

During the era of the empire's greatest expansion in the sixteenth century, the professional training of the slave janissaries, who in 1527 numbered almost 30,000 men, offered the sultan unparalleled service, especially in the utilization of the latest firearms technology. Stationed in the strategic garrison towns throughout the empire, prohibited from marrying in order to enhance their steadfast dedication, and afforded promotion on the basis of merit, the janissaries were the essential guarantors of political order in the empire. Janissary garrisons were not subordinate to any local authority figure; they took their orders directly from the capital, thus emphasizing the power of the centralizing state. Some of these special Christian slaves were also trained for administrative work at court. The *devshirme* system afforded unique opportunities for the children of humble Christian parents to rise to positions of talent and power; indeed the meritocratic principle was reserved for those who were enslaved, an odd inversion of Western ideas and eventually an increasing irritant to free-born Muslim fighters.

This unique slave system thus served to buttress the power and security of the imperial officeholder. Unlike Western-style plantation slave systems which were based on the physical exploitation of those in bondage, Ottoman slaves served in key military and administrative capacities at court; some even became framers of state policy. Mehmed the Conqueror, for instance, chose all of his chief ministers from among his personal slaves, and this practice was adhered to by his immediate successors.[36] By the sixteenth century even the office of Grand Vizier was reserved for unfree servants. Many sultans were in fact the sons of slave mothers who had become part of the royal harem. Slaveholders were most likely to utilize their unfree servants as personal bodyguards and as household servants, and the market for slaves who would function in such capacities remained strong while the work on landed estates continued to be carried out by free peasants. Indeed it was not unusual for the quality of life enjoyed by slaves to exceed anything experienced by a tax-burdened free peasant farmer. By the late sixteenth century, the empire's strength rested on the loyalty of thousands of slave soldiers and administrators whose highest allegiance was to a half-slave head of state. Governors, tax officials and executives in many administrative departments all lived and worked as bondsmen, serving as counterweights to the influence of the free *ghazis* warriors. There was nothing in Europe to compare with such a monarchical system.

One other notable feature of the Ottoman monarchical order which served to enhance the absolutist claims of the sultan concerned the absence of a hereditary landed aristocracy.[37] Notions of family background and a reliance on inheritable estates as the basis of power and influence were much less pronounced in Ottoman culture when compared to Western Europe. Landholders never displayed the type of social cohesion and political identity of interests that was so much a part of the Western tradition. The free-born and landholding members of the sultan's military establishment were normally away from their estates for half the year, and as a result the level of provincialism amongst the aristocracy was markedly lower. In turn the financial obligations of the peasantry near the centre of the empire were rarely burdensome to the point where rebellion was a possibility.

OTTOMAN FAILURE

By 1580 the ruling elite of the Ottoman empire looked to the future with optimism. Tax revenues were secure, the economy was self-sufficient, and the bustling capital city was adorned by numerous fine works of architecture. To the visitor it appeared as though the Ottoman rulers were poised for a long tenure as leaders of the Mediterranean world.[38] Yet the fundamental challenge facing the absolutist system created by the Ottoman monarchs after the victory at Constantinople involved controlling the most turbulent elements of a society whose cultural expectations were built on the premise that military expansion and the expropriation of an opponent's wealth and land were normal activities to be encouraged by the state.[39] Formal institutions of government and law, taxation and permanent bureaucracy – these were concepts alien to the *ghazis'* way of life. One scholar has aptly described the Ottoman political order as 'a circular system in which everything depended on an inexhaustible supply of slaves, booty and land'.[40]

Ottoman sultans normally granted land to soldiers as a reward for bravery in battle; thus the constant acquisition of new territory was imperative if the military establishment were to remain loyal. The slave element in the army was normally more trustworthy, but even here new infusions of personnel required military aggression against peripheral populations. In large measure the revenue collected by the court during the period of growth came in the form of taxes on land and booty from war. As a result the empire remained on a constant war footing throughout the centuries of predatory conduct, 'a vast encampment rather than a state in the European sense'.[41] In a very important respect the notion of non-aggression was antithetical to the very survival of the sultanate. Called into existence by the search for plunder, the Ottomans never made a successful transition to an alternative model of state authority where wealth creation and public revenue were centred on commercial instead of military development.

Following traditional Islamic practice, the sultans did not make grants of land to soldiers on a hereditary basis; since landholding was always at the discretion of the leader, the motivation for steady military action at the frontiers was great. And as rapid population growth – 40 per cent in the villages and almost 80 per cent in the towns – placed additional strains on the system, the government began sending thousands of landless peasants to Cyprus. With respect to lands under Ottoman control, a system of tax farming was established whereby private contractors would agree to provide a given amount of revenue in return for the right to hold whatever was collected in excess. Obviously the potential for abuse here was enormous, and corruption in this area became more pronounced during the later sixteenth century. While business and trade were not discouraged by the sultans, the key to Ottoman success rested on continuous territorial growth at the expense of immediate neighbours, and this was coming to a close after 1600.

Another factor contributing to the decline of Ottoman power during the course of the seventeenth century was the quality of leadership in an age of increasing bureaucratization. The calibre of monarchical authority had always been the key to Ottoman success. The first ten sultans who ruled from 1299 to 1566 all personally led their armies in battle, and their leadership skills were key to the overall stability and success of the military empire. Paul Coles has compared the leadership styles of the Holy Roman emperor Charles V with his Ottoman contemporary Suleiman, and the contrast speaks to the distinct conceptions of leadership embraced by each system of monarchy. Whereas Charles spent the bulk of his time moving from one provincial capital to another, holding court, receiving petitions, conducting correspondence and showing himself to his subjects, Suleiman could be found at the frontiers with his armies, often far from the administrative centre of the empire.[42] Around the age of 14, designated heirs were normally assigned to duty as provincial governors in order to gain valuable administrative experience. This practice continued so long as the sultan himself was a competent and dedicated ruler.

After Suleiman, however, the quality of leadership deteriorated, both at the monarchical level and within the bureaucracy.[43] Designated heirs were no longer seasoned military leaders who had served apprenticeships as provincial governors. Rather they were now relegated to a life of seclusion within the private apartments of the palace where educational objectives were increasingly set by influential eunuchs and powerful female members of the royal family. The ugly practice of killing all potential male rivals to the throne was abandoned in the early seventeenth century, but in its place factions and conflicts developed among the brothers and sons of the sultan, each building their own power bases and coalitions in an effort to acquire the throne for themselves.[44] Within the administrative hierarchy, the practice of affording slave children from Balkan peasant villages opportunities to reach the highest levels of government through their own merit was slowly abandoned. Whereas slave bureaucrats generally worked to curb landholder exploitation of peasant populations, the reverse was true when court favourites and prominent landholders held top military and administrative posts. Appointees to government positions were expected to pay large gifts to the sultan and other high officials, and recouping these costs often involved the regular abuse of office.

The expansion of the empire effectively stopped in the late sixteenth century, and as opportunities for additional land began to wane parallel with the rise of European nation states in the West and rival Muslim states to the East, the ability to maintain a large military and bureaucratic establishment declined. Between 1578 and 1606 a series of military conflicts on two fronts – against the Persians in the east and the Habsburgs in the west – exhausted the resources of the empire. Naval mastery in the eastern Mediterranean and in the Black Sea was lost after 1600, and by 1613 Dutch and English pirates had penetrated the Red Sea. After 1600 the English ceased purchasing spices in Ottoman-controlled Cairo, preferring instead to import directly from India. Similarly, in 1617 the English entered into an agreement with the shah of Persia to purchase silk directly. The Ottoman state ceased to be the main transit route for goods destined for Europe.[45]

These unfavourable economic developments were compounded by a serious currency disruption occasioned by the flow of cheap American silver into the empire. As prices rose and currency was depressed, the allegiance of soldiers on fixed salaries declined. Revolts by janissaries became commonplace, while the ranks of bandits and rebels, many of whom had lost their lands during difficult economic times, grew at a disturbing pace.[46] Corruption increased at all levels, and peasants, who had long been the backbone of the system, were exploited and alienated. The resulting social dislocation and abandonment of productive lands only magnified the difficulties facing the empire. A more basic economic reason for the decline of the empire (not unique to the Ottomans) involved the leadership's failure to encourage or advance a manufacturing sector. A tiny elite of rulers and large landowners presided over a brilliant high culture, but the vast majority of the subject populations did not share in the affluence.

Within the empire, traditional guilds enjoyed the support of the powerful janissary corps, thus making it difficult for alternative forms of production to gain a foothold. Those Muslims interested in commerce and manufacture were discouraged from innovating by a system of tax farming which targeted and fleeced commercial leaders and potential investors.[47] Using their expanding merchant fleets, by the late sixteenth century European traders had largely circumvented the previous Ottoman monopoly over the flow of goods – and profits – from India and Asia. Even trade with the empire came to be dominated by Dutch, English and French middlemen. Market-oriented traders from the West penetrated African and Asian markets and displaced many of their Muslim counterparts. And later Ottoman rulers expressed little concern over these developments.

Unlike their European counterparts, most Muslim heads of state did not take as part of their charge the responsibility to foster the economic welfare of their subjects, a view which was, according to William McNeill, 'as old as civilization itself in the Middle East'.[48] Mercantilist policies were never adopted by the sultans, one result being the progressive takeover of the carrying trade of the empire by European merchants. Subjects were considered to be the *reaya* (supported flock) who in return for the sultan's protection were expected to produce the bulk of the wealth that the ruling class would exploit and defend.[49] Urban dwellers were exempted from military service and the forced labour requirements imposed on rural people, but there was no official state support for commercial ventures. The intellectual gap which existed between rulers and common subjects in the empire did not exist in the more fluid social system in the West.

Following the rise to power in Persia of the Shi'ite leader Ismail Safavi and his conquest of Baghdad in 1508, the Ottoman sultans and the Safavid shahs engaged in a protracted religious conflict not unlike the fratricidal conflicts which debilitated Europe in the wake of the Protestant Reformation. Supported by his fanatical followers and by the Shi'a theological community as the head of the entire Muslim world, Ismail's armies posed a serious threat to the leaders of Mughal India and the Ottoman empire alike, encouraging Shi'a sympathizers throughout the Muslim world to take up arms against their

Sunni rulers. A serious Shi'a rebellion broke out in eastern Anatolia in 1511, just seven years before Martin Luther would ignite a serious split within Western Christendom. The Ottoman sultan Selim I rallied his forces and defeated Ismail's forces at the Battle of Tchaldiran in 1514, but while briefly occupied the Shi'a state to the east was not permanently undermined. A climate of hostility every bit as intense as the one with the Christian West continued with the Safavids until 1639, coincidentally just one decade before the close of Europe's last major religious conflict, the Thirty Years War.[50]

THE MUGHAL INTERLUDE, 1509–1720

The third of the great early modern Muslim kingdoms was located in a land where centralized political authority was very much the exception to the normal state of affairs. It was also a land where the followers of the Prophet constituted but a tiny minority of the population, and where Muslim control was by definition rule by recent invaders, by Turkic outsiders hailing – like so many previous encroachers – from the north-west (contemporary Pakistan and Afghanistan). We are referring, of course, to northern and central India, a 750,000 square mile territory bounded by Afghanistan in the north-west, the great Ganges basin in the east, and the Deccan plateau in the central uplands.

On only three occasions in India's long history, specifically under the Mauryan emperors (322–185 BCE), the Guptas (320–c. 550 CE) and briefly under King Harsha (606–647 CE), had a large portion of the subcontinent been under any form of effective centralized monarchy, and even in the case of the Guptas and Harsha there continued to exist local dynasties which owed only nominal allegiance to the centre. Hinduism's indifference to the pretensions of the material life, the powerful assertion that all within the realm of the senses was simply *maya* or illusion, placed the demands of the territorial state well beyond the concern of those seeking to fulfil their duty or *dharma* in this life.[51] This is not to say that peaceful conditions always obtained in an India dotted by tiny Hindu kingdoms;

rather incessant and debilitating warfare seems to have been the rule throughout the subcontinent. But with a population estimated at some 100–140 million during the sixteenth century, and where cultural priorities placed the problem of the transmigration of souls well above the importance of socio-political matters, the task of forging a single territorial state in the Hindu subcontinent dwarfed all similar undertakings in Western Europe, Ottoman Turkey and Safavid Persia.

India's previous centralizers Chandragupta Maurya from 313 to 300 BCE, his grandson Asoka from 269 to *c*. 232, and the Gupta monarchs of the fourth to the sixth centuries CE, were born and raised in the Buddhist and Hindu traditions. Islam's first contacts with India occurred during the seventh century along the western coastline, where Arab traders, few of whom were violently anti-Hindu, made a series of commercial contacts. In 712 Arab armies attacked and conquered Sind, and while border skirmishes continued over the next 300 years, it was not until the eleventh century that fierce Turko-Afghan raiders, soldiers of Allah whose casteless egalitarian religious ethos was so very different from that of their Hindu opponents, broke deep into the expanses of northern India. Between 1000 and 1027, for example, Mahmud of Ghazni led a series of vicious attacks with the dual purpose of plundering the countryside while conducting holy war against the Hindu infidel.[52]

At the close of that century additional Turkic peoples (all recent converts to Islam) invaded and formed regional states in Punjab, and by the early thirteenth century the Muslim sultans at Delhi ruled over the entire Ganges basin. The great fourteenth-century Muslim traveller Ibn Batuta described the capital as 'a vast and magnificent city, uniting beauty with strength'.[53] These Delhi sultanates later broke up into separate – and quarrelsome – dynasties in Bengal, Kashmir, Gujarat and the Deccan, but all continued to dominate a variety of indigenous tributary states for upwards of 300 years, just as the Mongols tolerated tributary powers in Russia.[54] Indeed much of the explanation for this Muslim success can be found in the surprising inability of native Hindu *rajas* (kings) to cooperate against a common enemy.[55] Still, as a practical matter the scant number of Muslims in India necessitated the delegation of considerable power to a wide variety of defeated Hindu rulers. Timur Lang's devastating invasion of north India at the close of the four-teenth century shattered the Delhi sultanate, but Islamic influ-ence was not completely extinguished. Another century would pass before a renewed effort to impose rule by an Islamic elite over the Hindu majority was attempted by yet another wave of Turko-Afghan horsemen. However by 1500 'Hindu society in nearly every region of the subcontinent save the extreme south was conditioned to accept the authority of an Indo-Muslim ruler – whether foreign or of Indian origin'.[56]

The first of the great Mughal[57] emperors, Babur of Kabul (1483–1530, r. 1495–1530), was the Sunni Muslim leader of nomadic raiders and adventurers based in Afghanistan, and a descendant of Timur (Tamerlane) on his father's side and of Genghis Khan on his mother's side. We know a good deal about him thanks to an autobiography assembled from notes composed throughout his life.[58] Like so many of his predeces-sors, Babur and his followers first entered the Indus Valley solely with the intention of carrying out a brief pillaging expe-dition. The summer heat of northwest India disinclined Babur's roughly 12,000 Central Asian mercenaries from any desire to lay permanent claims, but the leader was determined to consolidate his forays and to build a lasting empire in the divided lands of the north.

Employing cannon and matchlock guns acquired from the Ottoman Turks, Babur's outnumbered army defeated the incumbent sultan of Delhi, Ibrahim Lodi, at the Battle of Panipat in 1526 (50 miles north of Delhi), and after occupying both Delhi and nearby Agra on the Jumna river, the victor pro-claimed himself emperor of Hindustan. For the next four years until his death in 1530, the autocratic Babur fought a series of successful campaigns against indigenous Indian armies and extended his rule from Kabul in Afghanistan to Bihar in north-east India. There was no time to forge even a rudimentary bureaucratic system; Babur's empire was very much of a piece with his dynamic personality. Unfortunately his indolent and dissolute son Humayan (1530–56) managed to lose most of his inheritance to rival Afghan warriors. Eventually the erstwhile emperor had to seek refuge in Persia at the court of Shah

Ismail, and at this crucial juncture it appeared as though the incipient empire of the Mughals might wane as rapidly as it had risen.[59]

However when Bairam Khan, the able and loyal regent for Babur's 14-year-old grandson Akbar, defeated an Afghan competitor at Panipat in 1556, the process of political consolidation was restored, and the roots of what would become one of the most extensive centralized war-states in the pre-modern world were planted. For the next 175 years, the wealth and power of India's Muslim emperors was rivalled only by the Ming of China. During the larger part of Akbar's extended reign (1542–1605, r. 1556–1605), military operations against a variety of opponents were ongoing, and the capital of the empire was often situated wherever the massive tent encampments of Akbar happened to be situated. The emperor served as his own commander-in-chief after the dismissal of Bairam Khan in 1560, and his repeated if hard-fought victories on the field of battle secured the submission of the Muslim warrior grandees.[60]

As a rule Muslim leaders who had been defeated by Akbar lost their territories, but Hindus – and especially Rajput princes in Rajasthan – who accepted defeat were granted nominal authority over their former domains and an acceptable position at court.[61] As the Rajput military elite, together with the clerical castes (Brahmins and Kayasthas), slowly opted for alliance with Akbar and with it entry into the noble (*amir*) rank, the Hindu masses came to accept Mughal government as their own. More than any other previous Muslim ruler, the illiterate Akbar understood that the security of his kingdom required the support, or at least the acquiescence, of the non-Muslim majority of his subjects.

As an emperor who represented a minority religious tradition in India, Akbar had tolerated Shi'a Muslim immigrants from Persia, as well as native Hindus, Buddhists, Jains, Parsees and Sikhs. In 1579 he abolished the hated *jiziya* or poll tax on non-Muslim adults, and he even welcomed a delegation of Jesuits to visit his court in 1580. Hindu warriors were grateful to Akbar for abolishing an offensive assessment which had been imposed on Hindus on pilgrimage to holy sites such as

Mathura. The emperor and his court also celebrated important Hindu festivals like Diwali, the festival of lights. In 1579 an important step in the direction of theocratic absolutism was taken when Akbar issued an imperial edict stating that the emperor's prerogative included final arbitration of religious affairs within the realm, overriding the claims of Muslim jurists and scholars – the *ulema*.[62] According to the emperor's trusted friend and chronicler, Abu Fazl, Akbar insisted that 'the status of a just king is greater before God than the status of an interpreter of the law'.[63] Finally in 1582, in an effort to bridge the varied religious traditions of India, and thus to solidify the unity of the empire by calling attention to the sanctity of the imperial office, the emperor established a new syncretic belief system which he called *Din-i-Illah* (divine faith). All of these actions deeply alienated the conservative Muslim *ulema* who believed that doctrinal purity required zealous orthodoxy on the part of the emperor.[64]

It is nonetheless exceptional that at the very time when Western Europe was beginning its long descent into Protestant–Catholic religious warfare, Akbar was advancing a unique model of autocratic rule in India, one where toleration was promoted and where voices from all religious quarters would be respected by the crown. Perhaps not surprisingly, the divine faith did not win acceptance outside court circles, but it did solidify loyalty to the emperor as the symbol of divine action in the world, an idea ultimately rooted in Persian precedents. According to the 'Institutes of Akbar', an account of the entire reign composed by Abu Fazl, 'No dignity is higher in the eyes of God than royalty and those who are wise drink from its auspicious fountain.'[65] Even official art and architecture was placed fully at the disposal of the movement to embellish and elevate the status of the ruler. It was during the reign of Akbar's son and successor Jahangir that the Western Christian nimbus or halo began to appear around the imperial head in Mughal paintings, many of which were completed under the auspices of a department of court painters. The divine right to rule was confirmed in eulogistic poetry, in official correspondence, and in court ritual and protocol. Rituals of submission were a daily experience for those in attendance at the Mughal court.[66] The semi-divine associations reinforced the injunction to unquestioning obedience as the will of God.[67] In an effort to forward the process of political socialization, Hindus were represented, albeit as a minority, in both the military and in Akbar's bureaucracy, and the emperor himself took as his principal wife a Hindu Rajput princess. He actively encouraged Muslim members of the imperial court to follow his example and intermarry with Hindus. In addition to recruiting Hindus for court service, Akbar patronized Hindu artists and writers, and granted endowments to Hindu temples.

The administrative offices established during Akbar's long reign would mature over the next two centuries, just as European traders (who as a rule were welcomed by the cosmopolitan Mughals) began to make initial direct contacts with the subcontinent. Instead of appointing one chief minister who might become the focus of possible opposition, Akbar established four specialized departments: finance and revenue, military, household and judicial/religious affairs.[68] Each of these posts was occupied by an imperial servant who in turn supervised a large staff of clerks, auditors and messengers. The empire was divided into separate provinces under military governors, some of whom were subordinate Hindu rajas, but all of whom were directly responsible to the emperor. The majority of provinces were placed under the control of Muslim officers, but in all cases these *mansabdars* or holders of commands were paid a regular salary in place of the traditional practice of making permanent land grants, and every governor was rotated on a regular basis in order to prevent the establishment of regional power blocks.

The post of mansabdar was not hereditary, thus each of these officials served at the pleasure of the crown. Mansabdars were ranked and remunerated on the basis of the number of troops which they provided for imperial service, but in essence it was a system which afforded opportunities for new men of talent irrespective of their religious affiliation. The emperor also created a domestic administrative system under the leadership of the *diwan* or finance minister. The Hindu Todar Mal held this important post during much of Akbar's reign, and each provincial capital was assigned a fiscal officer who reported to the *diwan*. A royal mint was established and tri-metallic coins of silver, copper and gold were circulated throughout the kingdom. The key source of revenue was the land tax, an assessment which amounted to roughly one third of the value of the annual crop. Akbar had begun his reign by calling for a general survey of holdings down to the village level in order to determine average yields. The actual assessment and collection of land taxes were carried out by *zamindars* (landholders) who in some instances contracted with the government as tax farmers. In return the zamindars were permitted a measure of autonomy over their own territories. Territorial expansion and solid financial management meant that under Akbar revenues always greatly exceeded expenditure.[69]

The power of the Mughal emperor, theoretically limited by the *Qur'an*, was in fact largely unrestrained. Akbar kept around 12,000 cavalry troops in regular pay and readiness, and these units monopolized control over artillery resources.[70] The emperor also enjoyed the services of troops raised by higher-ranking mansabdars. These well-paid warrior aristocrats headed fighting contingents ranging in size from several hundred to several thousand men. Akbar promoted a wide array of men to noble status: Rajputs, Afghans, Indian Muslims, Persians and Uzbeks.[71] As a result no one ethnic group was able to pose a serious threat to the imperial government.

Persians and Central Asians made up the largest percentage of the imperial bureaucracy during the sixteenth and seventeenth centuries. In fact the official language of the court was Persian (although Turkish was also employed) and Hindus were obliged to learn the language in order to serve the caliph. The mixing of Turko-Persian culture with the indigenous dialects of north India led to the formation of a language known as Urdi (camp language). Written in Arabic script but employing Hindu grammar, urdi became the vernacular of northern India and a testimony to the assimilative powers of the two cultures. Muslims were subject to Islamic law as administered by *ghazis* or law officers, but under Akbar Hindus were permitted to settle legal disputes following local precedents and Brahmanical practice. The village authorities handled most cases of lawbreaking. Akbar recognized that Hinduism provided the only underpinning of an all-India social structure and philosophic outlook on life, and the emperor was loath to tamper with this ancient set of ideas.

Government functions under the Mughals were limited essentially to the collection of taxes, the maintenance of order through a large standing military force, and the building of strategic roads and bridges. Like its Ottoman counterpart, the Mughal empire was essentially a state on a constant war footing, one where the leadership ethos was governed by a strong military tradition.[72] Mughal troops were regularly engaged in operations designed to extend the authority of the emperor. Since the Muslim invaders were few in number, a very large military establishment was maintained, both as a bulwark against other central Asian peoples and, if necessary, to over-awe the 90 per cent of the population which remained Hindu. A solid communications network was maintained throughout the empire by relays of foot-runners who carried official notices, orders and reports to and from provincial towns and cities.[73] There was very little concern demonstrated by the Mughal monarchs for the relief of poverty or for internal economic improvement. The early seventeenth-century English ambassador Sir Thomas Roe was not the first to comment on the enormous disparity between the wealth of the court and the abject poverty of the population as a whole. In fairness, however, it must be said that Europe's approximately 80 million peasants struggled for survival under conditions not unlike those experienced by India's 100 million villagers.

Most tax revenues were devoted to the support of the military and for a lavish court lifestyle, while essential irrigation projects and transportation infrastructure were often neglected. Mansabdars at the provincial level emulated the lavish lifestyle of the Mughal court, while craftsmen and artists found ample sources of employment and patronage. By the close of Akbar's reign in 1605, mansabdars and their households (including military personnel) consumed over 80 per cent of the entire annual budget of the empire. By contrast the royal households expended less than 5 per cent of the total budget.[74] The Mughals never demonstrated the concern for public welfare that was, for example, so much a part of the political culture of Chinese monarchy. The emperors lived lavishly with hundreds of servants, many of whom were domestic slaves. Akbar, for example, had a spacious new imperial residence constructed at Fatehpur-Sikri, 20 miles west of Agra. Finished in 1578, it featured a palace, mosque, extensive gardens, and housing for the court staff. It is estimated that his harem alone numbered 5,000.[75] But after much expense and long years of construction, the emperor spent only fourteen years (1571–85) in residence before relocating to Agra.

Akbar's grandson Shah Jahan (r. 1627–58) built two new capital complexes at Agra and Delhi. Upon completion, these cities were among the world's largest in terms of population. Agra was home to some 600,000 residents, and the city boasted 70 mosques and 800 public baths. In Delhi or Shahjahanabad, where construction was begun in 1639 and completed in 1648, an enormous imperial palace and mosque was housed inside the large Red Fort, and this would remain the official royal residence until the city was taken by the British in 1857. Here sat the famous Peacock throne, inlaid with precious stones and whose value has been set at more than $5,000,000.[76] The eighteen years and 20,000 labourers involved in the construction of the Taj Mahal at Agra, a mausoleum and memorial for Shah Jahan's favourite wife Mumtez Mahal, is yet another example of the funding priorities of the government.

And the culture of excess was built into the Mughal administrative system itself. Akbar had paid his top officials in cash instead of land, and while his son reverted to land grants in lieu of salary, the governing nobility did not enjoy the right to bequeath property to their offspring. At death the property of the noble was resumed by the crown, and this encouraged the sorts of ostentatious display and spending that became one of the hallmarks of the Mughal elite.[77] While the architecture of the Mughal period illustrates a fine interaction between Islamic and Hindu styles, the considerable resources of the state were always narrowly employed for the greater glorification of the ruling nobility. The intellectual vigour and excitement of the court had little impact on the rhythms of village life, while the architectural treasures which remain so much at the centre of

India's artistic tradition were but tiny archipelagos in a much wider expanse of rural poverty and caste exclusiveness. Those millions situated in the latter circumstances knew the state mainly as an agency of extraction. The historian Percival Spear was very close to the mark when he concluded that for the average Hindu 'it did not matter much who ruled in Delhi – Mughal, Maratha, or Englishman. His concern was with his crops, with the next monsoon, and with the annual visitation of the collecting officer.'[78]

Traders and textile producers worked unhindered in India under the Mughals, and the commercial wealth of the empire was much envied by the less affluent Muslim kingdoms to the west. Cotton textiles, muslin, calico and rugs were manufactured and exported, while pepper, indigo, and opium were also among the many profitable commodities sold outside of India. Most of these goods were transported to the coast along the river networks due to the fact that the monarchy did not engage in extensive road building in order to facilitate the movement of goods destined for export. As a result trade added only moderately to the overall prosperity of the empire as a whole, or to government revenue in particular. Similarly, despite India's strategic location at the centre of a large east–west trading network, the Mughals never encouraged the formation of either a merchant or a naval fleet. Most of the export commodities were carried in foreign bottoms.

Foreign traders included Europeans, and in particular Portuguese, who as early as the 1490s had established direct contacts with Indians at Malabar, followed in 1510 by the establishment of a trading station at Goa on the west coast. Unlike the Chinese, the Mughals permitted European traders the right to travel freely throughout the empire. The Portuguese presence along the west coast grew during the troubled years of Humayan's reign (1530–56) and remained a force throughout the course of the sixteenth century. In 1604 the first representative from the British East India Company was received at Akbar's court, and with the death of two great monarchs, Elizabeth of England in 1603 and Akbar of India in 1605, the dynamic and often troubled history of interaction between the two cultures began. In 1615 King James I dispatched Sir

Thomas Roe to the Mughal court of Jahangir, and the emperor granted the East India Company a trading station at Surat.

At the outset of the relationship with English traders, Mughal India was much the greater power, with a larger population, a wealthier court, a bigger army and clear sense of cultural superiority over the barbarian westerners. Nothing at the time would suggest that James I's small island kingdom had the potential to succeed the Mughals as the effective rulers of the Indian subcontinent. Indeed while literate Europeans acquired a detailed picture of Mughal society thanks to popular travellers' accounts, Mughal society showed little interest in European culture in general and its technology in particular.

The English had secured a trading station at Madras on the Bay of Bengal (Fort St George) in 1639 and at the end of the century additional concessions were won at Bombay in the west and at Calcutta in the northeast. By 1700, annual profits of 25 per cent from the Indian trade were commonplace. In addition, the French had chartered their own East India Company in 1664, and their merchants were soon to pose a strong challenge to English interests. Lost in most of this activity was the development of India's economic infrastructure. Mughal monarchs always, and in retrospect unhappily, preferred focused display over broad-based improvement.[79]

But it is clear that the arrival of the Europeans was nothing more than coincidental to the fall of Mughal authority. Internal weaknesses associated with monarchical absolutism and religious intolerance were the fundamental causes of the breakdown. The loyalty of the majority Hindu population may have been a possibility under the tolerant Akbar and his immediate successors, but once the ruling elite set their course on a narrow sectarianism, the hopes for long-term stability evaporated. Akbar's personality was both engaging and focused. He was an exceptional leader of men who, according to contemporary Jesuit sources, 'endeavours to show himself pleasant spoken and affable rather than severe toward all who come to speak with him'. At the time of his death in 1605, the emperor had acquired 'an aura of near-divinity and mystery which further reinforced popular perceptions of Mughal infallibility'.[80] The image was not sustained by his successors. The Mughal ruling elite were essentially consuming parasites upon an enormous society of peasant producers who received next to nothing in return from their unwelcome overlords.[81] Convinced of the intractable nature of Hindu culture, the Muslim monarchs had no deep-seated commitment to altering this colonial relationship. For their part Hindus had never turned to government as an institution key to the established Hindu social order. The caste system provided an unshakeable rationale for the hierarchical social structure, and as long as discreet caste groups were successful in managing their own affairs at the village level, loyalty to caste and community always took precedence over allegiance to an abstract state or a personal emperor. In times when taxation was not onerous, the Mughals were an irrelevancy to most of India's population.

Akbar's seventeenth-century successors, Jahangir (r. 1605–27), Shah Jahan (r. 1627–57) and Aurangzeb (r. 1659–1707), continued the tradition of autocratic – and expansionist – rule which was emblematic of all successful Islamic states in the early modern period. Not unlike their Ottoman counterparts, war was the chief concern of every emperor; the territories under direct Mughal authority increased until all but the southern tip of India and Ceylon were embraced. But the instability attendant upon a monarchical order lacking a formal rule of succession seriously compromised the Mughal tenure in India. Akbar's eldest son Selim revolted against his father in 1602, thus setting a precedent which would be followed by subsequent competent heirs. Selim, who became the emperor Jahangir after Akbar's death in 1605 and reigned for 22 years, may have poisoned his father in order to wrest authority from a long-serving autocrat. In turn, Jahangir's 17-year-old son Khusrau organized a series of coup attempts against his father, and in response the emperor finally had the young man blinded and imprisoned for the rest of his life.[82]

Shah Jahan's ascent to power in 1627 was marked by the murders of most of the emperor's male relatives, another gruesome hallmark of Mughal succession ritual. In the bloodiest of struggles, in 1657 Aurangzeb revolted against his father and seized the throne. He had Shah Jahan imprisoned and proceeded to kill his three brothers in what can only be described as a form of civil struggle and fratricide unique to the Ottoman and Mughal monarchical systems. Sadly, Aurangzeb, who ruled almost as long as his grandfather, also reversed Akbar's enlightened policy of religious inclusiveness. In a reign equal to Akbar's in duration (1618–1707, r. 1658–1707), Aurengzeb set in motion policies which in the end nullified the achievements of his predecessors in creating a strong centralized state.

The Muslim *ulema* had been vehemently opposed to Akbar's efforts at a syncretic religion, and his son Jahangir (the offspring of a Hindu mother) did not continue his father's plan to promote *Din-i-Illah*. In response to Sikh complicity in Khusrau's revolts, Jahangir had the leader of Sikhism, the Guru Arjun, executed. This inaugurated a protracted conflict with the Sikhs of the Punjab. Artists, poets and scholars had been patronized by the early court, but even this support waned during the seventeenth century. Jahangir's addiction to alcohol and opium resulted in a pattern of reclusiveness and the delegation of military command which weakened the sacral authority of the ruler. Aurangzeb, who was a man of extreme Muslim exclusivity, set about proscribing Hinduism, lifting the ban on cow killing, destroying a number of Hindu temples and building mosques in their place, and reimposing the hated *jiziya* or poll tax on non-Muslims. The emperor also removed Hindus from high public office and appointed censors of public morals in all of the major cities, while efforts were redoubled to enforce Islamic laws against gambling, drinking and prostitution. Aurangzeb also further exacerbated relations with the Sikhs.

Corruption in the military and civil administration grew markedly in the mid-seventeenth century as the accustomed pattern of military victory and territorial expansion slowed. Military commanders failed to maintain the armed forces stipulated by their rank.[83] Under Aurangzeb the land tax was increased to one half of annual yield in order to pay for the emperor's ongoing military enterprises in the south, and unscrupulous landowners oppressed peasant producers with impunity. Parallel with these tax increases for the general population was the emperor's decision to grant tax-free lands to Muslim *ulema* and their dependants.[84] As Aurangzeb's armies moved across the country against rebellious Sikhs, Marathas and Rajputs, the vision of multi-religious political unity under Muslim domination eroded with it. One French observer, François Bernier, observed that the country's ruin was the direct result 'of defraying the enormous charges required to maintain the splendour of a numerous court, and to pay a large army maintained for keeping the people in subjection ... the cudgel and the whip compel them to incessant labour for the benefit of others'.[85]

In the Deccan a Hindu revolt against the Mughals, beginning in 1681, provided a serious drain on the emperor's time and financial resources. Led by Maratha fighters, the rebels formed a separate Hindu state in central India, one which the traders of the English East India Company in Bombay took seriously. Similarly, Sikhs in the Punjab rebelled against Aurangzeb's harsh rule and established their own territorial enclave in the northeast. Akbar had granted the Sikhs, who under their founder Nanak had articulated a faith system which fused elements of Hinduism and Islam, territory in and around the city of Amritsar. Here they had erected the Golden Temple, a holy site and repository of sacred texts. Aurangzeb had the Sikh leader Tegh Bahadur executed for refusing to convert to Islam, and what had originated as a gentle non-violent movement was pushed into acts of aggression against an intolerant Mughal master.

At his death in 1707, the emperor's three sons immediately fell to disputing the succession to a state whose human and financial underpinnings had been recklessly dissipated by their father. Not surprisingly the victor in the struggle, 63-year-old Muazzam, killed his two brothers but only reigned for five years himself. During the next few decades increasing numbers of provincial mansabdars failed to heed the commands of the quarrelsome emperors, preferring instead to shape new relationships with European, particularly British, traders. But the Westerners did not yet represent the most pressing threat. In 1739 a Persian raider named Nadir Shah invaded India from the north and defeated a large Mughal army. Ignoring all notions of Muslim brotherhood, the invaders looted Delhi, massacred 30,000 inhabitants, and removed the imperial

Peacock throne, commissioned by Shah Jahan, to Persia. This incursion was followed by attacks from Afghanistan under Ahmad Shah Abdali, who after freeing himself from Persian rule, raided northern India on four occasions between 1747 and 1757.[86]

In the aftermath of these experiences no Mughal emperor was able to restore political unity to a land where deep religious animosity and mutual suspicion had been fostered by their predecessors. Following the reign of Aurangzeb, Hindus had little reason to associate their Muslim monarchs with notions of political legitimacy. European commercial interests would inherit the dilemma during the second half of the eighteenth century when several hundred Hindu and Muslim kingdoms and chiefdoms dotted the Indian landscape. In 1765, when forces of the British East India Company defeated the provincial governor (*nawab*) of Bengal and received from the puppet Mughal emperor the right to collect revenues in the province, the effective close of the Mughal interlude was confirmed. After some 200 years, and despite an auspicious beginning under Akbar, the Muslim monarchs of India had failed to procure the allegiance of the majority population. In the end the English would fail as well, but not before bringing India squarely, and permanently, into the arena of world history.

RECESSIONAL

Monarchy in the Islamic lands had become by the midpoint of our survey a form of government characterized by chronic instability and individual capriciousness. While Ottoman Turkey, Safavid Persia and Mughal India reached considerable heights as territorial empires during the course of the sixteenth century, their long-term viability as strong centralized monarchies was severely compromised by three factors: (1) economies built largely around the need for constant military aggrandizement; (2) the failure to formulate and implement an agreed mechanism for the peaceful transition of royal power; and (3) a general reluctance to encourage either the development of new technologies or the ambitions of an entrepreneurial class of merchants and traders. In addition to these major liabilities, the later caliphs, sultans and emperors sadly forfeited the initial strong association of the caliphate with the work of the Prophet Muhammad. Although it can be argued that all Muslim rulers viewed themselves principally as defenders of the Islamic faith in their respective kingdoms, by the time of the Abbasids in the eleventh century the linkage between the office of caliph and the spiritual side of Islam had deteriorated beyond repair. Extravagant and formal court life, personal excess borne of abundant wealth, the bellicosity of an earlier nomadic Turkish tradition, and Persian-Byzantine habits of autocracy all propelled Muslim heads of state in the direction of a type of personal monarchy devoid of the sorts of institutional anchors which ensured the longevity of the Chinese imperial system.

To be sure there had always been conflict over the caliphate; from Abu Bakr onward the mantle of authority had been claimed by competing – and combative – interest groups. But while disputes over the succession characterized even the first century of Arab rule under Islam, it was assumed by all parties that the true caliph enjoyed the power to direct the entire community of the faithful. By the sixteenth and seventeenth centuries, however, this theory stood in awkward juxtaposition to the harsh reality of chronic internecine warfare, Sunni Ottoman against Shi'a Persian, Mughal minority against Hindu majority.

That the ideal of a single Islamic polity had been difficult to sustain in practice should not surprise us given the enormous geographical sweep of the empire as early as the eighth century. But when the political fragmentation of the Islamic nation was compounded by leadership figures who eschewed the mundane work of creating stable mechanisms for the orderly transfer of power, the consequences could be profound. As Paul Kennedy observed in one particular context, 'An idiot sultan could paralyze the Ottoman Empire in the way that a pope or Holy Roman emperor could never do for all Europe.'[87] When the printing press was forbidden for fear that it would facilitate the spread of dangerous ideas, and when a state observatory was destroyed in 1580 on the assumption that the activities undertaken there had somehow contributed to the onset of plague, the deleterious side of personal monarchy in its Ottoman incarnation was brought into very sharp relief. Monarchs who identified their prerogatives with the successor to Muhammad had become expensive parasites, collecting taxes from an increasingly impoverished base and embracing a form of cultural and technological conservatism which would not withstand the challenges presented by their ambitious inferiors to the west, monarchs who, while less powerful with respect to internal matters, were soon to usurp the authority and prestige of their much-loathed Muslim counterparts. Theocratic monarchy was about to succumb to the forces of modernization led by Europe's constitutional monarchs.

4 The Holy Roman Emperor Henry IV (kneeling, foreground) with relations and supporters, just before his submission to Papal authority at Canossa, 1077.

FOUR

The European Anomaly, 1000–1500

As we have seen, most of the world's major civilizations – in China, Byzantium, South Asia, the Islamic lands – had endowed their temporal rulers with a sacral role as head of the religious community. Governed by these theocratic priest-kings whose divine or semi-divine status precluded the creation of effective plural authorities, the work of state building proceeded apace in these lands without significant internal threats to the hegemonic claims of the ruler. The one major exception to this all-encompassing model of governance over heterogeneous peoples was located in the far northwest corner of the Afro-Eurasian intercommunicating zone. For unlike their counterparts elsewhere in the global community, there were no monarchs in what we call Western Europe who ruled alone over Church and state in the year 1000. Indeed there were no states to speak of by this date, if we associate state authority with uncritical loyalty to a recognized ruler, common notions of subject status within a single political community, and the existence of impersonal institutions of law and administration.

European kings ruled over peoples and not over fixed territorial units. According to Antony Black, the notion of a secular king 'as princeps in the Roman-law sense, entitled to make laws without consent, was stoutly resisted by most'.[1] Although it was widely accepted that the Christian head of state derived his authority from the one true God, and while the coronation of a new monarch had become a quasi-sacramental rite by the start of the ninth century, this did not translate into any broadly based movements to make the ruler an unlimited theocratic sovereign. Legitimate kingship in the

West involved temporal power alone and 'rested on the consent of a king's subjects' whether through public acclamation or by election or by an explicit royal promise to uphold established law and tradition.[2] In a manner unique to the West, no functioning monarch in Europe could carry out executive and legislative responsibilities without regular consultation with a wider politically active community of churchmen, nobles and leading townsmen.

What accounts for these anomalous developments? How did Europeans manage to embrace monarchy without succumbing to the lure of absolutist rule (at least until the seventeenth century) and why did constitutional or limited monarchy become the norm solely in this small northerly portion of the Eurasian land mass? There was a time when medieval scholars were content to point to the 'consensual' Germanic features of kingly rule as the answer to these difficult questions. The westward migration of peoples whom the Romans called Huns, Visigoths, Goths, Angles, Ostrogoths and Franks had resulted in the emergence of a host of small tribal and territorial kingdoms after 500 CE, each controlled by largely illiterate warrior elites and their chosen leaders. The Germanic word for king was associated with kindred, and kingship originally represented the authority of an entire clan instead of an individual ruler.[3] It was the clan unit which was believed to possess spiritual power to heal, lead in battle and preserve crops, and the most successful of the clans normally elevated their leader to the position of king over a host of other groupings. The king would in turn select the most promising of his offspring to succeed him, and this act was subsequently affirmed by the popular acclamation of the allied peoples. As long as success in battle and sufficient harvests continued – sure signs that the leader was indeed endowed with special potency – the mandate to rule remained relatively secure within one family. At the foundation of Germanic kingly authority, then, was the implicit understanding that supreme power was contingent upon the enduring good fortune of the leader and his heirs. The magical or sacred qualities associated with early kingship began working against the ruler at the moment that communal belief in his extraordinary powers, and his access to the world of the spirits, abated.[4]

In this early Germanic society, local customary law quickly replaced the old Roman law, while the oath of allegiance to a personal military overlord took the place of fidelity to a wider abstraction: the imperial state. Most importantly, the lord–vassal relationship between the king and his supporters emphasized the need for cooperation and consent when efforts to extend the royal dominions were undertaken. Given these conditions, Germanic kings were obliged to rely upon a variety of devices in order to maintain their power. The appeal to sacred function and consecrated office, constantly impressing upon those who would challenge personal rule the importance of the monarch as a conduit of divine support or favour, clearly had a constraining influence on disgruntled subjects. The threat of force was perhaps the most obvious asset to the ruler, but any resort to violence by these early monarchs was rarely successful without the material support of landed elites who were in agreement with the royal agenda. And such support was almost always connected to the generous bestowal of royal favours, concessions, grants and privileges.[5]

The difficulty with the Germanic 'exceptionalism' thesis is that it is not sustained by what we now know of early peoples elsewhere around the globe. Indeed it has been amply demonstrated by historians and anthropologists that the practice of consultation and the employment of customary law were rather commonplace features of many primitive societies irrespective of geographical setting. We can find some of the best illustrations of this model on the African continent prior to the arrival of the Europeans in the late fif- teenth century. An alternative, and sometimes complementary, explanation involves the place of feudalism in early European political culture. The core of the feudal 'system', we are informed, was built around the principles of common defence and reciprocal understanding of shared needs. But while notions of mutual obligation and reciprocity were at the heart of this localized form of government in Europe beginning with the Germanic invasions, we must ask why other civilizations which adopted feudal practices (such as Japan) failed to follow the limited monarchical model. It appears that when all of the comparative variables are assessed, the one political feature unique to Europe during the centuries before 1000 turns out to be the existence of a powerful, independent and sometimes rival religious establishment – a papal monarchy with universalist pretensions – capable of providing a serious counterweight to the always extensive claims of temporal princes.[6]

Before we look at this special relationship, however, it is helpful to note that in a study of the institution of monarchy in Europe, beginning with the year 1000 is particularly appropriate. Not because there were no kings or emperors in the western reaches of the Eurasian land mass before this date, but rather due to the striking fact that one cannot speak of conventional 'states' over which these monarchs ruled. Fixed territorial boundaries, formal bureaucracies, trained administrators, a stable judicial system with written codes of enforceable law, central control over the instruments of violence, the power to tax and to organize large-scale human and natural resources, a sedentary populace using a common language, and the ability of the political structure to survive changes in leadership – none of these features of civil society which we associate with the modern territorial state could be found in the personal Germanic kingdoms which governed and misgoverned Europe between the fall of Rome and the year 1000. In fact if we exclude Anglo-Saxon England, we must move well into the twelfth century before we can discern marked changes in the institution of monarchy, changes which begin to anticipate some of the more important features of the bureaucratic territorial state.

Unlike their Christian counterparts in Byzantium, the Western monarchs of the early Middle Ages (c. 500–1000) never really succeeded in establishing kingdoms which were anything more than temporary and unstructured coalitions among a like-minded warrior aristocracy. The source of power and wealth in Germanic society was land, and rulers looked upon their lands as private possessions to be used in order to reward loyal servants. Often the royal patrimony would be divided up among the surviving male offspring, thus reducing the authority of the monarch in relation to his most powerful subordinates. Not until the early tenth century was the widespread practice of sharing or dividing kingdoms between sons ended, thus helping to enhance regnal power.[7]

Allegiance to family, community, Church, village, local lord and manor: these were the objects of highest temporal import for the peoples of the early Middle Ages. Across almost 500 years, Europeans largely failed to distinguish between public and private authority, nor for that matter would they have erected separate spheres for politics, religion and morality in the *populus Christianus* or community of Christian peoples. Kings could claim authority solely over lands with loose and shifting boundaries, and most often that authority was only as stable as the relationship between lord and warrior was firm, as long as personal horizontal ties were respected by both parties. Not unlike leaders in stateless African societies, Europe's early medieval monarchs lacked the economic, administrative and intellectual resources needed for the emergence of stable governments.

During the course of the ninth century, in the aftermath of the collapse of Charlemagne's experiment in continent-wide neo-Roman unification, the Latin West was beset by a new wave of invasions – pagan Vikings from the north, Muslims from the south, and Turkish Magyars from the east – the impact of which furthered the process of political fragmentation and decentralization. According to one recent historian, these ninth-century invasions constituted 'one of the principal limitations on the development of a powerful European empire'.[8] Charlemagne's grandsons cleaved the Frankish empire into jurisdictions which would later emerge as separate kingdoms in France and Germany, but the trend towards territorial dissolution did not conclude at this level. The move in the direction of local rule by independent castle lords and their retainers (often referred to as feudalism) was most pronounced in the western reaches of the former Carolingian empire, while in the east a series of Saxon kings managed to retain a small measure of authority while preserving title to a now much-diminished imperial crown.

In 919 the imperial office in Germany passed to Henry, duke of Saxony. Saxony was one of the four great duchies in East Francia, and in 962 Henry's son Otto soundly defeated the Magyars in what signalled the decisive end to pagan threats from the East. Accorded imperial status by Pope John XII, the Saxon dynasty prevented the complete collapse of the German kingdom, but it was but a pale reflection of the old Carolingian empire embracing Germany, Burgundy and northern Italy. With the one exception of Anglo-Saxon England, ineffective monarchy and the absence of central public authority was very much the norm in the Latin West during these centuries; national kingdoms where monarchs oversaw enforceable laws had to await the conclusion of hostile in-migration of new peoples into Europe and the emergence of more settled patterns of life and economic activity. And even then, in places like northern Italy, the penchant for localism outweighed the incipient trend towards centralized monarchy.

ST PETER'S BEQUEST

Into this troubled and fluid political environment one prince alone could lay claim to a measure of universal jurisdiction, but even he faced serious difficulties in translating principled assertion into unencumbered fact. Unlike all other major world civilizations, Europeans during the Middle ages owed their allegiance to two distinct monarchs, each of whom ruled as head of a divinely ordained government and neither of whom was willing to concede superiority to the other. This anomalous situation was due originally in no small part to the gradual disintegration of Roman imperial authority in Western Europe during the fourth and fifth centuries. The first of these monarchs was the temporal head of the empire (*imperium*) or kingdom (*regnum*). In the descending model of government endorsed by leading Church authorities from Augustine to Aquinas, original political power over secular affairs was owned by God. The divine King of kings delegated this authority to a viceregent who was in turn responsible to no one but the supreme lawgiver in heaven.

This theocratic model was in the West set against an ascending theory which located original power in the people or community who subsequently delegated it to a chosen leader. One sees the contours of this model in early Germanic society after the cessation of Roman control in the West. Implicit in the ascending view was a right of resistance should the king exceed the specific powers granted to him by the popular assembly. Before the emergence of an educated lay population in the twelfth century, however, the vast majority of writing about politics was carried on by clerics and canon lawyers for whom the descending model of original power was without serious rival. Filling most of the positions in royal chanceries and other court offices, ecclesiastics actively promoted the notion of royal authority hedged by divinity.

Indeed the metaphor of royalty bulked very large in medieval theology. 'Christ the King' was a commonplace but puissant description of the structure of universal government beyond the earthly realm. Throughout the Middle Ages Christian theology taught that all human authority originated with God, thus legitimizing the rule of one as the best mirror of the divine model.[9] For the influential thirteenth-century Dominican theologian Thomas Aquinas, monarchy was most in accord with nature since

> every natural governance is governance by one. In a multi-tude of bodily members there is one which is the principal mover, namely, the heart; and among the powers of the soul one power presides as chief, namely, the reason. Among bees there is one king bee, and in the whole universe there is One God, Maker and Ruler of all things. And there is a reason for this. Every multitude is derived from unity. Wherefore, if artificial things are an imitation of natural things and a work of art is better according as it attains a closer likeness to what is in nature, it follows that it is best for a human multitude to be ruled by one person.[10]

After Roman authorities officially embraced Christianity in the fourth century, churchmen commonly referred to the king as the protector of the faith who acts in God's name and who exhibits the divine qualities of virtue, honesty, justice and mercy.[11] Indeed the emperor Constantine was often referred to by churchmen as the thirteenth apostle, not least for his precedent-setting decision to grant toleration to Christians in 313, but also in view of his role as protector and chief advocate for the Church.

The second monarch was, of course, the bishop of Rome, successor to St Peter and, following one interpretation of Matthew (16:18–19), monarchical representative of Christ on earth in all matters touching the moral and spiritual realms. In these two areas, the orbit of which often intersected and at times appeared to be coterminous with the temporal sphere headed by individual kings and emperors, the pope claimed plenary judicial power. For a Christian society where murder, robbery, assault and indeed most other crimes were also categorized as sins against God, the boundaries between the jurisdiction of the universal Church and individual kings were more than a little fluid. How to clarify and define the relationship between pope and king so that sharply delineated areas of authority might be set was, in the end, an insuperable challenge.

The Protestant Reformation of the sixteenth century finally settled the issue, sadly, through a very messy divorce in which the autonomous princely state clearly emerged the winner. But the political impact of this thousand-year commingling of the two forms of government had already been felt long before Luther broke with the papacy, with consequences for the future that neither party to the initial disputes could have anticipated or desired. According to Brian Tierney, the existence of two competing power structures during the Middle Ages 'greatly enhanced the possibilities for human freedom' in the West during succeeding centuries. Even after the Reformation elevated the Protestant prince to something greater than a mere layman in the religious affairs of his country, monarchy in Europe would never reach the heights of absolutism witnessed in other major civilizations. Having once been challenged by spiritual monarchs in Rome, Europe's secular kings would next find their ambitions hedged and curbed by their own recalcitrant subjects who demanded a very wide range of corporate liberties and rights to assembly.

This unique, and for the institution of monarchy, momentous conflict with the Church had very deep roots extending back to the fourth and fifth centuries. At first it might seem exceptional that the nascent faith would take any interest in secular matters, especially given both the ambiguous position of the New Testament authors towards the Roman state and the expectation among the first Christians that the end of time was near. While St Paul conceded that some form of coercion was necessary in a world of sinners and counselled obedience to Caesar in the things of this world, there was no hint of according pagan temporal rulers any special relationship with the one true God. The general harassment and periodic persecution suffered by Christians at the hands of the Roman authorities over the first three centuries of the common era did little to foster Christian support for the imperial structure. In the second century, the great Church father Tertullian took the bold and politically dangerous position of referring to Christ as Emperor – an obvious affront to the imperial incumbent – but the majority of early Christian writers used the less charged word 'King' in describing Jesus and 'Kingdom' in reference to His eternal home. Still, all such references were doubtless aimed at emphasizing the universality of Christ's rule as opposed to the temporary and circumscribed jurisdiction of human kings and emperors.[12]

Suspicion turned to alliance after the Roman empire under Constantine recognized Christianity in the early fourth century, but with society now increasingly based on a spiritual framework, the Church in the West pointed with renewed vigour to the contingent nature of temporal authority and claimed for itself an unusual directive role in a universe replete with inveterate sinners. Forgotten was the classical Greek idea of man as a political animal who can only realize his highest ideals within the context of active citizenship, and in its place emerged the picture of temporal political authority as a regrettable response to humankind's sinful nature. Crucial to this formulation was the thought of Augustine, bishop of Hippo (354–430) in North Africa. The impact of St Augustine's thinking on the subject of temporal rule both assisted and undermined the secular monarchical idea. Writing in the early fifth century when the Christian Roman empire in the West was under attack by Germanic tribesman, the bishop of Hippo encouraged Christians to use their talents in the service of the imperial state. In this age of crisis he also counselled obedience to the emperor so long as his actions and mandates did not violate divine ordinances. Resistance to the lawful head of state was sinful, even if the ruler should become a tyrant.

More importantly in terms of its lasting influence, St Augustine emphasized that in the end even the intelligent Christian monarch is doing work of little consequence in comparison to life in the eternal city of God. When rulers neglect their charge to advance the interests of this latter city, then their work on earth is entirely without merit. The fleeting city of man must be governed, and preferably by a monarch who attends to the questions of human nature and human destiny, but for subjects the condition of the soul deserves pre-eminent and enduring attention. And it was the Church which guided the Christian community in the crucial work of life; the secular ruler's subordinate duty was to enforce decisions made within the jurisdiction of God's ordained representatives on earth.[13] Augustine's other-worldly emphasis contributed to the promotion of papal claims to sovereign power in this world, if only in the sense that earthly government was concerned exclusively with the ephemeral, the fleeting affairs of the pilgrim who lives 'like a captive and a stranger in the earthly city', while the divine government of the Church was always focused on the lasting home.[14]

The Augustinian perspective influenced a number of concrete Church actions during that first century of official state toleration and conversion. In 390, for example, when the emperor Theodosius I ordered an indiscriminate attack on Thessalonica after residents there had murdered the garrison commander, the influential bishop of Milan (St Ambrose) excluded the emperor from communion until he completed a public penance. Surprisingly, Theodosius complied with the demand, asking forgiveness and acknowledging the sinful nature of his attack. The entire episode was referred to by later popes as an illustration of the superiority of the Church over secular authorities of all ranks.[15] Ambrose declared that the emperor 'is within the church, not above the church' and that where issues of faith were involved 'it is the custom of bishops to judge Christian emperors, not for Emperors to judge bishops'.[16] A century later Pope Gelasius (492–96) attempted to divide the responsibilities of Church and state so that both institutions were mutually supportive, but even he, in a letter to the emperor Anastasius, concluded that of the two 'the responsibility of the priests is more weighty in so far as they will answer for the kings of men themselves at the divine judgement'.[17]

As Roman power shifted to the East beginning with Constantine's reign in the early fourth century, political authority in the increasingly Germanic West was apportioned in a *de facto* fashion to the bishops of Rome, men who now faced the unenviable task of negotiating with the warlike pagan invaders as best they could. The image of Pope Leo I bargaining with the notorious Attila the Hun in 451 in an effort to save the city of Rome from attack is perhaps most suggestive of the expanded duties associated with the papal office. In the West the Church was emerging as the one true state, and while the pope continued to solicit the support of the emperors in Constantinople, imperial authority was normally exercised under papal auspices.[18] Missionaries were sent north by subsequent popes in order to convert the new Germanic inhabitants, and bishops in these unsettled lands often served *ex tempore* as governors, judges and protectors of the local populations. The difficult work of conversion and administration continued for centuries, but it was not until the emergence of a strong Frankish kingdom in the mid-eighth century that the papacy secured a dependable ally to take the place of the distant – and for purposes of Western security, ineffectual – emperor in Constantinople. The Franks had conquered the whole of Roman Gaul in the early sixth century, and their acceptance of orthodox Christianity (most of the other Germanic peoples were either pagan or Arians) identified them as suitable allies of the papacy. That alliance was solidified in the mid-eighth century when the patriarch of the West endorsed the usurpation of the Frankish throne by Pepin the Short in return for Frankish military assistance against the Arian Lombards of Italy.

Pepin's son and heir Charles the Great or Charlemagne cultivated the support of the papacy in the work of political consolidation and sought to find accommodation with the leaders of the Church whenever possible. Engaged throughout his 32-year reign in almost constant and brutal warfare against a number of 'heathen' peoples – Muslims, Lombards, Avars, Saxons – on behalf of Catholic Christianity, Charlemagne became the indispensable protector of the bishop of Rome, the very embodiment of expansive Roman Christianity during the late eighth century. In a dramatic incident on Christmas Day in the year 800, Pope Leo III placed a crown on Charlemagne's head and acknowledged him as the new emperor of the Romans. The word *emperor* was normally used to designate a king who controlled neighbouring peoples and kingdoms, as Charlemagne did from his Frankish base in Aachen.[19]

For the first time acclamation by the Germanic warrior elite was confirmed by the rite of holy coronation, an act which suggested to many within the Church that headship of the temporal empire – at least in the West – itself was in the gift of the Church. By performing the acts of anointing and coronation, intended to buttress the authority of the crown by marking the king off from other men by supernatural sanction, the papacy had taken an important step towards the claim that secular political authority was to be wielded on behalf of a more spiritual kingdom.[20] The militia of St Peter, under the immediate direction of Charlemagne but subordinate to the directive offices of the Church, would advance the cause of universal Christianity without reference to the Roman emperor in Constantinople.

Not surprisingly, it was at this important juncture that one of the more significant forgeries of the Middle Ages was produced. The so-called 'Donation of Constantine' alleged that the first Christian emperor, before departing for his new Eastern capital at Constantinople in 330, had made the bishop of Rome temporal ruler over central Italy in particular and over the whole of the West in general. In an important respect, the coronation of Charlemagne represented the papacy's declaration of independence from its centuries-long acknowledgement of Byzantine suzerainty in the now largely Germanic kingdoms. In 865 Pope Nicholas I encapsulated this sentiment when he questioned the right of the Byzantines to have a Roman Caesar who no longer spoke Latin and who no longer ruled Rome itself.[21] It was the start of an estrangement between the Roman Christian West and the Orthodox Christian East which would reach tragic proportions in the early eleventh century.

But whatever papal intentions may have been in the year 800, the coronation of a Germanic leader as emperor, performed by the Western patriarch, also served to enhance the dignity and authority of the secular head who was prior to this event little more than a successful warrior king. Now monarchs were often described in Old Testament terms as the Lord's anointed in a fallen world. Like his Byzantine counterpart in the East Roman empire, Charlemagne took a very active interest in clerical appointments, the convening of Church councils and the promulgation of religious doctrine. The religious element in the sacrament of coronation was after a manner described in the Old Testament, where priests applied holy oil to kings and prophets. And the symbolism which developed around the ceremony itself, where a sword, sceptre, ring and crown would be presented, and vestments and sandals worn, was not unlike the ceremony involving the consecration of a bishop.

If nothing else, the involvement of the Roman Church in the elevation of the secular ruler indicated that something more than the merely mundane was involved in the office of head of state, and that the actions of the emperor were akin to the will of the divine.[22] During those early centuries when many Germanic kings, including Charlemagne, were illiterate, the personnel of Church and state typically overlapped. Charlemagne actively recruited these scholar-bureaucrats to his palace school at Aachen, and in addition to preserving much of the learning of Latin antiquity and the early Church, these men contributed to the conscious identification of

Charlemagne's imperial project with the heritage of the Christian Roman empire. One of these scholars, Alcuin of York, told the king that

> Our Lord Jesus Christ has set you up as the ruler of the Christian people, in power more excellent than the pope or the emperor of Constantinople, in wisdom more distinguished, in the dignity of your rule more sublime. On you alone depends the whole safety of the churches of Christ.[23]

OPENING CONFLICTS

Unfortunately for fully fledged supporters like Alcuin, by the mid-ninth century Charlemagne's brief-lived empire came apart under the joint impact of new external invaders and the fratricidal misrule of his contentious grandchildren. As central authority frayed in the face of Viking, Magyar and Muslim attacks, local princes and lesser landed elites came to play an unprecedented role in the religious and political life of an increasingly feudal society. In addition to organizing defences at the local level, powerful laymen arrogated to themselves the right to designate and invest bishops, abbots and other clergy with their Church offices, for these churchmen more often than not functioned as officers of now much diminished units of royal government. Church buildings and property were not infrequently provided by powerful patrons who expected to appoint clergy. With bishops receiving the symbols of office (staff and ring) from lay lords while paying homage to lay rulers for the use of feudal lands, the historic claim of the papacy to oversee the spiritual direction of temporal rulers was deeply compromised. In addition, the accrual of large estates by bishops and abbots in the service of landed elites associated the Church with an unseemly penchant for wealth seeking and material ambition.

The untoward practice of laymen selecting bishops, abbots and other clerics persisted for a very long time before an important reform movement within the Church, begun by Pope Leo IX and forwarded by Pope Gregory VII (c. 1020–1085, pope

1073–85) at the start of our period, envisioned a revitalized and autonomous Church where all leading appointments were once again made without the interference of noble, king or emperor. In an age when the levers of secular government were often in the hands of men whose first obligation was supposedly to the spiritual realm and its head, the implications of such a reform for the authority of secular rulers were enormous. For those kings and princes who resisted the reform initiative within the Church, the protracted struggle known as the 'investiture controversy' was really about the papal monarchy's quest for international hegemony, a papal theocracy or world-monarchy.[24] Between the years 1000 and 1300 the debate over what has been called the 'proprietary Church' found contentious voices across the continent.[25] In the process new ideas about the proper scope of royal political authority found expression.

The papacy had not been immune to the forces of disintegration and decay which afflicted so much of European political life after Charlemagne's death. The city of Rome, for example, was repeatedly threatened by Muslims based in Sicily during the later ninth century, and the office of the Holy See had sunk to the level of a sordid prize pursued by rival factions within the Roman nobility, none of whom was particularly zealous about their religious charge. The venality and incompetence of many of these pontiffs led increasing numbers of Church officials and monasteries to ally themselves even more firmly to their respective lay lords. It was, ironically, a temporal head who appointed the personnel destined to inaugurate the papal reform movement. In 1046 the devout and conscientious emperor Henry III (1017–56, r. 1039–56) travelled to Rome for his imperial coronation and found there three rival claimants to the Holy See. Working alongside a group of sympathetic reform clergy, Henry deposed all of the candidates and intruded his own German nominee into the office. After two brief pontificates, another of Henry's choices, a kinsman of the emperor who took the name Leo IX (pope 1049–54), began the task of consolidating the power of the papal office over its own personnel, the *sacerdotium*. Synods were organized and the practices of simony (selling Church offices), clerical marriage and concubinage were condemned, while the pope undertook a series of trips through France and Germany, where additional councils were held and troublesome prelates disciplined. For the first time in centuries, the pontiff's direct authority was felt north of the Alps.

Further reforms adopted shortly after Leo's death by his successor Nicholas II (1058–61) included the claim that future popes must be elected by the cardinal clergy and not simply installed by royal fiat. According to this 1059 decree on papal election,

> When the pontiff of this universal Church dies the cardinal bishops shall first confer together most diligently concerning the election; next they shall summon the other cardinal clergy; and then the rest of the clergy and the people shall approach to give their assent to the new election, the greatest care being taken lest the evil of venality creep in by any way whatsoever.[26]

That same year a Church synod formally prohibited the practice of lay investiture whereby a newly appointed bishop or abbot performed an act of homage to the emperor (or another lay lord) in return for the symbols of his office, but no specific enforcement mechanism was established.

When the popular reforming cardinal Hildebrand was elected Pope Gregory VII in 1073, however, the theoretical foundations of an autonomous Church which had been laid in the previous decades were now translated into policy. For the new pope the true design of Christ's kingdom on earth necessitated a spiritual ordering of temporal life under the direction of the successor to St Peter. To this end he directed his subordinates to research and organize earlier claims on behalf of papal authority, and these claims were subsequently integrated into Church or canon law. On 7 March 1076 Gregory excommunicated and deposed Emperor Henry IV (1056–1106) over the investiture issue. The immediate cause of the conflict involved Henry's choice for archbishop of Milan, an important imperial office in northern Italy. Reform clergy in Milan rejected the imperial appointee, and Pope Gregory backed his clergy.

From the pope's perspective the continuation of lay investiture violated the ancient practices of the apostolic Church and undermined the spiritual monarch's efforts to restore a measure of discipline and control over religious personnel, not to mention the pontiff's ability to further the reform movement. Henry's position was equally compelling. During his long minority much of his power had been usurped by rival German princes, and now to forego the practice of appointing bishops and abbots jeopardized his plan to mould a united monarchy embracing all German and north Italian lands. Churchmen may have been compromised in their role as spiritual leaders while serving the emperor, but lacking an educated lay bureaucracy, kings throughout Europe needed loyal clerics who were dedicated to the royal agenda. Since German bishops were also powerful feudal lords exercising jurisdiction over lands belonging to the emperor, Henry believed that it was imperative for the temporal monarch to continue the custom of appointing men whose first loyalty was to the crown.

The pope's deposition of an emperor was an unprecedented act which extended the traditional papal claim of spiritual leadership to one of political headship as well, for in the letter of deposition the pope released 'all Christian men from the allegiance which they have sworn or may swear to him' and forbade anyone to serve Henry as king. 'For it is fitting that he who seeks to diminish the glory of thy church should lose the glory which he seems to have.'[27] Although many German bishops were troubled by Gregory's barbed line of attack, the pope's sweeping assertion inspired a number of disaffected German nobles to propose the election of a new emperor, and in the face of this incipient revolt Henry asked the pope's forgiveness during a meeting at the castle of Canossa in Tuscany. This dramatic stand down occurred in January 1077, and for a brief moment Gregory seemed to have vindicated his claim to supreme power in Christendom, including the right to depose temporal kings.

The pope's actions against Henry further destabilized an

already precarious political situation in the empire. Despite Gregory's forgiveness, Henry's opponents went forward with the election of an anti-king, triggering a civil war which raged for three years. In the end Henry defeated his rival Rudolf of Swabia and turned his armies against Rome. The imperial synods of Bamberg and Mainz in 1080 renounced all allegiance to Gregory, and by the time of the pope's death in 1085 the emperor had driven the successor to St Peter from the eternal city and appointed an anti-pope. After further conflict and negotiation, in 1122 a compromise was reached between Pope Calixtus II (1119–24) and Henry's son with the signing of the Concordat of Worms. It was now agreed that bishops and abbots would be elected according to the rules of canon law, but the emperor reserved the right to be present at these elections and to receive homage from those prelates who held lands as vassals of the crown. In effect the provision gave secular rulers ongoing influence in the appointment of all bishops within their realms, and this tangled situation endured throughout the remainder of the medieval period. Powerful churchmen continued to concern themselves with the material realm as wealthy landholders under kings and as clerks within their courts, and the fundamental issue of the Church's relationship with the world of perishable goods was left unresolved. The anomalous European practice of dual monarchy and dual allegiance would remain at the core of political culture for another 400 years.

RESURGENT MONARCHIES

The struggle between Pope Gregory and Henry IV took place at the start of the period covered in our survey, and the affair was emblematic of a deeper sense of crisis affecting all aspects of European society during the eleventh century. We therefore open our survey of monarchy in Western Europe with the unpleasant fact of widespread public disorder, with security for the bulk of the peasant population contingent upon the effectiveness of private authority subject to no higher order of civil organization. It was a society in which the bond of allegiance between lord and vassal took precedence, or in some cases replaced, the ostensibly higher bond between king and subject. The case of Capetian France is illustrative of the difficult situation. Elected king by the great magnates of the realm after the death of the last Carolingian in 987, Hugh Capet, along with his immediate successors, lacked the material resources necessary to intervene effectively in disputes between the great vassals of the crown and those who in turn had taken oaths of allegiance and fealty to holders of large fiefs or landed estates. In such a situation personal allegiance to the monarch was anything but firm; in practice the most powerful tenants-in-chief of the king of France continued to adjudicate disputes on their own feudal estates while commanding significant military strength by virtue of the primary oaths pledged to them directly.

Private jurisdictions, in other words, hampered the ability of the monarch to enforce obedience to the dictate of the crown; the king might issue calls for his vassals to appear before the royal court, but it was the exceptional vassal who complied with the request when it was not in his interest to do so. The strongest bonds of social cooperation, or what we might term 'public authority', continued to be private unwritten agreements (largely based on sacred oaths) between members of the nobility, lord over vassal, landowner over peasant. In such a society there was little room for abstract notions of the common weal.

By most accounts the experience of political localism was not a salutary one, and popular lay revulsion at the lack of security and continued exploitation at the hands of powerful elites would be a key factor in the revival of strong monarchies during the twelfth century. Endemic warfare between rival estate holders with their complement of knight retainers not infrequently disrupted what little economic and social order could be found in the European countryside. So pronounced was the instability that a Church council meeting at Charroux in France in 989 condemned any person who attacked the poor. Subsequent prohibitions against attacking certain classes of people resulted in formalizing what became known by the mid-eleventh century as the

'Peace of God'. It was followed by the 'Truce of God', pronouncements which were meant to stop violent activities first on holy days and later from sundown on Wednesdays until sunrise on Mondays.

These were something more than pious declarations, for by 1050 a number of regions, particularly in France, witnessed the emergence of popular mass-movements led by clerics and designed to put an end to the indiscriminate violence.[28] The Holy Roman emperor Henry III made a public appeal for peace at Constance in 1043, and by the close of the century the sight of monks leading peasants in what amounted to private self-defence organizations testified to the high level of frustration that common people felt regarding local lawlessness. The peace movements also reflected the incapacity of kings to do much about the problem of pugilistic nobles. And while the Church by the tenth century possessed many of the features of a state, with its formal bureaucracy and staff of literate administrators, it too was lacking the coercive power requisite to the enormous task at hand.

At best the Church could encourage a redirection of noble violence away from orthodox innocents and against the heretic who demurred from official theology. By the close of the eleventh century this penchant for constant warfare on the part of the feudal nobility was being employed in a new struggle against the Muslim infidel. At the Council of Clermont in November 1095, Pope Urban II (1088–99) called for a general peace in Christian Europe and the redirection of feudal military activities eastward. In advocating an armed pilgrimage to Jerusalem, the Church would supervise and control the violence of Europe's lay warrior class against non-Christians. Lacking any practical alternative, Europe's spiritual leaders were keen to harness traditional patterns of violence in the broader interests of the Church militant.[29]

The return to strong temporal monarchy, if it was to be realized, needed to be coupled with an appeal to the divine nature of the executive office, especially if the movement had any reasonable hope of curbing the abuses of local strongmen. Widespread support, both lay and clerical, for such an exalted office in the face of the continued depredations of feudal magnates provided the essential ingredient in the reconstruction of monarchical authority, in endowing monarchy with the requisite moral authority to back its claims to legal supremacy. In 1066 William the Conqueror succeeded in convincing the papal curia that Harold Hardrada was a usurper and that Archbishop Stigand of Canterbury was a schismatic, and as a result the Norman invaders entered England carrying a papal banner. And in 1155 the only Englishman to serve as pope (Nicholas Breakspear or Adrian IV) made a formal grant of Ireland to King Henry II. In France during the twelfth century the Capetian kings began the process of consolidating their power base around Paris and Orleans with the support of the Church, thereby setting the stage for future encroachments on the assumed prerogatives of the semi-independent feudal nobility, but the process of centralizing authority, and of inculcating the notion that the preservation of the state was a positive good, was both slow and arduous.[30]

But while it may have been difficult for contemporaries to recognize any substantive changes in the overall quality of their lives after 1000, by the end of the eleventh century Western Europe was beginning to recover from the worst difficulties occasioned by the failure of the Carolingian political-religious project. As the threat of outside invasion receded and fixed population centres evolved, agricultural production increased on reclaimed lands, towns and cities re-emerged, long-distance trading connections were established, and the overall population of the continent began an upward trajectory which would continue until the demographic disaster of the Black Death in the mid-fourteenth century. Each of these developments contributed to the formation of monarchies dedicated to the idea of centralized administration, uniform justice and religious orthodoxy.

Improved agricultural technology, including the use of windmills, water mills, heavy wheeled ploughs, horseshoes and the tandem harness, all boosted agricultural output to the point where surpluses were available for sale in growing urban areas. The most significant social, cultural and political developments after 1000 occurred in the towns, where for the first time since the collapse of Roman rule in the West a strong merchant class developed which was very keen to see the enhancement of royal authority if this meant greater security for long-distance trade. In turn the growing affluence of the mercantile class translated into a quickening of intellectual life centred around the cathedrals and the newly formed universities. The expanding wealth of the towns provided kings with a unique opportunity to build a more stable political structure.

Seeking a steady source of income which might be employed in curbing the excesses of the feudal nobility, monarchs began focusing on better estate management, the collection of tolls and the assessing of fines in royal courts, and negotiating agreements with local urban elites whereby greater self-government was granted to cities and towns in return for an annual financial grant to the crown. Merchants sought the right to own property and to move goods unhindered, to execute commercial contracts, to be tried by peers in a town court, while monarchs took the opportunity to confer these rights in return for crucial economic assistance. The enhanced monetary and military status of the crown made possible by such arrangements enabled kings to bring potentially rebellious vassals into greater cooperation with the royal centralizing programme.

ENGLAND FIRST

Many of these developments occurred initially in Anglo-Saxon England. At the very time when the French kingdom was spiralling downwards into a myriad of troublesome private jurisdictions, the kings of Wessex in the south of England were creating institutions of centralized authority which would be adopted and further developed by the Normans after their successful invasion of the island kingdom in 1066. England before the ninth-century Viking onslaught consisted of three competing monarchies – Wessex in the south, Mercia in the midlands, and Northumbria in the north. But the

Danish attacks after 800 eliminated all but the authority of the West Saxon kings, and even here it was only at the close of the century that King Alfred of Wessex was able to rebuff the invaders. West Saxon propagandists successfully linked the heroic victories over the pagans with Christian rulership, and subsequent West Saxon territorial gains over other Anglo-Saxon peoples were conveniently represented in terms of a religious *reconquista* against pagan Norsemen.[31]

Beginning in the 880s the Wessex kingdom extended its influence across most of southern England, and by the middle of the tenth century not only did local royal officials (counts of the shire or sheriffs) enforce internal order, but a network of royal courts adjudicated disputes throughout the kingdom and prevented the growth of private jurisdictions. A national army (*fyrd*) instilled a sense of common purpose even at the local level, and the Anglo-Saxon kings won support for each of these innovations in a deliberative assembly known as the *witan*.[32] In 973, King Edgar, in an elaborate consecration ceremony at Bath, a city with firm links to the Roman imperial past, was crowned king of the entire English people.[33] Even the Danish king Canute, having defeated an incompetent English monarch in 1017, continued to uphold the legal and administrative apparatus created by Alfred and his immediate successors. England's monarchy was very much what Jeremy Black has called an 'administrative kingship' where the roots of political centralization went much deeper than anywhere on the European continent.

Rather than abandon these helpful precedents, the Norman kings affixed their own particular brand of the lord–vassal relationship on the extant institutions. In particular, the introduction of a unique model of seigneurial feudal governance in England after 1066 enabled William the Conqueror to avoid some of the more crucial difficulties inherent in the rule of kings with the support of oath-taking vassals. After his victory over Harold, earl of Wessex, William proceeded to claim all of England by right of military achievement and inheritance. He expropriated Anglo-Saxon estates and assigned them as fiefs to his French-speaking vassals, but vast stretches of territory remained in the royal demesne.

Whereas in the majority of feudal relationships vassals of the king were permitted to recruit their own allied subordinates whose contractual dependence was to their immediate superior, the Norman monarchs insisted that all vassals, irrespective of their oaths to an immediate local lord, had to accept that they were finally accountable to the king of England alone. Private war was prohibited, and all castle building had to be licensed in advance by the crown. The preservation and expansion of the Anglo-Saxon governing institutions facilitated the inculcation of this new view of the feudal relationship where the object of highest temporal allegiance, and the font of justice, was the king and the various royal courts of law.

Soon after his arrival in England, William I commissioned a wide-ranging survey of landholdings, and the resulting Domesday Book enabled the crown to better estimate what was owed in taxes and fees to the central government. Under William's successors, royal courts of justice and departments of state such as exchequer (for finance) and chancery (for the coordination of royal business foreign and domestic) became permanent features of the central bureaucracy. The employment of writs issued in the king's name for the purpose of initiating proceedings at law, together with the widespread adoption of jury trial where one's peers played the key role in deciding guilt or innocence, further advanced popular support for strong monarchy.

Under Henry II (1154–89) the old feudal formula of royal grants of land in return for services performed gave way before a developing money economy where royal servants became the paid agents of the crown. Henry was especially eager to extend the impact of royal justice, not only for the greater revenues that such a system was capable of generating through the sale of writs and the assessment of fines, but perhaps more fundamentally for their ability to cement the loyalty of a growing population to the person of the king. During his reign the notion of a common law, administered by itinerant royal justices who completed regular circuits throughout the countryside, superseded the jumble of local law and custom and fostered a sense of common, kingdom-wide identity.

In France the state-building enterprise had to begin around the circumscribed royal estates near Paris and the Île de France. And in a country of much larger size than England, with a wider diversity of local customs and traditions, the task of royal centralization was inevitably much more difficult. Although he was in theory overlord of the great princes – the dukes of Normandy and Burgundy, the counts of Anjou, Chartres, Blois, Champagne and Flanders – the Capetian king Louis VI (1108–37) spent the better part of his long reign attempting to curb the independent power of these vassals in adjacent regions, and in these efforts he enjoyed the blessing of the French clergy. Abbot Suger of St Denis served as a close adviser to the next king, Louis VII (1137–80), and even endorsed the monarch's call for the excommunication of his disobedient vassals as one weapon in the drive for monarchical supremacy.[34] The Church's support for the royal programme was greatly enhanced by Louis' leadership in the Second Crusade (1147–49), and by the king's support for Pope Alexander III in the papacy's conflict with the Holy Roman emperor Frederick Barbarossa.[35] By the time that Louis' son, Philip II Augustus (1180–1223), went on crusade in 1190, there were in place some basic elements of a system of royal administration over ever-larger districts, a system that by 1300 would oversee the largest and wealthiest monarchical state in Western Europe.

Under Philip Augustus, salaried *bailli* who were recruited from the lower nobility looked after the king's estates, collected tolls and assessed fines in local courts created under the king's name. The bulk of this activity took place within the royal demesne, thus providing the king with a source of considerable wealth separate from the still semi-autonomous provinces ruled by his vassals. Each *bailli* was responsible to the king's council, and three times each year a report was made to this body in Paris.[36] Revenues collected by the *bailli*, who in certain respects can be compared to the itinerant justices in Henry II's England, enabled Philip and his successors to reduce the independence of the great feudatories. Not least of these was the Norman king of England. When King John refused to acknowledge a royal summons to answer complaints made against him by another powerful vassal, Philip declared John's substantial fiefs forfeit to the crown. By 1205 the duchies of Normandy, Anjou and Maine were in the hands of the French crown, and no collective action on the part of the various counts and dukes to resist this aggrandizement of power emerged. The customs, laws and local institutions of these territories were left intact by the king, except for the fact that men from the Ile de France, all agents of the crown, took control of the key offices. In this manner particularist cultural sensibilities were in the main respected while the presiding officials were chosen by the monarch.

Provincial officials were constantly mediating between local authorities and the agents of the crown in Paris, but in the event the solution proved workable given the patchwork and divergent character of feudal tradition. Subsequent attempts by John to retake his feudal estates in France led to a series of unprecedented financial exactions on the most powerful of his English subjects, and their refusal to accept John's methods provided the background to the Great Charter or Magna Carta of 1215. The kings of France were not able to develop a system of common law like their Anglo-Norman rivals, but while French provinces continued to maintain their distinct legal customs, the lack of a common law or common tradition actually inhibited the type of collective resistance to the centralizing efforts of the crown that emerged in England and was epitomized in Magna Carta.[37]

King Philip Augustus was succeeded by his son Louis VIII (1223–26), who before his death after only three years on the throne allied the crown with the Church crusade against Albigensian heretics in southern France. The violent elimination of the Albigensians marked the extension of royal authority into new territory, but the king's death also marked the start of a long period in which the Louis' widow, Blanche of Castile, was the real ruler of the kingdom. Royal institutions of government continued to develop under Blanche's supervision, and when Louis IX (1226–70) took control of the government in the 1240s further reforms were inaugurated. In particular, Louis' concern for impartial justice within his own domains led to the formation of a new group of royal inspectors (often Dominicans or Franciscans) known as *enquêteurs* whose task was to investigate local grievances against *baillis* and other royal officials. Canonized as a saint by the Church at the end of the thirteenth century, Louis' crusading activities and general support for the Church has often overshadowed his significant work as an administrator. When he died at the age of 44, the territory and wealth controlled by the king of France were without rival in Europe, and the image of the crown as the focus of justice informed by religious idealism facilitated the decline of localism and provincial particularism, at least among those who were subject to the oppression and caprice of the landed elite.[38]

At the close of the thirteenth century, the government of Philip IV (1285–1314) accelerated the growth of royal authority, but the new monarch struck a different note from the pious Christianizing mission pursued by his grandfather Louis IX. The king's chief judicial council had become a group of professional judges known as the *Parlement*, and a central office of royal finance, the *Chambre des Comptes*, was created in Paris. In increasing numbers of districts throughout the kingdom a royal proctor or professional advocate watched over the king's interest in all local litigation. Perhaps more importantly, the new men who held these posts were students of Roman civil law. Trained at places like Orleans and Montpellier, they brought to their task a more secular approach and a predisposition to advance the royal prerogative throughout the country.

LAW AND MONARCHY

The initial stages of the investiture struggle had resulted in the failure of each of the two principal branches of the same Christian society to make good its claims to theocratic monarchy, and the implications for the future of monarchical institutions – and for human freedom – in the West were enormous.[39] The tension was sometimes complicated, sometimes ameliorated, by the fact that both institutions employed the services of overlapping personnel. As we have seen, the clerks who served in the chanceries, treasuries and courts of the king were more often than not ordained churchmen whose first allegiance, theoretically at least, was to the universal Church of Rome. However by the end of the twelfth century many of these churchmen were being trained in the growing fields of canon law and/or Roman law, and the impact of this training on ideas concerning the legitimate power of monarchs was transformative for Church and state alike.

Prior to the revival of legal studies in the decades before 1100, law in the Germanic tradition consisted mainly of an unwritten inheritance, prescriptive norms that were thought to be fixed and eternal but also particular to one people. By and large Germanic unwritten law and feudal custom focused on the contractual nature of relations between king and subject, where the king was expected to defend the inherited customs and laws of each of the communities under his jurisdiction.[40] While occasionally these laws might need adjustment, they never required fundamental reworking. One 'discovered' the law instead of legislating it into being. In opposing the Gregorian reformers in the Church, for example, the supporters of Emperor Henry IV appealed to custom when attempting to defend practices like investiture, and they did their best to allege 'innovation' against the papacy for its reform programme.[41]

But as monarchy came to be linked with the restoration of order and justice in the feudal and anarchic countryside, as kingship was increasingly associated with the administration of Church-defined notions of justice, a greater number of laymen and clerics began to take an interest in higher learning, both in jurisprudence as it was embodied in the sixth-century *Corpus Iuris Civilis* of Justinian, and in Church law as it had been assembled by Gratian around 1140 and set forth in his *Concord of Discordant Canons* popularly known as the

Decretum. The language of men trained in civil law (*ius commune*), the jurists who studied the ancient Roman legal system as codified under the sixth-century emperor Justinian, provided a key ingredient to political discourse and practice after 1000, one basically sympathetic to a strong monarchical ideal, especially the king's right to make new law through royal promulgation. Stressing universal principles rather than the particularist and local traditions of Germanic law, together with the value of strong central government with powers to tax and legislate for the common good, the law faculties at early eleventh-century Bologna and later at northern universities stressed this comprehensive picture of governing authority.[42]

Classical jurisprudence tended to stress the divine origins of kingship and the sacral nature of the imperial office. Those texts which appeared to accent the will of the prince before the consent of the wider political community greatly assisted the programme of centralizing monarchy during the High Middle Ages. At its most basic level, Roman law re-introduced Western Europe to the idea of the state, and of monarchical government as a public enterprise involving the entire kingdom. No longer were private feudal magnates, whose authority came not from God nor from the people, accepted as legitimate law-making agents. Even in England, where the influence of Roman law was minimal, efforts at systematizing the laws were undertaken and twelfth-century Norman kings like Henry II worked diligently to sweep away a variety of archaic feudal jurisdictions, replacing them with common law as practised in the royal courts.

Canon law, on the other hand, provided a more diverse assessment of monarchical prerogative. Official interest in Church statutes had been aroused by the protracted investiture debate, but while various collections of Church law were extant by 1100, no uniform code was available to administrators whose primary interest was in shaping a consistent Catholic doctrinal practice and organizational structure throughout Europe. Gratian had set himself the enormous task of sorting out the many overlapping (and sometimes contradictory) papal decrees and council decisions from almost a thousand years of Church history. His goal was to provide the

Roman Church with a thorough structure of jurisprudence, one as complete in the area of Church affairs as Roman law was in civil matters. The scholars who followed in the footsteps of Gratian, known as Decretists or canonists, often worked to fuse concepts drawn from canon, Roman and common law traditions. By and large they offered support for the strong claims of the papacy to supreme authority over Christ's earthly kingdom, and indeed the Holy See became the court of final appeal when disputes arose within the Church on a wide range of issues, including marriage contracts, wills, oaths and vows, provision of poor relief, suppression of heresy and enforcement of contract. By the end of the twelfth century a great number of infractions involving laymen and clerks were being referred to papal authority for adjudication.

But the same canon lawyers who elevated the universalist authority of the pope also represented another view of Church polity which stressed notions of community governance, where papal supremacy was to be acknowledged when exercised in concert with the consent of Church leaders gathered together in a general council. Gratian's *Decretum* had mentioned several cases involving popes who were alleged to have sinned, and the prospect of the entire Church being undermined by one person's actions was deeply troubling to the lawyers. As early as the late twelfth century there were Decretalists who maintained that a heretical pope could be disciplined and even removed by general council, particularly when matters central to the faith were involved.[43] To prevent such disasters, the pope must be obliged to exercise his plenary authority within the state of the Church as a whole, the *status ecclesiae*. He might create law, but as head of the Christian community he could not alter the Church's organizational structure or change doctrines which had been established during apostolic times.[44] Thus the absolutist implications of the earlier Petrine theory were balanced by a strong model of the Church as a corporation, the congregation of the faithful, which flourishes best within the bounds of a broad governing consensus.

The impact of the canonists in this area was not restricted

to the Holy See, for their work later informed notions of parliamentary monarchy where the highest expression of secular rule was believed to be the product of the king-in-parliament. Thus community engagement and the principle of consent were key elements of stable and effective governance not just in the learned treatises of the canon lawyers. In fact by 1000 a wide range of lesser self-governing corporate bodies were functioning successfully throughout Western Europe. From cathedral chapters responsible for electing their bishop, to monks choosing their abbot, to members of guilds regulating their professional affairs, the principle of consent and collegial sharing had become a part of the intellectual fabric of everyday life across Western Europe. Universities, cities and towns, and religious confraternities also engaged in forms of governance which did not accept the premise of theocratic rule. Members elected their own officers, regulated their internal affairs without interference, and respected the equality of all who enjoyed a place in the corporation. Rule in the interests of the common good was instinctively linked with justice in the minds of lawyer and churchman alike, and monarchs who ignored this principle enjoyed scant support.

CENTRALIZING MONARCHIES, NATIONAL CHURCHES AND CONSENT

During the early Middle Ages, Church and kingdom were thought to be the two constituent parts of one larger society, the mystical body of Christ or the Christian community. Few people before the year 1000 would have drawn the sorts of formal distinctions between Church and state that we operate under in the modern West. But during the course of the eleventh century a variety of what we might call 'law states' began to emerge in the West, kingdoms whose primary function was the creation and enforcement of one rule of law for all subjects and in conformity with the Church's vision of Christian conduct. One impact of the investiture struggle between the emperor and the pope at the close of that century had been to highlight the monarch's duties with respect to the enforcement of law. The Gregorian reforms may have strengthened the Church's sense of institutional autonomy from the secular ruler, but as we have noted the Church had no coercive mechanism by which it could enforce orthodoxy on the wider population. Once the limits of proselytization had been reached, the papacy was obliged to turn to the secular head for assistance in the work of correcting the wayward.

But there was now a significant price to be paid for the cooperation of the temporal sword in the work of maintaining Roman Catholic orthodoxy. By the late twelfth century the monarchs of England and France were asserting the unprecedented right to discipline the clergy in their respective territories, and to tax the Church for the purpose of advancing the secular interests of the kingdom. The papacy instinctively resisted this innovation, but in the end had to concede that members of the Church must relinquish part of their corporate wealth to the magistrate whose control over resources of coercion was vital to the defence of the faith. It was a momentous transition, one where the prerogatives of the universal Church were now to be compromised by the financial exactions of the territorial state. And it is in this context that we see the development of the first permanent and impersonal departments of secular government whose jurisdiction transcended the myriad baronial and provincial practices of the feudal age. First in England, then in France, and later in the Spanish kingdoms, monarchs increasingly employed laymen and clerics whose training in Roman and canon law imposed a new sense of order and systematization on the routine of government. In particular, royal courts of justice, financial or treasury departments, and offices of administration or chancery begin to take control of the day-to-day operation of the royal court.

In twelfth-century England, for example, the office of Exchequer was responsible both for the collection of all crown revenues derived from widely dispersed sources – including the Church – and for auditing the accounts of the many royal officials who served the crown throughout the country. In terms of royal justice, the king's court served to adjudicate the disputes of the powerful, while circuit courts were established in order to bring royal justice into every county. By 1250 these courts were investing the local community in the justice system through the creation of inquest and trial juries. Gradually a body of precedent was developed so that judges could apply uniform rules and standards for the courts. In this way men who had for generations looked for justice from the manor, Church or baronial court now turned to the crown as an impartial arbiter of local conflicts.

King Henry II (1139–89, r. 1154–89) even attempted to bridge the traditional autonomy of the Church courts by bringing all religious under the jurisdiction of the common law. In particular, the right of clergy to be tried in Church courts for criminal acts, and to appeal cases to the Roman curia, was disputed by the crown. Henry's hand-picked Archbishop of Canterbury, Thomas à Becket, furiously resisted the attempted encroachment of Church autonomy at this juncture. The murder of Becket in 1172 by agents of the crown slowed Henry's efforts considerably, but by the end of his reign in 1189 the king had again managed to curb the overarching authority of the ecclesiastical courts. From the crown's point of view the expansion of a uniform justice system not only advanced the peace and security of the kingdom, but also greatly served as a key source of royal income. Profits from fines and the purchase of writs (secured from chancery and needed to initiate legal action in land disputes) all buttressed the image of the king as the source of unity and prosperity.[45] Henry created such an efficient administrative structure that it was able to function effectively during the largely absentee reign of his eldest son Richard the Lion-Hearted (1157–89, r. 1189–99).

Central to the consolidation of these law-based kingdoms was the role of extraordinary taxation. Ideally, the medieval monarch was expected to 'live on his own' or manage the affairs of the kingdom on the basis of revenues derived from his estates and from his traditional feudal prerogatives. In such a context, monarchs who attempted to wrest monies from their leading subjects without their consent, or for purposes at odds with the priorities of the landed elite, found themselves locked in stalemate and in some cases facing direct resistance. Developing out of the feudal compact where the vassal's performance of specific services was exchanged for royal protection and the use of land, kings could not arbitrarily usurp the property rights of their leading subjects without serious consequences. Most often in the feudal setting the king called together his leading vassals in order to solicit their advice and support. These unpretentious meetings, alternatively called *colloquia, concilia, conventus, curiae* or *tractatus*, featured both fluid membership and varied agendas. And as financial, military, economic and administrative problems became more complex, larger and more structured assemblies were called by the monarch.[46]

Formal representative assemblies emerged in most European countries – Spain, Sicily, Hungary, England, France, the Scandinavian countries, various German principalities – during the thirteenth and fourteenth centuries for a number of related reasons, but the key involved the need for monarchs to access sources of wealth not under their direct control as feudal lords. Increasingly after 1000 the cost of pursuing wider military objectives grew substantially across Europe. This was particularly true in the case of the thirteenth- and fourteenth-century wars between England and France, where monarchs on both sides were pressed repeatedly to find additional sources of income.

The word *parliamentum* was first coined in the thirteenth century, and by that time it was being applied to meetings of the unelected feudal council. Both the economic and social structures of European kingdoms were quite unique in comparison to the other major world civilizations, where nothing like Western parliaments ever emerged. Comparatively speaking, only in Europe were power and wealth distributed in a fairly diffuse fashion. The basic structure of medieval parliaments, including as they did representatives of clergy, nobles and commoners from towns and cities, was reflective of this important distribution of income and land.[47] It was in this context that the English king's royal council, for example, normally composed of important churchmen and aristocrats, expanded during the course of the thirteenth century to include new urban elites for the purpose of gaining consent to special taxation.

Another key influence on the emergence of secular parliaments involved the broader impact of consensual practices in the life of the Roman Church. Bishops were thought to represent their diocese whenever they were called to participate in provincial councils, and twelfth-century canon lawyers reinforced this practice in their theoretical work, especially when dealing with litigation involving corporations like monasteries and cathedral chapters. In these cases representatives of the corporations in question had to plead in court on behalf of their corporate bodies. The language of Roman jurisprudence, mediated by canon law, was also employed by proponents of parliamentary governance. The maxim 'what touches all should be approved by all', although originally formulated in reference to private law involving wardship and water rights, became, in the words of Antony Black, 'the commonest justification for parliaments and was used both by kings and Estates, to express both the duty and the right to consultation'.[48] In times of emergency, when the security of the kingdom was threatened, when military action was contemplated, or when conflict with the universal Church occurred, kings often felt constrained to enter into a relationship with their most powerful subjects whereby agreed public ends were to be advanced on the strength of common contributions.

The parliaments of medieval Europe were elective representative institutions. In each a small number of persons stood in the place of their larger constituencies and contracted with full power to bind their members to whatever political accommodation was reached with the crown. It was always within the monarch's prerogative both to call and to dismiss these assemblies, and in this important respect parliaments remained creatures of the crown throughout the medieval period. But these creatures were nevertheless very powerful supplements to royal authority. The English monarchy, for example, had traditionally found its greatest strength when pursuing policies agreed by a royally selected council. In Anglo-Saxon times that body was the *witanagemot* and after 1066 the Norman *curia regis*. The exact composition of these bodies was determined by the crown, and while the king's decisions were never subject to veto in a formal institutional sense, the approval of the leading barons was always key to the successful execution of royal policy in the countryside. During times of peace the king was normally advised by a small council consisting mostly of household officials, but in an emergency the important nobles of the realm were called together in a great council, normally at Westminster. By the thirteenth century the increasing wealth of urban areas led to the integration of townsmen into the large council, especially when the crown was requesting extraordinary taxation. The consent of the wealthy burghers reflected their greater ability to provide the king with the funding necessary for an expansive military policy on the continent.

During the reign of Edward I (1237–1307, r. 1272–1307) these councils or parliaments included knights of the shires in addition to increasing numbers of townsmen. The king made regular use of these meetings, experimenting with different combinations of nobles, churchmen and commoners, all designed to loosen the purse strings of England's most successful subjects. Edward's protracted military aggressions against Wales and Scotland, together with the need to garrison Ireland, necessitated frequent requests for special taxes. By the fourteenth century the barons and the commoners began to meet in separate assemblies, giving rise to the formal division of Lords and Commons. Parliamentary initiative always rested with the king, however, and the elected commoners did not consult with the king, as the bishops and nobles did, over non-financial affairs of state. Still, the precedent of calling representatives of a new social class had enormous implications for the future of royal authority.[49]

Over the course of the thirteenth century a profound transformation in the locale or focus of personal allegiance had been accomplished in England. During the aristocratic rebellions against King John in 1214, against John's inept son Henry III in 1258, and in rumblings against Edward I in 1297, what the nobles were seeking was the preservation of the administrative, legislative and judicial innovations of the previous century, not their destruction pursuant to a return to provincialism. It was the kings who were charged by their leading subjects with upsetting the agreed constitutional and administrative framework of the realm, not the barons. Unwise and selfish royal policies, not disdain for the centralizing project, motivated the landed elite to act in defence of an ideal kingdom. A sense of loyalty to the idea of the impersonal state, to law and consultative government, was gradually becoming a part of the monarchical system in the island kingdom.[50] More than anything else, this gradual relocation of baronial allegiance proved essential to the birth of the modern omnicompetent territorial state.

Unfortunately for the kings of France, their efforts at consolidation faced much greater difficulties simply because of the deeply entrenched tradition of provincial autonomy. Philip IV's wars with England (1294–1303) and Flanders (1297–1314) placed unique financial strains upon the kingdom which could not be met out of ordinary royal sources. Seeking to extract extraordinary revenue from his subjects, Philip called together representatives of the clergy, of the nobility of the provinces, and of the great commercial cities. In this Estates General the king's ministers explained the nature of royal policies in the hope of securing broad-based support. While the Estates General did not fix grants of taxation in the manner of the English Parliament, the support of this body was key to the success of crown negotiations with individual provinces over how the money which the king needed was to be raised. And while the Estates General did not formulate a set of theoretical limits to royal prerogative, when assembled it did forward a sense of common interest around the royal programme. Future resistance to crown authority in France would come from the individual provinces, not from a coordinated national body as in England.

The monarch's ability to engage the support of powerful elites throughout the realm is perhaps best observed in the quarrel with the papacy over the ruler's claim to tax the clergy for the defence of the kingdom. In fact this Church–kingdom struggle provided the occasion for the very first meeting of the Estates General in France in the year 1303. In rebuking the pope's power King Philip IV felt the need to go beyond seeking the support of his feudal vassals and instead called representatives from the Church, nobility and towns together in an effort to shape a national front against the papacy. The fact that there was no support for the pope's position in 1302, only a call for a special Church council to try the bishop of Rome for high crimes, indicates something of the strength of national ecclesiastical consciousness at the start of the fourteenth century. Loyalty to the temporal prince over against the universalist claims of the Church had become a reality in the politics of the later Middle Ages, thanks in no small measure to the role of this new instrument of consultative government.[51]

THE END OF PAPAL MONARCHY

The late medieval trend in the West away from a united Christendom and towards sovereign kingdoms was accelerated after 1300 by two parallel developments: the rise of religious mysticism and disarray within the papal office. Christian mystics tended to downplay the role of the official clergy and the place of the sacraments as channels of divine grace in favour of an immediate personal experience of union with God. Two important and widely influential Dominican mystics of the fourteenth century, Meister Eckhart (d. 1327) and Catherine of Siena (d. 1380), emphasized the value of personal contact with the divine unhindered by the intermediary role of the ordained clergy. Beginning in the third quarter of the fourteenth century, after the epidemiological disaster of the Black Death, a new lay organization called 'Brethren of the Common Life' took up the call of earlier Franciscans and committed themselves to charitable works and education. Taking no lifetime vows, however, these lay men and women set a powerful example of Christian action unencumbered by the administrative oversight of the increasingly bureaucratic Church in Rome.[52]

Both Martin Luther and Desiderius Erasmus received

their early educational training in schools organized by the Brethren. By the time of Luther's birth, one of the great works of Christian mysticism, Thomas à Kempis's *Imitation of Christ*, encapsulated the spirit of emerging personal religion. Here was a cogent and moving defence of inner piety and pure personal adoration taking the place of ritual and service under the direction of ordained superiors. The dissent from papal authority expressed by John Wyclif (d. 1384) in England and Jan Hus (d. 1415) in the Czech lands, so clearly anticipating the challenge posed by Luther at the start of the sixteenth century, found fertile ground in a wider European culture where Christian individualism came into conflict with the corporate Church ideal.

The intense spirituality of late medieval mysticism contrasted sharply with the political and personal disasters confronting the papacy during the course of the thirteenth and fourteenth centuries. The relocation of the papal office to Avignon (1309–77) and the subsequent 'Great Schism' (1377–1415) exacerbated divisions between the kings of France and England. Already engaged in the debilitating Hundred Years' War, England and its allies supported the popes in Rome while France backed the Avignon claimants to universal spiritual leadership. By the close of the fifteenth century, after the failure of the conciliar movement to redefine the relationship between pope and general council, the Italian noblemen who monopolized the papal office immersed themselves in the political squabbles of the Italian city-states. Leaving northern monarchs to influence Church appointments in their respective kingdoms, the Borgia popes abandoned the centuries-old papal claims to directive authority over a united Christendom. Instead they resigned themselves to the work of regional politics combined with a large dose of scandalous living and family self-aggrandizement. By the eve of the Reformation, the papacy had largely forfeited its claim to hegemony over a transnational Christian community, and Rome had become marginalized from new centres of political power north of the Alps. History informed by a providential message, where the Church militant guided Western Europe towards the climax of the Second Coming, where politics was infused with religious significance, now ceased to guide a new generation of monarchs.[53]

Into this power vacuum of the fifteenth century, where mere human ends replaced eternal ones, stepped the individual princes of nascent sovereign states. As early as 1302, the French Dominican John of Paris came to the defence of the sovereign monarchy by insisting that 'royal power both existed and was exercised before the papal, and there were kings in France before there were Christians'. Similarly in 1324, Marsilius of Padua argued in his *Defensor Pacis* (Defender of the Peace) that the secular state should enjoy complete authority over all of its subjects, lay and religious alike, unhindered by the power claims of the international Church. Christians must remain united in faith but obedient to their individual temporal princes whose task was now for the first time to be viewed as essentially separate from the end pursued by the clergy.[54]

This advice seemed to be heeded, at least at the level of the baronage, during the century-long conflict between Valois France and England. In the end the Hundred Years' War solidified the movement towards secular sovereignty, as English feudal claims to territories – and the crown – of France were decisively rejected by 1453. Frustrated in France, the English baronage continued to exercise their bellicose habits in a fratricidal civil war at home, the end result of which was to eliminate most of the strongest claimants to the throne during 30 years of intermittent conflict (1455–85). In the Iberian peninsula, political centralization under monarchical rule was first achieved only in the late fifteenth century. The three Christian kingdoms of Portugal, Castile and Aragon struggled both against the Muslim kingdom of Granada and against their own turbulent nobility throughout much of the thirteenth and fourteenth centuries. In Aragon the monarch had made important concessions to a series of regional political assemblies known as *Cortes* while in Castile chronic noble intransigence frustrated the royal drive for greater power.

Only with the marriage in 1469 of Ferdinand of Aragon to Isabella of Castile did the two largest kingdoms join forces and begin the process of creating a central administration. This work of centralization was furthered by the success of the 'Reconquista' against the Muslims and the incorporation of the kingdom of Granada into Spain in 1492. Royal support for overseas exploration was a chief characteristic of Europe's westernmost kingdoms of Portugal and Spain, as was the employment of the Holy Office of the Inquisition to enforce religious orthodoxy during the turbulent period of the Reformation. While the kingdoms of France and England, together with the Holy Roman Empire, were racked by religious turmoil during the sixteenth century, the Spanish monarchs ruled over a religiously united kingdom together with an American empire of unprecedented scale.[55] The stage was set for the beginning of global domination.

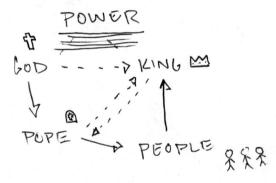

The King and Pope ALWAYS be fightin'.

5 Contemporary portrait of the Habsburg Emperor Frederick the Great (1740–86).

FIVE

Monarchy and European Hegemony, 1500–1914

Given the profile of the global community at the start of the twenty-first century, it is hard to deny that one of the major themes of human history over the past 500 years has been the emergence of the West as *the* dominant civilization. From the contours of political culture to the fabric of economic development, in standards of human rights to models of religious pluralism, on definitions of progress and in popular conceptions of material comfort – for better or for worse the values of the West have increasingly guided the agendas of governments and peoples around the world.

The year 1500 marks a useful starting point for the age of European overseas expansion, an unprecedented outward drive for trade and territory undertaken, paradoxically, thanks largely to Europe's relative backwardness and underdevelopment. Politically and religiously fractured, overwhelmingly rural and dependent upon subsistence agriculture, producing few finished goods or raw materials apt to attract the attention of potential trading partners elsewhere, Europe in 1500 was a very unlikely candidate for global power status.[1] Indeed prior to this date most of the world's major civilizations, while not totally isolated from their neighbours, developed their own cultural, economic and political structures in what can only be described as a high degree of regional seclusion. Important contacts there had often been between the peoples of Western Europe, the Middle East, Asia, South Asia and North Africa during the first 5000 years of human development, but in the main most of these junctions were both limited in number and brief in duration. Influential ideas and specialized techniques for managing the environment were exchanged, mostly in an east–west direction across the Eurasian land mass, but even here the cultural and trade links were fitful, often dependent upon the varied fortunes of empires.

The major civilizations 500 years ago – the Ottoman empire, Mughal India, Safavid Persia, and especially Ming China – each enjoyed significant advantages over the West, not the least of which involved climate. Western Europe was the northernmost and thus coldest of the major civilizations, and its overall population of roughly 80 million was modest when compared with that of India or China. The Ottoman Turks and the Persians also enjoyed longer growing seasons and controlled much of the trade in precious goods destined for Europe from the East. And as if this were not enough, in 1500 Europeans were still coming to grips with the loss of Christian Constantinople to the Turks. With the final collapse of Byzantium in 1453, the Habsburg rulers of the Holy Roman Empire scrambled to the defensive against the expansionist Muslim sultanate now based in Istanbul, a desperate holding action which may well have prevented the Spanish and Austrian Habsburgs from attaining the type of dominance over all of Europe enjoyed by the Ming over China and the Mughals over India. By the second decade of the sixteenth century the Ottomans had secured the Balkans and were closing in on Budapest and Vienna. With 14 million subjects under the absolutist rule of Suleiman (r. 1520–66), Eastern Europe seemed ripe for Muslim conquest, just as northwest India had succumbed to the forces of Babur. And at no point during the course of that pivotal century were the fratricidal Europeans able to unite in opposition to the tough janissary armies of Suleiman, a distressing commentary on the divided state of Western Christendom.

Despite these considerable disadvantages, however, over the course of the succeeding 500 years nearly all of the non-Western peoples of the globe would find themselves obliged to respond to the dynamic aggressiveness of the Europeans. With the start of Europe's overseas expansion in the late fifteenth century, the connections between peoples round the globe became more frequent and more sustained. First the western coastline of Africa, then the Americas and India, and ultimately

China, Japan and Australasia – all were drawn into the ever-expanding trade networks of Europe. Between the mid-fifteenth century and continuing to the start of the twenty-first, the world's great oceans have served as highways of exchange, and more than anything else it has been the export of European techniques, European ideas and European values which have made the greatest impact on global cultures.

EXPLAINING EUROPE'S RISE

It is more than a little significant that the West's dynamic ability to transform itself in very rapid order, becoming in the process less a peripheral outpost in a world of dominant non-western states and more an initiator of change and technological advancement, took place under political systems which remained monarchical in structure right through to the breakdown of European hegemony after the First World War. What adjustments in Europe's self-understanding of the royal office permitted such an unlikely development? How did a political system first formulated to address the concerns of largely traditional agrarian societies manage to lead Europe into the age of industry and political democracy? How did a competitive, entrepreneurial and expansionist economic environment secure the endorsement and support of an institution whose age-old loci of support had come from those who dominated land and labour? And if innovation and the setting of precedent strengthened the West's position relative to the other great civilizations after 1500, what explains the retention of what in an increasingly democratic age might be termed a political anachronism; why was the Eurocentric world system led by hereditary monarchs?

The answers to these questions are varied and controversial, but it is useful to begin with the divisions in Christian Europe precipitated by the early sixteenth-century Protestant Reformation.[2] What started as a reform movement within the Roman Catholic Church in the end accelerated the formation of hostile sovereign states and greatly enhanced the authority of centralizing monarchs over their subject populations. In the wake of the Reformation debate, distinct confessional states took up arms in defence of their respective spiritual convictions and put an end to the organizing principle of universal Christendom. To this day, no alternative unifying postulate has emerged to shape a common European identity.

The monarchs who dominated the European stage during the era of the Reformation were themselves products of a bellicist culture which equated a quick resort to violence with the noble pursuit of religious and dynastic objectives. The Habsburg emperor Charles V spent most of his long reign engaged in war against his own recalcitrant subjects, while his son King Philip II of Spain experienced only six months of peace during a reign which lasted almost 40 years (r. 1556–98). Indeed by 1650 most of Europe's dynastic families owed their thrones to the willingness of their predecessors to fight for their claims. We are less ready than our pre-modern forebears to accept the propriety of an immediate recourse to violence as a means of settling disputes.[3] No such inhibitions troubled early modern monarchs. The Tudors in England in 1485, the Bourbons in France in the 1590s, the Romanovs in Russia in the 1610s, the Austrian Habsburgs in Bohemia in 1621, the Braganzas in Portugal in the 1640s – all had to take up arms against rival claimants. And seeking by any means to buttress their claims to final authority, European royalty took upon itself the mantle of religious leadership.

Increasingly distinguished as protectors of the national Church in a climate of growing religious conflict, Europe's monarchs undertook to consolidate the material resources of their territories in an effort to preserve their respective kingdoms from religiously motivated aggressors.[4] By 1555 the Holy Roman Empire was irreparably split into hostile principalities, Protestant in the north and Roman Catholic in the south. An imperial Diet convened that year in the city of Augsburg confirmed the rupture, allowing individual princes to set the true faith for their respective territories. Luther's Reformation of the early sixteenth century emphatically confirmed developments already visible a century earlier: the work of priests and princes was no longer complementary; religious and political ideals were no longer one; the advancement of the otherworldly kingdom had ceased to be under the directive oversight of a single monarch in Rome. Thanks largely to the Reformation, the unity of Christendom ceased to function as the essential prerequisite to the advancement of God's kingdom on earth. Religious agendas continued to influence political action in very important – and often bloody – ways for the next 200 years, but directive authority was now focused on the individual monarchs who attempted to impose their own interpretation of the Christian mandate on neighbours and subjects alike.

Henry VIII of England made the strongest claims in this respect. Winning the support of Parliament for his break with Rome in the early 1530s, the monarch declared himself supreme head of the Church in England. The doctrine of royal supremacy opened the door to a wholesale looting and confiscation of Church (especially monastic) properties, and the subsequent sale of these lands by the king slowly enhanced the economic and political power of the English gentry. Still, the royal claim to leadership in religious affairs, affirmed by Henry's daughter Elizabeth and subsequently by her Stuart successors, represented a distinct trend in sixteenth-century politics across the continent. Between 1500 and the late eighteenth century the maintenance of confessional orthodoxy as established by the crown became one of the key functions of sovereign states across Europe.

Despite these theocratic developments, Europe's sixteenth-century kingdoms were not absolute monarchies in the mould of their non-western counterparts. It is important to emphasize at this point that no sixteenth-century European monarch wished to eliminate the traditional nobility or destroy its elite political and military status; kings, after all, were aristocrats themselves. Europe's feudal tradition of local authority under corporately organized elites (including the Church) posed significant challenges to monarchs who desired to create institutions of centralized power. Instead of antagonizing society's traditional leaders, monarchs in England, Spain, France and in certain German states hoped to replace private armies and feudal jurisdictions with new opportunities for the aristocracy at court. Leading royal armies, dispensing justice in the king's name, securing office in expanding royal bureaucracies: this

transition would help to anchor both the security of the kingdom in an era of intense religious and commercial strife while
guaranteeing the preservation of society's natural elite in the
service of the crown.[5]

While Lutheran dissent from the universal Roman Catholic
Church enhanced the power of Europe's temporal monarchs
by calling on them to reform the Church and clergy in their
respective kingdoms, Calvinist thinkers were much less prone
to accept any principle which accorded greater authority to
royal officeholders. Placing obedience to God's law before conformity to the will of the prince, political theorists writing
within a Calvinist theological perspective insisted that the king
who violated divine ordinances was not to be obeyed. Anti-
absolutist sentiment was decisively advanced by the emergence
of these religiously motivated resistance theories. Works such
as the anonymous *Vindiciae contra tyrannos* and George
Buchanan's *De jure regni apud Scotos*, both appearing in print in
1579, argued on behalf of religious minorities who found
themselves persecuted by their monarchs. In the midst of the
French wars of religion, the Protestant Philippe Duplessis
Mornay insisted that 'God's jurisdiction is immeasurable,
whilst that of kings is measured; that God's sway is infinite,
whilst that of kings is limited'. Mornay's *Defense of Liberty
Against Tyrants* was first published in Latin in 1579 but quickly
translated into French and finally into English just one year
before the execution of King Charles I in 1649 by his Calvinist
opponents.

Mornay employed metaphors drawn from the medieval
feudal tradition in describing the proper relationship between
subjects and their rulers. Since God created heaven and earth
out of nothing, he alone 'is truly the lord [*dominus*] and propri-
etor [*proprietarius*] of heaven and earth'. Earthly monarchs, on
the other hand, are 'beneficiaries and vassals [*beneficiarii &
clientes*] and are bound to receive and acknowledge investiture
from Him'. Facing religious persecution at the hands of a

Catholic monarch, this spokesman for the French Protestant minority took the bold step of denying kings any sacred or special distinction. Men do not attain royal status 'because they differ from others in species, and because they ought to be in charge of these by a certain natural superiority, like shepards with sheep'. Instead of lording over subjects, legitimate monarchs are those who protect the subjects in their care, both from the aggressions of individuals within the kingdom and from hostile neighbours. In language striking in its modernity, Mornay claimed that 'royal dignity is not really an honour, but a burden; not an immunity, but a function; not a dispensation, but a vocation; not license, but public service'.[6]

Another important factor in Europe's rise under monarchical rule involves the relationship between the monarchies of Europe and the commercial middle class. It has been the contention of some recent observers of global politics that non-European powers failed to maintain their strength relative to the West in part due to the persistence of all-embracing theocratic monarchy. Absolutist dynasties in China, India and in the Islamic kingdoms successfully opposed the development of economic and religious pluralism in their respective societies. In the Ottoman empire after the death of Suleiman in 1566, 13 incompetent successors undermined the expansionist agenda of the earlier sultans, naval and army readiness declined, merchants were heavily taxed, and the free exchange of ideas through print technology was forbidden.[7]

Europe, by contrast, was changing on a number of fronts and Western monarchs by and large adjusted their expectations and style of rule accordingly. Beginning in the late sixteenth century, population west of the Elbe river grew at a rapid pace, until by 1800 Europeans constituted one-quarter of the world's inhabitants. And as populations expanded and emigration to America became a viable life choice for common people, Europe's monarchs found themselves placing economic issues at the top of the agenda in matters of war and diplomacy. After 1700 long-standing religious conflicts were replaced by commercial ones. Questions of trade, of access to new markets and to raw materials now began to dominate relations between the kingdoms of Europe. Speaking in broadly comparative terms,

European merchants after 1500 faced little opposition from their governments in the drive for commercial and industrial development. Quite the opposite; as rivalries between European monarchs shifted out of the realm of religion and over into matters of trade and territory, Europe's more ambitious monarchs endorsed and in some cases even subsidized the activities of explorers and developers irrespective of the religious question.[8] Spanish and Portuguese settlement in the Americas was tightly regulated by the state, with a percentage of the profits of trade assigned to the crown. While less intrusive, the English empire in North America, although initially undertaken by private investors and dissenting groups, also became a royal enterprise by the second half of the seventeenth century.[9]

In China and in South Asia the reaction to Europe's heavily armed sailing ships was at first sluggish and even dismissive. The Ming and, after 1644, Qing emperors generally treated the westerners with sharp disdain, permitting trade relations only under tight imperial controls and refusing to establish formal diplomatic relations with their importunate visitors. Europeans were treated as subordinate tributaries until the mid-nineteenth century, when at last superior naval and military technology allowed the West to redefine the essential nature of the relationship.

China's reluctance to engage in trade on equal terms with the West was in part the product of its own earlier forays into global commerce. While sponsoring a series of overseas trade expeditions under the Muslim naval commander Zheng He in the first three decades of the fifteenth century, the Chinese Ming emperors ordered a stop to the construction of long-range cruising vessels in the 1430s. From this point forward Chinese mariners were restricted to coastal and river navigation, a reversal of policy which reflected both the economic autarchy of China's 100 million people, and the inherent conservatism of the large Confucian bureaucracy, whose thousands of highly trained administrators distrusted the culture of business and unfettered entrepreneurship. Having visited and traded with the inhabitants of Ceylon and East Africa long before the Portuguese rounded the Cape of Good Hope in

Southern Africa, the Chinese imperial authorities abandoned the prospect of global interaction and instead focused the productive efforts of native Chinese on internal commerce, technical development, and defence against the still-potent northern Mongols. In a kingdom where the emperor did not face any institutional counterweights to the bureaucracy under his command, where a million-man army ensured the security of the imperial lands, there was little opportunity for the development of a market economy anchored in overseas trade.

In India, by contrast, the gradual internal dissolution of the Mughal dynasty during the course of the seventeenth century was compounded by the invasive and persistent trade practices of European companies, particularly the British East India Company. This monopoly trading enterprise, sanctioned by the English crown and by Parliament, found itself taking on, often in a *de facto* manner, the responsibilities of local governance in ever-widening areas of the Indian subcontinent. The end result of the process of uncoordinated absorption and cooption of Mughal authority was the outright annexation of the subcontinent in 1857 as a colony of the British monarchy under the Queen-empress.

Europe's impact on the monarchies of Central and South America was much more immediate and dramatic than that experienced elsewhere. The inadvertent introduction of European diseases such as smallpox and typhus annihilated large numbers of indigenous peoples during the course of the sixteenth century. From an estimated population of 50 million inhabitants prior to the arrival of Spanish explorers in the Aztec lands in 1500, the overall population of what today constitutes the territory of Mexico was reduced to three million by the start of the seventeenth century. In the aftermath of these demographic disasters, European cash-crop planters inaugurated the horrific process of transporting African slaves across the Atlantic as a substitute source of labour. Plantation economies in the Caribbean, Central and South America, and by the seventeenth century in the southern colonies of British North America, contributed to a fundamental redefinition of New World culture, one where European norms were extended to transatlantic frontiers. And it was within this rapidly changing global context, where native cultures were being undermined and where West African cultures were transplanted to the New World, that European monarchs laid claim to hegemony over Amerindian lands. By the third quarter of the sixteenth century, King Philip II of Spain ruled over an empire in the Americas which dwarfed in size his European territories. And the wealth extracted from Spain's New World possessions provided the resources whereby the Catholic monarchs could pursue their Counter-Reformation military-religious agenda on the European continent.

ABSOLUTISM'S BRIEF MOMENT

Absolute monarchy in the West was both atypical in form and brief in duration. Emerging first in France after the mid-point of the seventeenth century, there were many European kings who sought to reduce the power of deliberative estates and assemblies in an effort to enhance executive authority. From the point of view of some observers, and in particular from the perspective of radical Whig politicians in eighteenth-century Britain and in Britain's North American colonies, European political life was falling victim to 'oriental despotism', the calamity of absolute monarchy.

At a cursory level, an inspection of political developments appeared to confirm these fears. In France the Estates General was not convened between 1614 and 1789, while the Cortes of Castile did not meet after 1667. Similar trends were to be observed in Sweden and Denmark at the close of the seventeenth century. In 1683 a Danish law asserted that the king exercises 'supreme authority to draw up laws and ordinances according to his will and pleasure, and to elaborate, change, extend, delimit and even entirely annul laws previously promulgated by himself or his ancestors'.[10] In Tsarist Russia, the autocratic penchants of the Romanovs, perhaps reinforced by Byzantine and Mongol influence, issued in the absolutist rule of Peter the Great (1672–1725, r. 1689–1725). Further west in Brandenburg-Prussia, civil and military affairs were securely under the direction of the royal house of Brandenburg. The

Electorate of Brandenburg in the Holy Roman Empire had begun the process of royal centralization during the mid-seventeenth century. Beginning in the 1640s, the elector Frederick William exempted the *Junker* aristocracy from taxation but in return these landed elites pledged themselves to regular military service. By 1688 an efficient army where promotion was linked to merit had grown to a well-disciplined force of 30,000 men, and by the middle of the next century some 80,000 were in military service. Consuming 80 per cent of Prussian revenues by 1750, King Frederick the Great (1712–86, r. 1740–86) used this well-trained army successfully against Austrian, French and Russian adversaries. The civil service was similarly organized along military lines, with the king enjoying complete power over the machinery of government while his *Junker* subordinates were permitted a free hand over their peasants, most of whom remained serfs.

Supporters of absolutism claimed to be interested solely in the larger well-being and security of the territorial state in a world of hostile neighbours. Following the Frenchman Jean Bodin's understanding of sovereignty as 'the most high, absolute, and perpetual power over the citizens and subjects in a Commonweal', they saw the dramatic enhancement of royal authority as essential to domestic tranquillity and international respectability.[11] Under this reading, noble privileges, local legislative assemblies, clerical exemptions and judicial power in the hands of landed elites all represented potential threats to the kingdom. These exemptions and privileges could no longer be tolerated if the state were to survive in a highly fractured international environment. According to the absolutist perspective, the unencumbered directive authority of the king was an essential factor in the social, religious and economic well-being of the country. Sound, responsible administration, economic prosperity, religious peace, the equitable delivery of justice, the promotion of trade and industry – none of these objectives could be secured without the enhancement and concentration of power at the centre under the directing hand of the prince.

Given the history of the Roman Catholic Church's opposition to the extended claims of temporal monarchs, it is ironic (but perhaps not terribly surprising) that some of the strongest voices of support for absolute monarchy after 1500 were to be found among the clergy of the dominant national churches. In France, Spain and Austria, Roman Catholic clergy willingly allied themselves with the authoritarian claims of the prince in an effort to staunch heresy. Further east the clergy of the Russian Orthodox Church became the principal bulwark of tsarist absolutism during the course of the seventeenth century. Peter the Great assumed the right to collect income from estates owned by the Church, and in 1721 the patriarchate itself was abolished by royal command and replaced by a state agency known as the Holy Synod. In England, where bishops had been appointed by the monarch since the early stages of the Reformation, support for the prerogatives of the monarchy echoed from the pulpits. When King James VI of Scotland (and after 1603 James I of England) published his *Trew Law of Free Monarchy* in 1598, the notion that kings 'sit upon God his throne in the earth, and have the count of their administration to give unto him', was not unfamiliar, and royalist clergy were quick to back the claims of their benefactor.[12] God's purpose in setting up an absolute monarch was to secure a type of harmonious political order which was impossible to obtain whenever conflicting interests were allowed to find voice in legislative assemblies.

Theoretical claims aside, the success of European absolutism depended largely on the monarch's ability to curb the power of the landed aristocracy and the Church. In France this goal was largely achieved by King Louis XIV (r. 1643–1715), but only at the very high cost of foregoing important potential sources of crown revenue. Under Louis the great French nobility were obliged to become courtiers to the crown at Versailles, the king's lavish Baroque residence located some fifteen miles outside of the city of Paris. Here the development of a rigid if lavish court culture emphasized the subordination of the high nobles to the crown. Government posts, sinecures, Church offices, military appointments – all were dispensed under the king's watchful eye, while in the old feudal provinces administrative assignments were made to loyal commoners called *intendants* who were in the exclusive employ of the crown. In return for their compliance with the royal centralizing project, the nobility were exempt from royal taxation. Similarly, the clergy or second estate of France contributed nothing to the financial well-being of the kingdom. This was a very significant concession, especially given that Church property yielded a total income of between 40 and 50 per cent of landed wealth in the kingdom.[13]

By excluding the first two estates from the burden of taxation, the crown was obliged to rely almost exclusively on the peasantry, those least able to pay, for the bulk of the revenues needed to sustain a very aggressive and expansionist military programme. Known as the *taille*, this annual tax was combined with an indirect salt tax or *gabelle* to create conditions of enormous hardship and resentment on the part of the labouring poor. Louis XIV's territorial ambitions, his persecution of enterprising Protestant dissenters known as Huguenots, and after 1667 his near-constant military conflict with a coalition of European powers led by England, bankrupted his absolutist state by the time of his death in 1715. Under Louis XV (r. 1715–74) attempts were made to reform the finances of the monarchy, but the Church and nobility stoutly resisted all attempts to link taxation with ability to pay. Wars on the continent and in the colonies pitted the French against England throughout the course of the 1700s, and the resources needed for these far-flung military engagements only heightened popular discontent with the absolutist state. By 1763 the French had lost their entire North American empire to the British, and French military support for the Americans in their colonial revolt against Britain further exacerbated the financial difficulties of the crown. Six short years after the successful conclusion of the American Revolution, the French would set about their own struggle whose result was the repudiation of monarchy and the institution of Europe's largest republic.

While the seventeenth and eighteenth centuries are often described as the 'age of absolutism' in Western Europe, the label is inappropriate for a number of important reasons. Even at the high water mark of royal power in Europe, no monarch could hope to govern effectively without the loyal support of aristocratic and monied elites. Even Louis XIV, for example, was always careful to cultivate the good will of the second estate, for the king realized that effective law enforcement in the countryside and obedience to the crown was in large measure dependent upon the power of the nobility both to enforce royal law and to collect taxes. The sale of key crown offices, each tax exempt, was the linchpin in Louis' plan to maintain the support of his powerful subjects.[14]

In Spain, where by the 1590s King Philip II commanded the strongest military force west of the Elbe while enjoying hegemony over an American empire larger than all of Europe, it appeared as though absolutism had reached its apex. But Philip's domestic power actually extended no further than his home kingdom of Castile. This was of particular importance when revenue issues were at stake. Of the 16 million Europeans under Spain's control in the early seventeenth century, only one-third of these, largely concentrated in Castile, bore the costs of imperial administration. Philip III (r. 1598–1621), was unable to coerce financial subsidies from the representative assemblies in Aragon, Valencia, Portugal or the Basque lands. And only one-quarter of total crown spending was provided for by wealth extracted from the New World colonies.[15] In England the story was not dissimilar. Despite attempts by the later Stuarts, Charles II (r. 1660–85) and especially James II (r. 1685–88), to emulate the absolutist pretensions of their contemporary Louis XIV, the strength of Parliament prevented any serious erosion of legislative autonomy or the rule of the common law.

MONARCHY AND NATIONALISM IN THE NINETEENTH CENTURY

A new and decisive period in the history of monarchy as an institution began in the West towards the close of the eighteenth century. For despite the fact that many Europeans still embraced ideas concerning political organization that would have been familiar to their predecessors in the late medieval period, fundamental reassessments were underway during the Enlightenment. And with the commencement of Europe's industrial and democratic movements, long-accepted standards of economic and political organization precipitately capsized. Centuries of economic underdevelopment in a comparatively cold climate, where agricultural production had been the mainstay of Europe's economy, now gave way before the rapid advance of machine production and manufacture. Steam, coal and iron rapidly became the chief weapons in concentrated efforts to manipulate the natural environment for human purposes. Throughout the course of the nineteenth century, all of Western Europe felt the transformative force of the machine and factory age.

Before examining some of these changes, however, we must be mindful not to ascribe too much influence to the eighteenth-century movement in ideas known as the Enlightenment. Indeed few of the *philosophes* had much faith in the malleability of the uneducated masses. Instead men like Voltaire hoped for a type of enlightened despotism where reformist monarchs would govern following rational and scientifically informed standards. Many of the Enlightenment figures hoped to replace the clerical estate with an abstract priesthood of reason, but their programme was limited both in terms of its demographic appeal and in its pool of potential supporters.[16] Irrespective of the fact that criticism of the *ancien régime* was growing among the educated bourgeoisie, mid-eighteenth-century Europe was still very much a Church-centred culture. The majority of published works continued to focus on religious subjects, higher education was still dominated by clerics, and functions that we would today associate with the secular state: public health, assistance for the poor, basic education, were in 1750 almost the exclusive concern of religious institutions.

And prior to the great political upheavals in America and France, the office of the monarch continued to be solidly grounded on religious moorings. Kings and queens ruled over status societies that were conceptualized by the ruling elite as organic, corporative and hierarchical. Subjects belonged to unequal occupational and social groups, and each group was governed by rules and legal sanctions unique to its membership. The enlightened enemies of 'priestcraft' and 'superstition', when at last the French Revolution consumed the monarchy with the execution of the king in January 1793, turned almost straightaway to a novel secular substitute, the nation state, as the focus of highest allegiance. The shift was symbolized during the period of the Terror, when the revolutionaries destroyed the holy vessel at Rheims Cathedral from which France's monarchs had been anointed since the Middle Ages. In their pursuit of the good society, the revolutionaries were determined to eradicate the venerable trappings of old-style monarchy.

Modern nationalism and an equal citizenry would in the end supplant divinely guided monarchs and a subject population, but at the outset incipient French nationalism did little more than plunge Europe into two decades of bloody conflict. The Enlightenment had been a truly cosmopolitan movement, and in the early days of the Revolution (before the execution of Louis XVI), Enlightenment ideals had succeeded in linking nationalism with human freedom and equality. Napoleon's establishment of an imperial throne for himself in December 1804, however, together with his military domination of much of the continent by 1810, recast enlightened nationalism into naked imperialism. And in one respect the Napoleonic wars, which always pitted the British against the French, represented a grand European struggle between two forms of monarchy: the British constitutional and the French absolutist.

The emperor of the French, when not actually removing defeated monarchs, treated them as leaders of petty vassal or satellite states. Despite the rhetoric of destroying the old feudal order while uniting all of Europe under a new structure featuring legal equality and secular, rational government, Napoleon's dictatorship in France and his imperial penchant for toppling adjacent dynasties only to establish new ones with his own relatives on the throne, succeeded in giving birth to rival nationalist sentiments in German-speaking lands, in Spain, Austria-Hungary, Italy and the Low Countries. Legal reform, the creation of a meritocratic civil service, the abolition of serfdom and the curbing of monopoly guild power – none of the changes introduced by Napoleon across Europe could induce the vanquished to accept French hegemony. In his 1790 *Reflections on the Revolution in France*, Edmund Burke issued a robust indictment of political action informed solely by abstract theorizing. In a sense, Burke's claim that society is nothing if not a rich historical product, a repository of collective wisdom and practice jettisoned only at the high cost of enormous human suffering and political instability, set the intellectual stage for the restoration of monarchy in France and elsewhere after the defeat of Bonaparte.

Still, the French Revolution had demonstrated that the institution of sacred monarchy, together with the whole feudal structure of privilege based upon the accident of birth, could be successfully challenged by an alternative ideology stressing the essential civil equality of men irrespective of birth. Napoleon had reconstituted the monarchical office, but he sought a popular, not a divine mandate for his actions. Frenchmen voted for monarchy and empire under Bonaparte. And they supported this ambitious ruler even as he exported the ideals of the revolution in campaigns across the continent. He needed them as much as they were beholden to him. Whatever the nature of his autocracy, it was not God-appointed dominion that Frenchmen accepted, but one that was in large measure self-imposed.

However with the emperor's final defeat at Waterloo in June 1815, a number of traditional dynasties, each dedicated to preventing the further spread of liberal ideology, were re-established across Western Europe. At the meeting of victorious powers held in Vienna, the principle of 'legitimacy' adopted by the delegates meant that Europe's old royal families, some living in exile, would return to their thrones. Respect for monarchy and aristocracy as the only conceivable constitutional form was the guiding precept of the principal architect of the peace settlement, Prince Klemens von Metternich (1773–1859) of Austria. The Bourbons in France, in Spain, and in the Kingdom of the Two Sicilies, the House of Savoy in northeast Italy, the Austrian Habsburgs in the remainder of north Italian lands – each of these dynasties, together with the Russian tsar Alexander I and the pope in Rome, struggled mightily to resist the infectious spread of revolutionary principles. For men like Metternich and his royal master Francis II, liberalism and nationalism represented mortal threats to multi-ethnic kingdoms like the Habsburg empire. When a revolution against the reactionary Spanish king Ferdinand VII occurred only five years after the Congress of Vienna, Russia, Prussia, Austria and Britain authorized the French to intervene militarily on behalf of monarchical legitimacy. Similar actions were taken by the Austrian crown against a liberal revolt in the Italian Kingdom of the Two Sicilies (1820) and by Tsar Nicholas I against Russian officers who called for an end to autocracy in 1825.

The precise legal nature and the powers exercised by Europe's monarchs after 1815 varied considerably, with the British and the Russian dynasties representing the two ends of the spectrum. Although lacking a written constitution, the British Parliament had secured the principle of cabinet independence of the crown. In fact since the Glorious Revolution of 1688 Parliament exercised the right to determine the succession to the throne. Two well-defined parties dominated the political agenda, and party leaders in the main set the legislative agenda. George III lived until 1820, but during his declining years, and especially during the decade-long reign of his son George IV (1762–1830, r. 1820–30), executive power was sharply diminished. When the dissolute and womanizing George IV died in 1830 *The Times* opined that 'there was never an individual more regretted by his fellow creatures than this deceased king'. After a brief period of popularity, his successor William IV (who at his brother's funeral talked constantly and walked out early), also earned the disdain of the political nation. *The Spectator* denounced him for his 'feebleness of purpose and littleness of mind, his ignorance and his prejudices'.

Queen Victoria's long reign (1819–1901, r. 1837–1901) was marked by the continued depreciation of dynastic strength in political affairs, and the queen failed to earn the admiration of her subjects until relatively late in her reign. Editorials in the press were normally hostile before the 1870s. This was largely due to Victoria's 20-year reclusiveness after the death of her husband in 1861. In the estimation of Walter Bagehot, who as a scholar of the constitution and supporter of the crown could not be accused of hostile bias, the queen 'has done almost as much to injure the popularity of the monarchy by her long retirement from public life as the most unworthy of her prede-cessors did by his profligacy and frivolity'.[17] Still, the enlarge-ment of Britain's global empire continued at a vigorous pace during these decades, and Victoria even assumed the title 'Empress of India' after the outright annexation of much of that continent in 1857. But crown functions had by the nine-teenth century become largely ceremonial. In the judgement of Russian Tsar Alexander III, Victoria's position was 'hardly to be counted as a monarchy, but rather as a Crown by election'.[18]

In Alexander's Russia, on the other hand, there was no national deliberative assembly to check the ambitious claims of the monarch. A large military and bureaucratic apparatus upheld the divine-right power of the Romanov tsar, and lawmaking was synonymous with imperial decree. A council of ministers advised the tsar, but he was in no respect bound by these subordinates. In a gesture packed with political and religious symbolism, tsars from the time of the empress Elizabeth in 1742 regularly placed the imperial crown on their own heads during the coronation ceremony in the Cathedral of the Dormition in the Kremlin.[19] Forming a partnership with the landholding class whereby nobles enjoyed unfettered control over their serfs in return for military service, the Russian monarchs successfully overcame the myriad problems associated with poor communications in a large territorial empire.

Traditionalist and conservative exertions notwithstanding, the bid by statesmen like Metternich to turn the clock back was, in the end, unsuccessful. The medieval Holy Roman empire, consisting of some 300 political units, had been dis-mantled by Napoleon and in its place a 38-state German con-federation was established. Some of the German princes permitted the creation of legislative bodies, and a small number of landed elites joined the political process. The leading state in the northern portion of the streamlined confederation was Prussia, and within 50 years its dynamic leaders would fashion a monarchy which would eclipse the power of Habsburg Austria and provide the core of a new German nation. Similarly in Italy, a robust national movement, led largely by students and members of the urban middle class, continued to mature despite the rigid opposition of Austria and the papacy. By 1871, after numerous setbacks and a successful war (1859) against Austria, the unification of the entire peninsula had been achieved under the king of Sardinia, Victor Emmanuel II (1820–78, r. 1861–78).

Even the restoration of the Bourbon monarchy in France failed to affirm the hopes of diehard Catholic aristocrats known as *ultras*. While the post-1815 French constitution declared that the monarch's powers rested on divine mandate, the document protected the constitutional rights of equal citizens to freedom of thought and religion. A bicameral legislature was established, and when Louis XVIII's (r. 1815–24) successor Charles X (r. 1824–30) attempted to ignore the will of the legislature and return greater power to the Church and to the aristocracy, a bourgeois-led revolution forced the king to abdicate. At his coronation ceremony at Rheims Cathedral in May 1825, Charles had revived all of the ceremonial of the *ancien régime*, including the medieval practice of touching for scrofula, but the whole affair, with its assumption of royal supernatural powers, was received with ridicule and alarm.[20] Charles X's successor studiously avoided all such associations. Between 1830 and 1848, a coalition of wealthy bankers and industrialists provided the main backing for King Louis-Philippe's government, a man who preferred dressing in the business attire of a middle-class gentleman to the traditional trappings of royal apparel.

As mentioned earlier, unprecedented social and economic forces were at work in Europe during the nineteenth century, and combined with the export of French revolutionary principles, these forces inflicted a serious wound on the institution of divinely ordained monarchy and the entire culture of aristocratic privilege. Although grinding poverty remained widespread across the continent, and while over 60 million Europeans emigrated overseas in order to escape that poverty, population growth was spectacular. It is estimated that some 190 million people inhabited the continent in 1800; by 1900 that figure had easily doubled. Industrialization and urbanization had an enormous impact upon the lives of those millions of Europeans who abandoned the centuries-old rhythms of rural life and work in exchange for the myriad hardships associated with mine and factory. For the industrial working class,

Marx's proletariat, traditional beliefs respecting the purpose of government at the highest level had little validity. In this dramatically altered social and economic milieu, European monarchies faced a broad array of new challenges to the political principle of rule by one. Nationalism, liberalism, socialism, republicanism, Marxism, representative democracy – each of these political ideologies reflected wider changes in the material and intellectual fabric of the industrializing West.

NATIONALISM AND POLITICAL RIGHTS

Two of these doctrines stand out in the century between the fall of Napoleon and the start of the First World War: the growth of nationalism at the expense of dynasticism as a key factor in promoting territorial unity, and the spread of representative forms of central government where ever-expanding numbers of male citizens were granted the franchise. Nationalism implied that a wide set of common interests, a collective personality which clearly transcended the ambitions of individual monarchs, should take pride of place in the policy-making calculations of political elites. Even the great nineteenth-century liberal John Stuart Mill declared that it was 'in general a necessary condition of free institutions that the boundaries of government should coincide in the main with those of nationalities'.[21] Protecting the public concerns of the nation, increasingly defined along economic, territorial, cultural and linguistic lines, became the fundamental duty of government, whether monarchical or republican in structure.

For some, nationalism became a spiritual force destined to replace traditional Christian otherworldliness, providing a sense of fellowship and historical identity which cut across class lines. The German historian Leopold von Ranke wrote in 1836 that the fatherland 'is with us, in us'. And as 'a mysterious something that informs the lowest among us' the idea of the nation 'precedes any form of government and animates and permeates all its forms'.[22] The nation state as sacred community became the focus of one's highest loyalty, and the successful monarch skilfully embraced a new identity as servant and chief advocate of the national will. It was now clear that if monarchy were to survive in a modern European setting, royal families had to position themselves not as God's agents on earth, but instead as servants of the nation state, and in no small sense as deputies of their subject populations. This disavowal of divine validation for the office of monarch represented a sweeping change in popular conceptions of legitimate governance. And yet for those skilled rulers who weathered the transition, the institution increased in popularity. Indeed monarchy remained the one form of government which was most comprehensible to innately conservative peasants whose family lives were regulated by patriarchal principles. The new centralized nation states which emerged over the course of the century in Italy and in Germany, for example, while both led by dynastic monarchs, predicated their political consolidation on a sense of common identity embraced by a wider public. For the inhabitants of these kingdoms, membership in religious, community, occupational and kinship groups became less important than wider linkages associated with a newly articulated sense of common national culture. By the third quarter of the century, nationalism had become an inward-looking and quasi-tribal movement which defined the nation, and not the individual citizen, as the essential good worth protecting at all costs.

The call for representative institutions of government was the second great formation of the nineteenth century. The individual's place in the political process began to compete with the interests of the status group as the middle class entered into the law-making process. By 1848, a series of revolutions across the continent, spurred by middle- and working-class discontent at their continuing disenfranchisement, signalled a new stage in the evolution of monarchical states. The sweep of the early liberal successes against monarchs in France, Austria-Hungary, Italy and Prussia was due in no small part to a 'cumulative failure of nerve on the part of monarchies and governments which were, in a physical sense, fully able to control events'. King Louis-Philippe in Paris, the incompetent Ferdinand III in Vienna, the dilatory Frederick William IV in Berlin (not to mention the papal monarch Pius IX) were all initially unwilling to use force against the students and urban intellectuals who demanded broader constitutional rights. But the military never abandoned the monarchs, and by the end of the year the revolutionaries had been crushed in every capital.[23]

Although these revolutions failed to achieve their more comprehensive objectives – written constitutions, free speech and press, more widely representative legislative bodies – the industrial and commercial bourgeoisie did secure for themselves a modicum of participation in the law-making process. The French constitutional charter of 1814 had allowed for an elected Chamber of Deputies, but under the property requirement only one in 300 Frenchmen could vote for delegates. After the ouster of Charles X in 1830 and the formation of a new national assembly, one in 40 French males could vote in national elections, and after the 1848 revolution universal manhood suffrage was established. In Britain an electoral reform bill in 1832 enfranchised many members of the new industrial middle class (one in five males could now vote), and it was the Hanoverian king William IV who guaranteed passage of the bill by threatening to create new peers who would support the legislation in the House of Lords. As one moves eastwards, this process of political liberalization abated, although even in Russia, Tsar Alexander II issued an 1861 edict granting 20 million serfs their personal freedom and the right to become landowners. By 1870 local governments were organized on the basis of a representative system and the judicial code was reformed.[24] All across Europe, parliamentary elective bodies with varying degrees of law-making power were in place at the start of the twentieth century, and governments led by monarchs worked to shape public opinion along nation-state lines.

With the emergence of party politics during the second half of the century, and with universal manhood suffrage achieved in most kingdoms by 1900, the monarch was increasingly viewed by many as the one person who could always rise above the provincial interests and political quarrels of the electorate and their representatives. Leading professional armies of largely peasant conscripts, it is not surprising that European kings after 1850 increasingly appeared in public in military dress.[25] The special guards regiments which were located in the capital cities often served as the training units for the heir apparent and other princes. And the officers in these regiments were almost always drawn from aristocratic families, while the military values which they represented were instrumental in promoting the monarch as paragon of national identity. Unlike elected party leaders, it was thought that the king could not ignore or compromise the national interests, but instead was obliged to consider the permanent and long-term concerns of the people when making policy.

Most European monarchs eagerly embraced the rhetoric of nationalism and constitutionalism while working to define their office as central to the enterprise. Thus liberal calls for representative institutions at the kingdom-wide level and broader political rights were skilfully managed within the context of monarchical rule, with rulers manipulating the emotional appeal of nationalism and rallying the citizenry to the royalist banner. With the exception of the Habsburg and Russian empires, no European monarchs after 1850 rejected the adoption of written constitutions and some form of parliamentary government. In fact a carefully cultivated façade of popular support was deemed essential to the flourishing of monarchy in the modern age. During the 1850s and 1860s, the rulers of France, Italy and Germany set the most compelling examples of this strategy.

After the 1848 revolution in France succeeded in exiling King Louis-Philippe and establishing a republic, universal manhood suffrage was introduced and Louis Napoleon Bonaparte (1808–73, r. 1852–71) was elected president of the Second Republic. But within two years strong monarchist and conservative sentiments reasserted themselves, as first the new Constituent Assembly severely restricted the universal suffrage provision and finally as the president, in a *coup d'état* on 2 December 1851, overthrew the republic and assumed the title of emperor. The coup was quickly followed by a plebiscite (in the tradition of his famous uncle) which ratified the extralegal actions of Bonaparte. The imperial regime combined political authoritarianism and press censorship with genuine administrative innovation in the areas of public service, education, health and worker rights, and the emperor's shrewd employment of nationalist rhetoric secured popular support for the regime until his forces were defeated in a war against the Prussians in 1870.

The unlikely origins of this conflict lay in the dynastic politics of Spain. In 1869 a popular revolt against the Spanish crown had led to the flight of the incumbent ruler, Queen Isabella. One of the leading candidates to succeed her was Prince Leopold of Hohenzollern-Sigmaringen, a distant relative of the Prussian king William I. To the French the choice of the Prussian candidate would be akin to encirclement by the Habsburgs in the sixteenth and seventeenth centuries. Thus the French demanded not only that Leopold withdraw his candidacy, but that the Prussian king provide a guarantee that it would not be revived at a later date. The humiliating defeat of French forces by an invading German army in 1870 was quickly followed by the refusal of republican and socialist Paris workers to accept either surrender in war or the legitimacy of the provisional government which had replaced Napoleon III. The result was a bloody clash between the Paris 'Communards' and the French army in which some 20,000 were killed. The provisional government was victorious and captured communards were treated as traitors to France and executed without trial. For a brief moment it appeared as though the monarchists within the provisional government would succeed in their design to re-establish royal authority, but while those in favour of the restoration of the monarchy held a majority of seats in the National Assembly, they failed to back a single candidate. Supporters of the House of Bourbon quarrelled with those who remained loyal to the House of Orleans, and as a result of the stalemate a presidential system was adopted which featured a bicameral legislature with a president chosen by the two legislative houses.

One important by-product of the French military defeat at the hands of the Prussians was the withdrawal of all French forces from Rome. Napoleon III had supported the papacy in its efforts to maintain its hold on the city, but when the Italian army took possession of Rome in triumph, Pope Pius IX, who only the year before had reaffirmed the doctrine of papal infallibility, lost significant ground in his struggle against temporal monarchy. Now restricted to a tiny enclave on the outskirts of

Rome, the pope forbade the Catholic citizens of the Italian state all association with political life. The directive had little substantive impact, however, for in 1870 the last remnants of the papacy's temporal power were extinguished by the new kingdom of Italy when the Church-controlled lands outside the Vatican were annexed. This in effect ended almost 1500 years of papal authority over matters temporal, a claim dating back to the Church's first alliance with the Merovingians in the late fifth century.

Italy had only emerged as a united kingdom in 1861, and over the next 85 years monarchs from the House of Savoy in northeast Italy succeeded each other on a throne which was limited by a number of significant constitutional restraints. The first king, Victor Emmanuel II, had already served as king of Piedmont, Savoy and Sardinia for twelve years before becoming sovereign of Italy in 1861. But republicans like Giuseppe Mazzini, men who had fought for decades in the hope of establishing a united Italy, were wary of the new monarchy. Under the terms of the first constitution (one actually issued in 1848 by Victor Emmanuel's father Charles Albert to his subjects in Piedmont-Sardinia) the monarch ruled 'by the grace of God' as well as 'by the will of the people'. A bicameral assembly was established with members of the upper house chosen by the king and the lower house elected on the basis of a very restricted franchise.

Victor Emmanuel retained the power to appoint and dismiss ministers at will, to dissolve the assembly, and to veto legislation passed by both houses. The king was also commander-in-chief of the Italian armed forces and conducted foreign affairs without having to account for his actions to the assembly. In addition, the constitution allowed the monarch to declare war and make peace on his own advice, and important national treaties could be kept secret if in the judgment of the king it was in the national interest to do so. The monarch could not be called to account for any of his official actions, and to even hint at royal responsibility for a failed policy was, under the constitution, a criminal offence.[26] But despite these considerable executive powers, Victor Emmanuel II was neither assertive nor particularly diligent regarding his executive duties. Ordinary administration tired him, a promiscuous private life harmed his public reputation, and his disagreements with his nine prime ministers over the course of a reign which lasted until 1878 thwarted the full employment of his legal prerogatives.

Developments in Prussia after the 1848 revolutions signalled the high water mark of royal authority adapted to the demands of a new industrial society. The 1850 Prussian constitution allowed for guarantees of individual freedom, thus ending the last vestiges of feudal obligation, but the king enjoyed both control over the armed forces and the right to choose his ministers without interference from elected representatives of the lower house or Landtag. In 1862, after having failed to secure the approval of the Landtag for a new three-year military service bill, King William turned to Otto von Bismarck, a conservative landowner who was serving as Prussia's ambassador to Paris, in order to break the deadlock with the assembly. When Bismarck ignored the liberal majority in the Prussian parliament and ordered the collection of tax revenues without legislative authority, the fact that most taxpayers complied suggested more than a little about the weakness of constitutionalism in the Prussian kingdom.

Loathed by liberals in the Prussian parliament when first appointed by the king in 1862, Bismarck's rapid military triumphs over Denmark (1864), Austria (1866) and France transformed the vast majority of liberal parliamentarians into militaristic nationalists. The consequences of this liberal capitulation to the nationalist faith would have serious implications for Europe into the middle of the twentieth century, but in the late nineteenth century the support of urban intellectuals and middle-class industrialists for the royalist programme was key to the unification of Germany. Bismarck himself was no simple apologist for unhindered royal prerogative, however, for he believed that absolutism 'demands impartiality, honesty, devotion to duty, energy, and inward humility in the ruler'. Unfortunately the influence of favourites, together with 'the monarch's own vanity and susceptibility to flattery' made unencumbered royal authority a deeply problematic system of centralized authority.[27]

On 18 January 1871 the Prussian king William I was

declared kaiser (emperor) by the German princes who had participated in the war against Emperor Napoleon III. The ceremony was conducted at Versailles just outside Paris and was symbolic of the great shift in political power taking place on the continent; for the next half century a federated Germany composed of 25 individual states would be the pre-eminent economic and military power in Europe; 23 of the 25 states were headed by princes, and it was as president of this federation of princes that the Prussian king held the title of German emperor.[28]

During the final third of the nineteenth century what has sometimes been termed 'the social question' rose to the forefront of government priorities in all of the Western monarchies. One result of the extension of the franchise in an era of industry was the emergence of credible socialist political parties. Supporters of monarchy like Bismarck were adaptable enough to take the lead in addressing many of the pressing social and economic concerns of the labouring class. Across Western Europe, royal governments began to take an active role in areas once off limits to the state: factory and housing inspections, health services for the poor, compulsory education at the elementary level. And as long as Europe's monarchs took cognizance of the changing role of public authority in a complex urban and industrial society, popular support for the political system would continue. Largely due to German leadership under Bismarck, by 1900 monarchy had ceased to be the bulwark of official religion and aristocratic privilege that had for centuries been at the core of the office. New tasks associated with the advancement of national interests, not particularist ones, had been embraced by rulers and ruled alike as the foundation of a new consensus about the purpose of civil society. Both in terms of the time span involved and the scope of the re-invention, it was an extraordinary departure.

When Kaiser William died in 1888, his successor William II undertook to expand German imperial power well beyond the confines of Europe, propelling the German monarchy to the forefront of global power while simultaneously making gestures towards the principles of parliamentary government and individual freedom. With a population of some 67 million in

1870 (double the size of Britain's) imperial Germany became an industrial powerhouse during the last quarter of the century. Electronics, chemicals, pharmaceuticals, armaments – Germany led the world in a variety of specialty areas. The Kaiser was keenly aware of the importance of promoting German industry and commerce, and his government consistently pursued policies likely to advance the material interests of the industrial middle class.[29] William II surrounded himself not only with *Junker* aristocrats but with bankers and industrialists who called for the extension of German economic and military power overseas. This was an astute and timely political move on the part of the monarch, and it was repeated in Britain and to a lesser extent in Nicholas II's Russia. The social differences between the old landed aristocracy and the industrial bourgeoisie were lessened to a degree as monarchs bestowed noble titles on the captains of industry and banking. In Britain the Rothschilds and the Sassoons, in Germany the Krupps and the Siemenses, in Austria the Gutmanns, in Italy the Franchettis – the wealthiest bankers and manufacturers successfully entered the ranks of the traditional nobility elite thanks in large measure to the willingness of the greatest landed aristocrat to embrace them.[30]

In terms of political organization, Bismarck's imperial constitution (1871–90) was an ingenious mixture of democratic and autocratic elements. One recent scholar has described the German Reich 'as a facade of a parliamentary monarchy superimposed upon the edifice of an authoritarian state dominated by the reactionary, militarist, landowning aristocracy of Prussia'.[31] Under the new federal structure, William II not only personally appointed (and dismissed) the chancellor and commanded the armed forces, but also enjoyed the right to call and dismiss the bicameral federal parliament. A lower house or Reichstag was elected on the basis of universal manhood suffrage, and this legislative assembly enjoyed considerable budgetary powers, but it was the emperor who officially initiated all domestic legislation. The upper house or Bundesrat consisted of delegates sent by the constituent states, and all national legislation had to be approved by both chambers. However, since the chancellor and his cabinet were responsible solely to the emperor, he and his government could remain in power even without the support of the parliament. In addition, the king-emperor exercised full authority over the armed forces and was the chief architect of foreign policy.[32]

By the early 1890s William had realized some of the more expansive ambitions of monarchs dating back to the sixteenth century: the crown enjoyed a monopoly of coercive power through a standing army and a dedicated bureaucracy. None of the major political parties in the Reichstag – the Catholic Centre Party, the Social Democrats or the National Liberals – opposed the authoritarian domestic structure or the aggressive foreign policy of the emperor's government.[33] And the young Kaiser's understanding of his prerogative befitted a personality at once boastful and insecure. After dismissing Bismarck in 1890, the monarch moved Germany into an aggressive and expansionist posture. In language reminiscent of eighteenth-century divine-right absolutism, he informed the Provincial Diet of Brandenburg in 1891, 'that I regard my whole position and my task as having been imposed on me from heaven, and that I am called to the service of a Higher Being, to Whom I shall have to give a reckoning later'. To Bismarck's successor William confided in 1892 that he was not interested in personal popularity (although his actions belied this), 'for, as the guiding principles of my actions, I have only the dictates of my duty and the responsibility of my clear conscience towards God'.[34] In 1900 William told the future George V of England that as Kaiser he alone 'was master of German policy and my country must follow me wherever I go'. In the judgement of one recent observer the emperor personified the dynastic culture of late nineteenth-century Europe:

> He was a monarch by Divine Right yet always the parvenus; a medieval knight in shining armor and yet the inspiration behind that marvel of modern technology, the battle fleet; a dyed-in-the-wool reactionary yet also – for a time at least – the Socialist Emperor who supported basic accident and retirement insurance for the industrial worker.[35]

But whatever these personal failings, in the short term at least this mercurial monarch, following in the path of

Bismarck, effectively co-opted the liberal agenda by delivering on the promise of national greatness.

THE HABSBURG DILEMMA

In Austria, on the other hand, the ruling family faced the daunting problem of trying to maintain control over a medieval land-based empire that was the very antithesis of the national ideal. At the Congress of Vienna, the Habsburgs made no effort to revive the ancient Holy Roman Empire which had been fractured during the Napoleonic wars. A successor Austrian empire had been declared by Francis II as early as 1804, and two years later, after Napoleon had forced western and southern German principalities to join a new Confederation of the Rhine, Francis resigned the title of Holy Roman emperor. Under Francis, who ruled until 1835, and his son Ferdinand I (r. 1835–48) the empire was governed in an autocratic fashion. Prince Klemens von Metternich oversaw a substantial network of internal spies and exercised a rigorous censorship over the press. During the early stages of the 1848 revolution Metternich fled to London while the emperor abdicated in favour of his 18-year-old nephew Francis Joseph I (r. 1848–1916). For the next 68 years the political fortunes of the Habsburg house would be in the hands of this man, a deeply conservative figure who had experienced popular urban revolution in the first year of his reign and who from that point onward struggled mightily to prevent a repetition of these events.

Germans, Magyars, Poles, Croatians, Slovenes, Ruthenians, Rumanians, Serbs, Italians, Czechs – the myriad peoples who inhabited the imperial dominions of the Habsburgs could not be insulated from the rumblings of nationalism born of the French Revolutionary experience. Habsburg armies had successfully defeated Italian and Magyar rebels in 1848, but after military humiliation at the hands of the upstart Piedmontese in 1859 and the Prussians in 1866, Emperor Francis Joseph was forced to concede domestic autonomy to the Magyar nobility of Hungary. A dual monarchy (under Francis Joseph as emperor of Austria and king of Hungary) was established, and this guaranteed that customs, foreign affairs and the army would remain unified, but the domestic autonomy won by the Magyars at the expense of their Habsburg monarch only fuelled the fires of nationalist sentiment among the other peoples of the polyglot empire. From this point until the collapse of the monarchy in the devastation wrought during the First World War, the Habsburgs were constantly at odds with a wide range of ethnic minorities within their far-flung domains.

The successful Piedmontese effort to oust Austrian forces from Italy, together with the Magyar achievement in securing domestic autonomy for the Hungarian portion of the empire in 1867, pointed up the remarkable extent to which dynasticism was the only variable linking a host of peoples who shared no racial, linguistic, social or historical cohesion. Austria-Hungary was an empire consisting entirely of minorities, a holdover from the medieval imperial idea of allegiance to crown and dynasty, not to abstract nation.[36] The only bond between the far-flung and varied provinces of the empire was the monarch himself, whose 68-year reign overlapped the decades when nationalism was becoming the strongest factor in the political life of Europe. Thus it should not surprise us that the principal powers enjoyed by the emperor, control over foreign affairs and the military, were constantly employed in the service of obstructing the realization of the nationalist agenda. In the view of one observer, 'foreign policy was the justification of the monarchy; almost every important change within Habsburg lands for a century or more had been the result of a need to meet a new crisis in foreign affairs.'[37]

And during the last 40 years of the monarchy's existence, questions of national rivalry within Habsburg-controlled lands constituted the key challenge to the ruler and his ministers. The ageing emperor felt a deep personal responsibility for the well-being and territorial integrity of his multi-ethnic inheritance. Unfortunately, concessions made to one group invariably spurred demands from another. What held the monarchical model intact into the twentieth century was, more than anything else, the sense of continuity represented by Europe's oldest dynastic house. Thus the celebration of the emperor's eightieth birthday in 1910 was every bit as significant for the empire as Queen Victoria's Diamond Jubilee had been for the British in 1897. The Habsburgs were associated in the minds of their subjects with the tradition of transnational Roman authority, the bold defence of Europe against the incursions of the Turk, and an almost exceptional sense of anti-parochialism.[38] The emperor was the heir of Charles V, apostolic king of Hungary and successor of St Stephen. Tradition still counted for something in this polyglot empire.

There were representative assemblies in both Austria and Hungary, and by the 1880s Austrians enjoyed freedom of religion, equality before the law and the protection of civil rights. In 1907 the parliament was elected on the basis of universal manhood suffrage, and a multi-party system was put in place. But government ministers were servants of the crown and not responsible to parliamentary control. Supported by an expanding civil service, army and Church, Francis Joseph was not a man predisposed to initiate change conducive to either a nationalist or constitutionalist agenda. The emperor did encourage state investment in certain infrastructure sectors like the railroad, and economic growth was led by industrial centres like Vienna and Prague. But raised in the intellectual climate of Metternich's Europe, and chastened as a young emperor by the memory of the 1848 liberal revolutions, the monarch placed the survival of the transnational dynasty above all other personal or political considerations.[39] One the eve of the First World War few of the king-emperor's subjects would have proposed the dissolution of the monarchy. Internally the crown still enjoyed considerable prestige. And the heir apparent to the elderly emperor, Archduke Franz Ferdinand, was known to be sympathetic to the South Slavs. In 1914 it was the nationalist ambitions of this minority group which posed what was perhaps the most serious challenge to the political well-being of the empire. But the archduke, it appeared, was poised to address this problem in a peaceful manner.

RUSSIAN INTRANSIGENCE

Monarchs in central and eastern Europe wielded the greatest level of personal authority over their still subject populations.

The Russian monarchy in particular emphatically resisted the influence of liberal and constitutional ideas throughout the course of the nineteenth century. It took a major military debacle in 1905 to shake the foundations of royal autocracy, and even then the tsarist system continued to oppose the sort of parliamentary model already established in Britain, France and to a lesser extent in Germany. In a very important sense the persistence of autocratic monarchy can be explained in relation to economic and material factors. Until the final decade of the nineteenth century imperial Russia remained an overwhelmingly agrarian state. The large majority of the tsar's subjects were indigent and illiterate peasants, and the hardships attendant upon landed labour were magnified by rapid population expansion and, paradoxically, by the abolition of serfdom in 1861 by Tsar Alexander II. Emancipation had left many peasants facing burdensome redemption payments to the former owners of the land. With the population expanding from 97 million in 1880 to 165 million in 1914, the government provided little in the way of social and educational services familiar to Western states.

Lacking a rudimentary industrial or strong commercial sector, the middle-class social base essential to constitutional change elsewhere in Europe was missing in Russia. The last two Romanov tsars, Alexander III (1845–94, r. 1883–94) and Nicholas II (1868–1918, r. 1894–1917) were dedicated if unimaginative autocrats who felt threatened by innovation and modernization. And they eschewed the type of personal connection with their subjects that had long been the symbolic hallmark of the dynasty. Earlier in the century, Tsars Nicholas I and then Alexander II often walked or rode through the city of St Petersburg without a convoy. The perceived accessibility of the emperor tempered the harshness of autocratic rule for many in the city which was home to the imperial court. But the 1881 assassination of Alexander II while riding to his weekly review of the guards of the capital changed this custom. After the killing, the Russian monarchs were never again seen in the streets without the benefit of intensive protection.[40] With an unwieldy security apparatus which by 1900 featured some 100,000 police, 5,000 security agents and a variety of spies and paid informers, liberal voices were quickly silenced.

Many would-be reformers chose exile while more committed radicals turned to terror as the only available tool for reform.

The last of the Russian tsars, Nicholas II, illustrates the extent to which the success or failure of autocratic regimes hinged on the personal characteristics of the ruler. As a young man Nicholas had imbibed the theory of divine right absolutism from his tutor Constantine Pobedonostsev, who was procurator or chairman of the Holy Synod (the committee directing the Orthodox Church) from 1880 to 1895.[41] Nicholas's entire tenure as tsar was informed by a passionate desire to pass this power on, uncorrupted, to his haemophilic heir. Throughout his reign the tsar was dominated by favourites, be it religious leaders or his wife and her confidant, the monk Rasputin. Capable administrators like Sergei Witte, who was the finance minister from 1892 until 1903, found themselves unable to secure the confidence of the monarch. Witte began a crash programme of state intervention in the economy in order to develop key industries like the railroad during the 1890s, and some success was achieved. In fact during the decade of the 1890s the Russian industrial sector grew at a faster rate than any other European counterpart.

But still the overall poverty of the population increased. Overwhelmingly rural and heavily dependent upon foreign loans and investment for nascent industry, Russia's enormous Eurasian land empire was put to the test in 1905 in a war with Japan. The result was defeat and humiliation at the hands of the upstart Asian power, and in the aftermath of the conflict Tsar Nicholas was forced to concede a national representative assembly called the Duma. The royal climbdown was neither extensive nor permanent, however. The newly established Duma could be suspended and dissolved at the will of the tsar, and its powers did not extend to military expenditure. In addition, a set of 'Fundamental Laws' issued in 1906 could be amended only by the monarch. On the eve of the First World War, the royal court was isolated and defensive, unwilling to make further concessions in the direction of constitutional reform and counting on the strength of Russian nationalism and residual loyalty to the dynasty to weather any future storms. In the event it proved to be an enormous miscalculation.

6 The wedding of King Hussein of Jordan and Queen Dina, 1955.

SIX

Endings and Remnants: Monarchy in the Twentieth Century

During the course of the twentieth century the institution of monarchy faced repeated challenges the world over. In Europe, despite the advance of democratic politics, the popularity of monarchy reached new heights at the turn of the century, only to be discredited during the course of the First World War. The Russian, Austrian, German and Ottoman empires were dissolved as a direct result of this unprecedented conflict, with democratic, secular republics emerging in all but the first country by the mid-1920s. Of all the major combatants, only Britain retained its monarchy at the end of the Great War, although by this juncture the royal family was reduced mainly to service in a ceremonial capacity, with the monarch obliged to support the policies set by the majority party in the House of Commons. As we noted in Chapter 1, a not dissimilar state of affairs obtained in post-Second World War Japan, where the emperor retained his office but disavowed both sacred status and political involvement. Twentieth-century Europeans abjured traditional monarchy, but by the 1930s a new and far more insidious version of rule by one had emerged to challenge the democratic paradigm. It would take another global war, and the deaths of upwards of 50 million people, before this modern repudiation of the dignity of the individual would be overcome. Elsewhere around the globe the forces of modernity continued to undermine the customary power claims of monarchs. China's imperial order was brought to a close by revolution in 1912; in India the world's most populous democracy replaced the British raj in 1948; and in Southeast Asia the Vietnamese monarchy collapsed in the face of communist insurgency. The one general exception to these wider global developments took place in the

Muslim world, where new monarchies were erected after the First World War, and where the discovery of oil resources gave some of these royal dynasties exceptional opportunities for the extension of royal power.

EUROPE'S APOGEE, 1880–1914

Europeans in general, and monarchs in particular, had cause for optimism at the start of the new century. Political democratization and constitutional, responsible government had largely been reconciled with hereditary executive power under kings and queens. By 1880 it was generally acknowledged in the West that the state and its traditional leaders should represent the nation, a people with a common cultural and historic identity. As we have seen, only Austria-Hungary, Russia and the Ottoman sultanate violated this pattern, and the situation would contribute mightily to the collapse of all three empires during the Great War. In Western Europe the old alliance of monarchs, churchmen and nobles was now expanded to include bankers and businessmen in the common defence of existing arrangements. Around the globe, sovereign nation states subject to no foreign power were emerging as the standard model of civil organization.

Scientific advances in industry, in biology, physics, and in the study of nature as a whole promised a future where mystery and obscurantism would be replaced by rational investigation and the empirical method. In terms of everyday life, advances in medicine had perhaps the greatest impact on the quality of life experienced by westerners. Queen Victoria, for example, was a key figure in the promotion of the use of anaesthetic in childbirth. Rail and bicycle transport, steam-driven ocean travel, the electrification of urban centres, better housing and a more varied diet presaged a new dawn in European life where material conditions would improve for all at an increasingly rapid pace. And of course there was also the comfort, more a matter of emotion than intellect, that the material and spiritual glories of European civilization were now being disseminated worldwide thanks to the expansion of empire into Africa and

Asia beginning in the 1870s.

At the start of the nineteenth century European monarchs headed kingdoms whose subjects controlled (and in some cases occupied) 35 per cent of the world's land mass. Just over a century later, in 1914, they controlled 84 per cent while directly colonizing a large portion of the world's peoples.[1] One-third of the planet's land surface on the eve of the First World War was dominated by two monarchies, the British and the Russian. By the 1880s Western Europe, consisting of approximately one-fourteenth of the habitable globe (excluding Russia's Asiatic lands) and home to one-quarter of the world's population (320 million), was clearly *the* dominant civilization.[2] Thanks to more than three centuries of innovation in the manipulation of the environment, Europe (and more recently the USA) possessed the ability to deploy enormous military force over most of the earth's surface. With superior economies and technology, transport and weaponry, European domination proceeded apace over women and men who in the main had for centuries been under the control of their own royal dynasties.[3]

The scale of the change is hard to overemphasize. Prior to the nineteenth century, colonialism had mainly been an affair involving European cooperation with local monarchs and their elite subordinates. Something of the Renaissance spirit of discovery and fascination with other, non-Christian, cultures still informed Europe's engagement with its distant neighbours. British India is perhaps the best case in point, for here the English East India Company sought to collaborate with the Mughal emperors and their subalterns for mutual economic advantage. The Indian sepoy mutiny of 1857 put an end to this informal relationship and introduced direct crown control over the majority of the subcontinent. It also marked the growth of a less generous view of non-westerners who had so obviously failed to keep pace with Europe's industrial development. More often than not after 1850, colonial peoples were viewed as benighted at best and biologically inferior at worst. The result was a dramatic acceleration of direct political takeover. In Africa by 1900 only two states, Liberia and Abyssinia, had managed to maintain their independence from Europe's control. Britain,

France, Germany, and to a lesser extent Italy, Portugal and Spain, together with Belgium, whose king Leopold II claimed Congo as a personal possession, completed the carve-up of the huge continent. In Asia only five kingdoms (Afghanistan, Japan, Persia, Siam and Tibet) remained free of European colonial influence.[4] For the imperialists, it was simply assumed that their values, techniques and idea systems were universally applicable, and that the 'backwards' peoples should welcome this gratuitous offering.

For the rest of the global community, the harsh choice at the end of that century was either to become clients of the Europeans or to employ European ideas and techniques in an effort to avoid imperial domination. From economic organization to educational ideals to medical techniques to the seeds of nationalism, the Western paradigm could no longer be ignored. But if things European sharply distinguished the Western imperialists from their involuntary subordinates around the world, and if the flattery of imitation was to be the lot of those who, like the Japanese, struggled to remain outside the orbit of Europe's direct or indirect control, then the institution of monarchy served as the one familiar bridge connecting the varied cultures of the globe. Rank and birth, social and political power linked to an ordered hierarchy – these elements of traditional societies worldwide helped to facilitate Europe's hegemony by allowing indigenous monarchs to continue to rule their kingdoms under Western oversight. This common institutional bond was put to immediate use in the nineteenth century by the more powerful Europeans in their ignoble quest to make empire pay.

The overlapping of European monarchy and non-western (and previously autonomous) kingdoms was pursued both at the level of symbol and substance. In colonial Africa, both the Germans and the British made broad use of the idea of imperial monarchy in representing themselves to peoples who were under the nominal rule of indigenous lesser kings. According to one scholar, 'the "theology" of an omniscient, omnipotent and omnipresent monarchy became almost the sole ingredient of imperial ideology as it was presented to Africans'.[5] African kings were informed by colonial missionaries and administrators alike that the European monarch took a personal and paternal interest in the well-being of all colonial subjects. Local rituals, all geared to the celebration of European rulership, were invented by the occupiers in order to enhance the status of the imperial incumbent. In her proclamation accompanying the Government of India Act of 1858, Queen Victoria assured her South Asian subjects that she 'was bound to the natives of our Indian territories by the same obligations of duty which bind us to all our other subjects'. Under the direction of Prime Minister Benjamin Disraeli, in 1887 Parliament bestowed the title 'Empress of India' on the queen, thus reinforcing the widespread assumption that what the British brought to India was better than what they had found there.[6] The head of British government in India after 1858 represented the Parliament in Westminster, but as viceroy he was the voice of the monarch who maintained a just relationship between the imperial crown and the many princes and peoples of the vast subcontinent.[7] The Indian princes were now accepted as feudatories of the sovereign imperial monarch, and the entire social hierarchy of India was organized in reference to the queen-empress.

POPULAR CROWNS IN A DEMOCRATIC AGE

In a work entitled *The Persistence of the Old Regime*, Arno Mayer argued that the First World War 'was an expression of the decline and fall of the old order fighting to prolong its life rather than of the explosive rise of industrial capitalism bent on imposing its primacy'. Whether or not Mayer is correct in viewing the war as the product of the *ancien régime*'s desperate attempt to hold on to power, the strength and durability of that regime can no longer be questioned. Monarchy stood at the centre of Europe's political order in 1914, and it was one of the institutions simply taken for granted by the overwhelming majority of people throughout the world. Even in Europe, where a market-based society was making inroads against traditional status-based culture, and where popularly elected parliamentary institutions of some sort existed everywhere except in Montenegro, the royal institution retained its popularity. Newly founded states in the Balkans – Serbia, Romania, Bulgaria, Montenegro, Albania – all established in nationalist wars at the expense of the Ottoman Turks, opted for a monarchical system of government.

Important alternatives there were in vast republics like the United States, more recently in France, and to a certain degree among the intellectual elite in China after the breakdown of the imperial order in 1912. But these cases were very much the exception. In the study of the past we tend to concentrate on advocates for change, on those who wished to reorder existing relationships and institutions. The result is that we overlook what Mayer calls 'the forces of inertia and resistance that slowed the waning of the old order'. Taking monarchy for granted, not defending the institution because it did not need much defence, is one of the implicit, indeed irreproachable facts of global history in the early twentieth century, but one which is often overlooked for lack of contention about it.[8]

A host of additional factors account for the persistence of the institution into the early twentieth century. The birth of universal military conscription, mandatory public education, the emergence of efficient tax assessment and collection systems, increasingly sophisticated rail and ocean transport, the abandonment of classical liberal prescriptions against government intervention in the areas of social policy and economic regulation – in so many ways the modern state played an unprecedented, and perhaps intrusive role in the lives of individual citizens. The personnel of government expanded greatly at the close of the century, and as civil service exams became the normal route of entry into government service, the state's regulatory abilities were enhanced. Clearly monarchs who supported the development of the service state where the social and economic well-being of the population became one of the key functions of government found that their popularity expanded along with their executive power.

Surprisingly, in an age of mass politics, industrial labour and geographic mobility, most Europeans continued to assume that society was best run by traditional elites. While commercial and industrial cultures based social and political power on competition in the free market, rank and birth continued to matter across Europe. In Britain, for example, landed elites still exercised considerable influence over the affairs of the House of Commons. In 1880 only 100 of the 658 members of the House based their income on commercial or manufacturing activities, while many MPs were relatives of hereditary peers who sat in the House of Lords. Yet there never emerged a popular movement to dissolve the monarchy, the House of Lords, or the ascriptive service nobility. Aristocratic and deferential assumptions about political leadership continued to bulk very large, even in the most industrially advanced nations. European society was slowly being transformed by bourgeois values, but the most successful elements of the commercial and industrial middle class continued to ape aristocratic style, buying country houses, sending their sons to elite schools, marrying their children into the titled nobility.[9]

The institution of monarchy in Europe also benefited from a late nineteenth-century backlash against the advent of mass democratic politics. The track record of republics, after all, was not terribly impressive. In France, for example, fragile coalition governments were the norm after 1871, and corruption scandals undermined more than one ruling alliance. Between 1890 and 1914 there were 43 different governments and 26 prime ministers in republican France. Universal manhood suffrage had been achieved in most countries by 1900, but for some the record of parliamentary politics was less than inspiring. In France, defeat at the hands of the Germans in 1870 and the subsequent loss of French-speaking Alsace-Lorraine provided the occasion for an outpouring of nationalist and anti-parliamentary thought. Monarchist opponents of the republic were convinced that France's decline relative to Germany was due to the lack of an authoritarian regime. Corruption, venality and incompetence – these were the primary characteristics of democratic republics where political elites manipulated the votes of the masses in a never-ending pursuit of party advantage.[10]

According to this line of thought, liberal democratic culture featured political power under the direction of men of inferior moral and intellectual endowment, ambitious parvenus who sought only to manipulate the electorate for their own narrow ends. The inefficiency and corruption of popularly elected governments provided the strongest evidence of the need to return to rule by one. In 1914, the theory that monarchies provided stability while republics were home to unsteadiness and insecurity appeared to be borne out by the fact that none of the great powers had fought one another since the Franco-Prussian war of 1870. There was scant thought given within diplomatic or military circles to the possibility of the break-up or removal of one of the great monarchies, even ones devoid of national identity like Austria-Hungary. A balance of power seemed to be the ongoing objective of all states.

Seeking to place national and corporate interests before the ambitions and centrifugal tendencies of party, writers like Maurice Barrès (1862–1923) and Charles Maurras (1868–1952) aimed to reinvigorate monarchy as the only viable model of governance in an age of industry. In his *Inquiry on the Monarchy* and in articles published in the review *L'Action française*, Maurras argued that political democracy and party politics as a rule ignore the greater national interest. The national tradition is best represented by a strong prince who can override the selfish ambitions of individual political figures.[11] Authors like Maurras wrote that monarchy, Church and army were essential features of successful government in the modern age.[12] The paramountcy of the state, and the failure of democratic republics to ensure the security of the state, was forcefully articulated by Heinrich von Treitschke (1834–96) in Germany. In his posthumously published four-volume *Politics*, von Treitschke argued that the unity of the state was best served when all legislative, judicial and executive authority was concentrated in one office. Not surprisingly the newly established German empire was the model state under this definition, where the chancellor was not responsible to the popularly elected legislative assembly.[13]

THE PLACE OF SYMBOL

One result of these developments was that monarchy in Europe experienced a distinct upturn in popularity at the close of the century. While the formal political influence once exercised by royalty abated, support for the crown as the symbol of national unity and permanence in a world of rapid urban and industrial change seemed to multiply. Even Britain's Edward VII, a man who came to the throne late in life after the death of his mother in 1901, and who had little commitment to hard work, found himself the object of deep respect. In a very real sense, European royalty in the year 1900 constituted one large extended family. Members of ruling dynasties were expected to marry members of other dynasties, unless of course the principals were willing to forego their status as hereditary elites. In Britain members of the royal family might marry commoners with the permission of the monarch, but even with this exception most royals married into other princely families. Catholic princes tended to marry within the Habsburg and Bourbon families; Protestants and Eastern Orthodox Russians preferred to pick from the numerous German dynasties. The fruits of this tight circle of marriageable partners was made clear in the first decade of the new century. Thanks to the fecundity of Queen Victoria, her son and successor was uncle to the German emperor William II and to the wife of Russian tsar Nicholas II. The sixtieth jubilee of the reign of Europe's senior monarch, Habsburg Emperor Francis Joseph, was occasion for an international gathering of dynastic rulers and their entourages at Vienna in the year 1908. To a certain degree this network of personal and familial relationships provided Europeans with a sense (misplaced as it turned out) that a greater solidarity of European interests was possible thanks to royal collegiality.[14]

In addition to blood relationships, the pageantry of monarchy, the marriages, coronations, state visits and funerals all provided enormously popular spectacles for an increasingly literate mass audience. The theatre or 'symbolics' of power in society, the varied manner by which hierarchies of dominance inherent in all forms of government are created and maintained, always involves the effective and didactic use of ceremonial and pageantry. In the modern American republic, ceremonies surrounding the inauguration of a president, the annual 'state of the union' address to Congress, and the celebration of national holidays all comply with carefully formulated protocol. In mid-twentieth-century authoritarian and aspirant totalitarian systems, the glorification of the arbitrary leader followed carefully scripted and stage-managed formulae. In monarchical systems, on the other hand, the rituals of royalty focus greater attention on the traditional aspects of governance, on linkages with a valuable past and the human embodiment of a particular tradition. Their main purpose was, and is, to emphasize consensus, disguise conflict, and promote deference and obedience to polities where the distribution of power is at all times unequal.[15] Just as the physical instruments of coercion have sustained political regimes throughout the last thousand years, so too pomp and pageantry have for centuries been in every society at the core of the effective exercise of power over subject peoples.

More monarchs may have adhered to what might be termed bourgeois values of family respectability by 1900, more may have dressed like businessmen, but idealized images of the monarch and his office were still principal concerns of the state. King Edward's coronation was the occasion for the meeting of important delegates from throughout the empire, as well as a great stage for European royalty. The monarch revived the state opening of Parliament after 40 years in abeyance, and this elaborate spectacle, complete with procession in the state coach to Westminster and the reading of an opening speech, has continued to the present day. George V's (r. 1910–35) coronation was followed by a visit to India and another elaborate ceremony (durbar) designed to celebrate the global reach of the English throne. At the funeral of his father in May 1910, a queue of citizens wishing to pay their last respects extended for seven miles to the entrance of Westminster Hall. The actual funeral procession, attended by nine monarchs, was witnessed by an estimated two million people who lined the streets of the capital city.[16]

In relatively new kingdoms like Hohenzollern Prussia (established as a royal kingdom in 1701), the invention of custom and tradition occupied the energies of the royal court through to the First World War. The 25th jubilee of the reign of William II of Germany in 1913, for example, was an occasion of enormous spectacle. Public forms of royal ritual during the nineteenth and early twentieth centuries were skilfully designed to identify the monarch with time-honoured corporate values in the face of rapid and often unsettling social and economic changes. During these ceremonies the king was portrayed as a man at one with his subjects, reconciling regional and religious differences, embodying the core of cultural identity.[17] Even architecture reflected the renewed interest and veneration for the crown. The construction of the Victoria Memorial in front of Buckingham Palace, like the King Victor Emmanuel monument built in the city of Rome, was but one outcropping of a broader sense of pride in and commitment to the hereditary office, irrespective of whatever personal weaknesses owned by the monarch. The images of royalty were disseminated in print, photography and ceramics for an audience keen to maintain the connection with hierarchy in an otherwise democratic era. At the close of the century, Russian soldiers still carried into battle pictures of their tsar, an emotional attachment to dynasticism quite remarkable for its resilience.

Thus on the eve of war in August 1914, the kings and emperors of Europe could rightly boast that they had not only weathered the profound social and economic changes wrought by the Industrial Revolution, but that in many respects their power over their respective citizens had increased tremendously. At a time when political rights were being extended to every adult male irrespective of circumstances, when a popular press was disseminating news to millions of literate working people, and when basic educational opportunities were for the first time available to the masses at public expense, monarchs in Germany, Austria-Hungary, Italy, Spain and Russia commanded more coercive might than any of their *ancien régime* predecessors.

THE CONFLICT

The First World War was to a certain degree the outcome of the failure of monarchy, at least in terms of the immediate events which precipitated the conflict. In 1908 Austria-Hungary had infuriated the Russians by annexing Bosnia, a land legally still under the control of the Ottoman Turks and inhabited by South Slav peoples. Emperor Francis Joseph and his government in Vienna feared that the Serbian monarchy had designs on Bosnia, and if these ambitions were ever to be realized then the Slavs inside the Dual Monarchy would push for integration into a Serbian-led greater South Slav state. For his part, Nicholas II was determined to assert Russia's centuries-old support for its Orthodox neighbours in the Balkans, and this meant opposing both Turkish resurgence and Habsburg expansionism. Defeat at the hands of the Japanese in 1905 only heightened the tsar's eagerness to reassert Russian influence in southeastern Europe. And in Berlin, Kaiser William and his military advisors were intent upon supporting the Habsburg position even if this meant war with Russia. 'The final decision in the South-East of Europe', the Kaiser reportedly informed an Austrian diplomat in 1913, 'may, we know, call for a serious passage of arms and we Germans will then stand with you and behind you.' William II had been close to the heir apparent to the Habsburg throne, Franz Ferdinand, and in the immediate aftermath of the assassination he wrote that 'The Serbs must be disposed of and that right soon.'[18] Guided by advisers who were themselves members of the nobility and not beholden to party or legislature, William II, Nicholas II and Francis Joseph I led Europe and then the wider world into the first of two mass slaughters which would, in less than 30 years, destroy Europe's primacy in global affairs. In one sense both world wars involved what was, at bottom, a great European civil war, for while there was no political unity in Europe, the combatants shared a broadly common culture and economic structure, a common civilization and sense of superiority over other non-western peoples. By 1945 the damage inflicted would put an end to Europe's military, economic and political leadership.

Few would have anticipated such a precipitate and demoralizing fall in the summer of 1914.[19] The assassination of Franz Ferdinand, heir to the Habsburg throne, had not been the first time that royalty had been targeted by opponents of the established political order at the turn of the century. In 1900 King

Humbert of Italy was assassinated, in 1906 an attempt was made on the life of King Alfonso XIII of Portugal during his wedding procession; the following year the king and his heir apparent were both killed.[20] And while the death of the Habsburg archduke precipitated a wider European conflict, a general sense of euphoria gripped leaders, combatants and civilians alike during the first months of the war. Writing to Empress Alexandra in late September 1914, Russian Tsar Nicholas II expressed confidence that 'with God's help here all will go well and end gloriously, and it has lifted up spirits, cleansed the many stagnant minds, brought unity in feelings and is a "healthy war" in the moral sense'.[21]

The tsar's sentiments respecting the cleansing effects of combat were echoed by the French philosopher Henri Bergson, who spoke of 'the moral regeneration of Europe' in supporting the Entente powers.[22] A Prussian officer stationed in Brazil wrote to a friend in Berlin that people were now attributing to Kaiser William II more greatness than either Bismarck or Napoleon Bonaparte. William was at the outset of the conflict 'a Jupiter, standing on the Olympus of his iron-studded might, the lightning-bolts in his grasp. At this moment he is God and master of the world.'[23] Artists, poets, university students rushed to the volunteer centres in search of spiritual renewal, community, excitement, and an escape from the hum-drum materialism of bourgeois existence. Even the leaders of Europe's emerging socialist parties, ostensibly committed to the solidarity of the working class across national boundaries, came to the defence of king and country.

Experience stimulated rash forecasts. After all, there had been no general conflagration on the continent in over a hundred years, and those wars which had been fought were, by and large, relatively brief affairs where movement and decisive victory were achieved within months (few Europeans took proper account of America's protracted and bloody mid-century civil war). In fact pre-established battle plans, predicated on the existing alliance system, called for the employment of speed combined with overwhelming force. In Germany the Kaiser's top military advisers, convinced that a general European conflict was inevitable, impressed upon their leader the need to act immediately while the military situation was favourable.[24] Even though the two opposing alliance systems which had been formed complicated the ability of one nation to strike a decisive blow against a range of enemies, no one expected a protracted conflict or a stalemate. In the event that a knock-out blow could not be delivered, victory was bound to lie with the alliance best able to combine military and financial resources over the long term.

The minority of Europeans who resisted the impulse to endorse this mass display of patriotic ardour were voices in the wilderness. One of the sceptics, Romain Rolland, observed sadly that 'there is not one among the leaders of thought in each country who does not proclaim with conviction that the cause of his people is the cause of God, the cause of liberty and of human progress'.[25] The misplaced fervour of those early months was reflected in the whole military approach to battle. Despite the many advances in weaponry brought about by the Industrial Revolution – the long-range cannon, the machine gun and breach-loading rifle, mechanized motor vehicles like the tank, poison gas – anachronistic practices such as the employment of brightly coloured uniforms continued to exist. In August 1914 French soldiers would march against the Germans wearing blue coats and bright red trousers, while British officers were ordered to sharpen their swords in preparation for attack in the age of the machine gun.[26] In August 1914, war seemed like a romantic quest for national renewal, and many monarchs symbolized the bellicose qualities inherent in the culture of a people.

It did not take long for the ordeal of trench warfare to temper this credulous perspective. 'War is hell, and those who institute it are criminals' was the poet Siegfried Sassoon's conclusion from the trenches. By the end of 1916, the tsar's imperial army had suffered 3 million dead or wounded, while an additional 2.1 million had been taken captive by the Germans. All of the combatants suffered in a similar fashion. In one five-month battle at Verdun, French and German casualties totalled 600,000. During the first day of battle at the Somme in the summer of 1916, 20,000 British soldiers were killed and 40,000 were wounded. As the prospect of rapid victory faded for all of the principals, government leaders took measures to curb critics of the war effort, measures which more often than not involved the abridgement of hard-won political freedoms. In September 1915 Tsar Nicholas II suspended the Russian Duma for the duration of the war, while in Germany the military general staff prosecuted the war effort without recourse to the Reichstag. Even in Britain and France, Prime Minister Lloyd George and Premier Georges Clemenceau governed through war cabinets which set policy in secret. Official censorship, internment, and massive propaganda rounded out the efforts to stem the tide of opposition to the stalemated conflict.[27]

None of these measures could effectively address the real domestic difficulties associated with total war. By the start of 1917 the tsar's war machine was in complete disarray. Inadequately supplied, short of food and ammunition at the front, demoralized by repeated reverses and the lack of qualified officers to lead them in battle, widespread desertion in the field and civil unrest in the cities was the result. In March 1917 revolution broke out in Petrograd and the tsar, unwilling to accept a popularly elected government, abdicated in favour of his brother Michael (who in rapid order abdicated himself). In the words of Marc Ferro, Nicholas had always rejected the legislative principle and withdrew concessions which he had been forced to make whenever provided with an opportunity to do so. 'He did not want a Duma, and all this supervision, all this dialoguing with the government, were for Nicholas an infringement of the prerogatives that God had conferred on him.'[28] The first of the great European dynasties had fallen victim to the horrors of war, but as the new government decided to continue the fight against overwhelming odds, radical opponents of the war like the well-disciplined, if numerically small Bolsheviks, were provided an opportunity to seize power with the promise of bread, peace and land.

Austria-Hungary had gone to war in 1914 in order to preserve the integrity of the multinational empire. The emperor and his government had few disagreements with France and Britain, although tension with Russia over the Balkans had long been a source of disagreement.[29] The Habsburgs certainly had no compelling reason to support the Kaiser's territorial ambitions on the continent or overseas. But by 1916, when the aged Francis Joseph died, the empire had become very dependent upon its German ally both economically and militarily. Because of the protracted and costly nature of the fighting, in two years the crown 'had been reduced from being an independent, if relatively weak, Great Power in 1914 to a helpless if resentful satellite of Germany'.[30] The new emperor, Karl I, and his foreign minister Ottokar Count Czernin were eager to see an end to the conflict, but they had little freedom for diplomatic action without the consent of their German partners. Fear of revolution at home, particularly after the fall of the Russian tsar in March 1917, was made more compelling by the general despair of the population, by food shortages and even reports of starvation, and by intensified Slav calls for the break-up of the state. In April, after the abdication of Nicholas II in Russia, the emperor wrote to Kaiser William that 'we are fighting against a new enemy, which is more dangerous than the Entente – against international revolution, which finds its strongest ally in general famine'.[31] By January 1918 there were only two months' worth of grain supplies left in Austria, and a wave of strikes triggered by a reduction in the flour ration further destabilized the government.

The First World War not only signalled the demise of three powerful and centuries-old monarchies, but also inflicted psychological wounds for which there was no treatment. Behind the fall of ancient institutions was a much deeper loss of confidence in the very principle of hereditary leadership. At the outset of the conflict none of the belligerents sought to overturn the entire political system of the enemy, but into the fourth year of the unprecedented conflict the war had clearly become an ideological struggle between authoritarianism and dynasticism on the one side and democracy and constitutionalism on the other. The Russian Revolution of March 1917 and America's entry into the war one month later finally afforded the allies a measure of ideological consistency in their publicly stated war aims. President Woodrow Wilson of America brought to the war effort not only the considerable economic resources and vast military potential of a rising industrial power, but also a strident opposition to autocracy in all of its forms, thus emphasizing a new moral justification for the war effort.

From 1917 onward the allied cause would be inextricably associated with a form of democratic idealism inconsistent with the monarchical principle. At the end of December 1917 Wilson asked all of the belligerents to state their aims in pursuing the war. And while British Prime Minister David Lloyd George stated publicly in January 1918 that 'the destruction of Austria-Hungary does not form any part of our war aims', the allied response to Wilson's request made direct reference to the 'liberation' of Italians, Slavs and Czecho-Slovaks from 'foreign domination'. Throughout the war the allies had called for federal reform of the empire where national minorities would enjoy greater autonomy, but by the last year of the conflict, even the most Austrophile elements in the West were no longer interested in the preservation of the Habsburg monarchy as part of a general peace. By May 1918, American Secretary of State Lansing had convinced President Wilson that 'Austria Hungary must be wiped off the map of Europe as an empire'. The French and British had officially concurred by August, and by early autumn 1918 the fate of the ancient monarchy had been effectively decided by the elected leader of the American republic. After the failure of the final German offensive in the West in July 1918, President Wilson informed the leaders of Germany that he would negotiate only with a genuinely democratic government. This was in October; by 9 November the Kaiser had abdicated and the German Social Democratic leader Phillip Scheidemann proclaimed a German democratic republic. The following day the Kaiser slipped quietly across the border into exile in Holland. The institution of monarchy in the German lands, inaugurated upon the fall of Rome, was at an end.[32]

THE CONSEQUENCES

The four years of war had witnessed not only the deaths of 20 million men, women and children, but also a massive transfer of wealth from Europe to the United States. Sustained allied borrowing transformed the American republic from a debtor to a creditor of Europe, and this fact allowed the American president to exert significant influence at the Versailles Peace Conference. For Wilson one of the major causes of the conflict had been the existence and malign influence of autocratic rule. He believed that national self-determination and democratic, constitutional government provided the only viable route out of the cycle of European rivalry and military conflict. The destruction of the four great empires which had ruled over hundreds of million people was therefore preliminary to the establishment of a peaceful, prosperous and democratic continent.

Ironically, although four traditional monarchies collapsed in the final two years of the war, perhaps the greatest casualty was the very principle of democratic self-government which had stood at the centre of the allies' high hopes for a post-war reconstructed Europe. For while the hereditary principle was discredited by military failure, by the early 1920s a new pattern of anti-democratic rule by one had gained numerous adherents across a war-torn continent. The physical destruction caused by four years of modern, mechanized warfare had been unprecedented, and the repercussions for the common people were immense. All across Europe, manufacturing output was down by an average of one-quarter of 1914 levels, thousands of acres of farm lands were destroyed, unemployment and inflation were high and, to add epidemiological disaster to material hardship, a harrowing global influenza epidemic struck in 1919, claiming the lives of more people than the war itself. Bewilderment and disillusionment affected vanquished and victors alike, while the promise of economic and civic renewal seemed remote. And in the face of this enormous set of rebuilding difficulties, Europe's freely elected political leaders appeared irresolute at best and inept at worst.

The Great War had signalled the end of traditional autocratic kingship in Europe, but the impulse towards strong leadership, a ruler who embodies the national will and is committed to the restoration of national greatness, remained very much alive in the gloomy post-war environment. This was especially true in Germany, where the defeated and much-demoralized nation had never been invaded or occupied during the war, where in fact the fighting had ended with German troops still on enemy soil. Saddled with unrealistic reparations payments and forced to accept blame for the Great War, Germany's newly established Weimar Republic never managed to deflect the criticism lodged against it by the radical right that it was a civilian government, not the Kaiser or the military, which had capitulated to the allies. Much the same general sense of resentment at the outcome of the conflict gripped Italy, where even alliance with the victorious powers meant very little in terms of securing post-war territorial claims along the Adriatic coast. Despite the rhetoric of national self-determination and democracy coming from the negotiators at Versailles, and irrespective of the founding of new republics in Germany, Austria and Hungary, all across Europe the immediate post-war situation was grave. In Soviet Russia, in Italy, and finally in Germany, powerful and insidious forms of autocracy took root in the aftermath of the fall of monarchies.

And these anti-democratic regimes were not without their admirers in a time of enormous self-doubt regarding the viability of popularly elected representative systems of government. In Spain Ortega y Gasset, in Germany Oswald Spengler, in Britain George Bernard Shaw and Evelyn Waugh, in America Walter Lippmann – all expressed deep reservations about the competence of free democratic institutions of government to grapple successfully with the economic challenges of the post-war world. After the Bolsheviks came to power in November 1917, the only freely elected constituent assembly that Russia had ever known was dismantled by Lenin. Men like Benito Mussolini in Italy felt compelled to replace 'the lie of universal suffrage' with the vigorous, heroic leader of the national community, however that community might now be defined. In Germany it was increasingly defined along pseudo-racial lines, in Soviet Russia along class lines, but never in terms of the primacy or dignity of the individual. Subordinating the recently achieved constitutional rights of the individual citizen to the overriding need of the state was, according to both fascists and communists, essential to the solution of pressing economic problems.

The story of the rise of European fascism and Soviet communism during the 1920s and 1930s cannot be our focus here. But it is worth taking note of certain elements which infused both movements, if only to identify some of the more important underlying, and perhaps enduring, psychological features of rule by one. The post-war fascist appeal to emotion and national pride, the need for charismatic political leadership, the willingness to use force against one's domestic opponents, and contempt for liberal democracy can all be traced back to tendencies inherent in European culture during the late nineteenth century. But they were now to receive their most successful increase in the economically depressed circumstances of post-war Europe. Many of the policies and techniques employed by governments during the war – the use of propaganda, censorship, management of the economy, suspension of key civil liberties – all returned under the malevolent leadership of fascist rulers in Italy and Germany, and under Bolshevik rulers in the Soviet Union. In addition to the shaping of dictatorships in Germany, Italy and the Soviet Union after the war, by 1930 two of the new states created at Versailles, Lithuania and Yugoslavia, had become dictatorships, while eight years later additional authoritarian governments had emerged in Bulgaria, Romania and Greece.

NEW MYTHS FOR A NEW CENTURY

The monarchies which remained in place after the devastation wrought by the First World War were by and large those which had already been divested of substantive political power prior to the opening of the twentieth century. In Britain, Norway, Sweden, Denmark, Luxembourg, and more recently in Spain, the reigning dynasties had forsaken all pretensions to the exercise of political authority independent of their respective legislatures. Those kingdoms in 1914 where royalty continued to wield real political and military power, on the other hand, were abolished in rapid order during the final years of the Great War. Survival of the monarchical principle has therefore entailed an unprecedented redefinition of the royal office, its broader purpose in civil society and the expectations associated with royalty.

The four twentieth-century British monarchs who followed Edward VII, all of whom sought to balance a scrupulous impartiality with respect to politics with their constitutional duty to advise, consult and warn the leader of the party in power, provides us with the clearest example of this trend. A reputation for personal integrity, public probity and attention to ceremonial detail has, by and large, enhanced the standing of monarchy in its British context, and in the one instance where both of these qualities were lacking, the king (Edward VIII) was obliged to abdicate the throne. In the increasingly democratic, war-torn and economically volatile twentieth century, the monarchy emerged as the rallying point for national consensus and common purpose. In the aftermath of two world wars, as royal dynasties around the world made their exit from the political scene, the politically powerless British monarchy continued to embody an ancient tradition in odd juxtaposition with the emerging welfare state. No longer considered to be uniquely linked with the divine, removed from any substantive role in the coercive power wielded by the state, still the monarchy retains its unique bond with the wider culture. Dignity having replaced divinity, the head of state now exercises her authority by dint of example and personal activity.

CONSTRUCTING NEW MONARCHIES: MUSLIM KINGDOMS IN THE TWENTIETH CENTURY

Unlike the emergence of democratic forms of government during the 1990s in lands formerly under the command of the Soviet Union, the Muslim world has remained largely resistant to calls for political pluralism, popular participation, and freedom of expression. In a *hadith* or saying attributed to Muhammad, the Prophet described sovereignty in the following terms: 'After me, there will be caliphs; and after the caliphs, amirs; and after the amirs, kings; and after the kings, tyrants.'[33] Although probably apocryphal, the attribution reflects something of the evolution of many Muslim states in the twentieth century. Unhappily, political instability occasioned by the lack of an orderly succession process has been endemic to most of the Middle East throughout much of this period. Autocratic regimes masquerading as democratic republics in countries like Syria, Libya, Sudan and Iraq make a mockery of the democratic ideal, while traditional monarchies in Saudi Arabia, Kuwait, and other Persian Gulf states continue to insist that the Western model of governance is inappropriate for countries where Islamic law forms the core of the constitution. Indeed in the United Arab Emirates, Bahrain, Oman and Qatar, the affairs of government continue to be organized in accordance with ancient tribal practices and Islamic precepts.[34]

Leaving aside the rise of authoritarian 'republics' under the rule of military strongmen, how do we explain the survival, indeed the expansion of the institution of monarchy in the Muslim world during the twentieth century? The most important variable doubtless involves a continuing commitment in Islam to the notion of civil government as part of a larger religious focus on the whole of life. We recall that in the Islamic tradition there is no equivalent to the Church as an ecclesiastical organization. For Muslims there cannot be a rigorous compartmentalization of life, an area of human experience outside the religious law and beyond the jurisdiction of those who uphold that law. To argue that there is an autonomous secular realm and a political class which tends solely to the affairs of that realm is a betrayal of Islam itself. In the Western tradition, on the other hand, the experience of the eighteenth-century Enlightenment advanced the view that political and economic institutions were to be differentiated from religious concerns. As we have seen, the history of the West to 1500 was marked by the existence of two authorities, *sacerdotium* and *regnum*, Church and state, each with its own laws and personnel, and for most of this period neither was prepared to acknowledge subservience to the other. Religion over the past few centuries in the West has been reduced to one corner of life, shifted from the public to the private sphere, and uncoupled from the collective agenda of civil society.

In Islamic societies, by contrast, economic and technological modernization has thus far not been accompanied by the sorts of socio-cultural shifts, the demystification of human relations, witnessed in the industrialized West since 1800. In the Muslim world, the political legitimacy of the ruler is derived not from dynastic or nationalistic claims, or by popular mandate, but rather by virtue of the fact that the ruler is the effective leader of the religious community of the faithful. The head of state is obliged to enforce *shari'a*, the Holy Law of Islam, which covers all aspects of human activity. Thus the purpose of government and those charged with the power to rule is to promote conditions under which each person can live as a good Muslim. Islamic jurists and *ulema* assist the ruler in his work of governance by formulating rules derived from the Qur'an and the traditions of the Prophet Muhammad. Given this intellectual framework, the subject is under a religious obligation to obey the sovereign authority.[35]

A striking continuity of historic political structures alongside sometimes rapid economic change distinguishes much of the Islamic world today. Even as increasing numbers of Western-educated Muslims take up key positions in the bureaucracies and governments of Islamic kingdoms, the values of an overarching religious ideal continue to shape thinking about appropriate forms and ends of government. In these kingdoms, as long as problems related to economic development, education, health care, employment and the defence of the faith are successfully met by the respective ruling families, there seems little prospect that Western-style pluralistic democracy will gain widespread support. Broadening the base of political decision-making in these monarchies will doubtless be avoided so long as the material base of the state remains secure.

As a form of civil organization, monarchy has always corresponded quite directly with a strong religious understanding of the purpose of civil society. But unitary monarchy has been an elusive goal for the adherents of Islam over the centuries, and during the past hundred years the multiplication of royal households has immensely complicated the effort to realize a single religio-political community, even among the first Muslims – the Arab peoples of the Fertile Crescent. In principle, there could be only one caliph, one successor to Muhammad, one supreme leader of the Muslim polity, for the office began with the death of the Prophet and assumed that unified leadership of the faithful was essential to the right ordering of life. At the start of our period, however, the non-Arab Abbasid caliphs based in Baghdad were being challenged by the North African leaders of a rival caliphate, the Fatimids. The leaders of this movement denied the legitimacy of the Abbasids and sought to supplant them as the legitimate head of the Islamic community. Another local caliphate was established by the Umayyad ruler of Cordoba, Spain in 929, but it disappeared from the scene in 1031. By 1258, when the Mongols captured Baghdad and executed the last Abbasid caliph, the era of single caliphal authority had come to a bloody close.

Although the ideal of a lone ruler would be maintained into the modern era, the office was never again universally acknowledged by Muslims. The Ottomans, for example, claimed caliphal dominion, but their status as non-Arab upstarts and recent converts to Islam prevented them from resurrecting the office in any meaningful sense. Still, the claim to be leaders of the entire Islamic community was made as late as 1876 in the Ottoman constitution of that year, and it remained official Ottoman doctrine until the dissolution of the caliphate by the Turkish republic in 1924.[36] When a descendant of the Prophet Muhammad attempted to assert his right to the office of caliph in the wake of the Turkish abnegation, a rival Arab leader attacked him and destroyed his power base around the holy cities of Mecca and Medina. That rival, Ibn Saud, would go on to establish the modern monarchy of Saudi Arabia.

Such internecine conflict within the Arab community is not untypical. For while sharing a common language, culture and religion, the Arabs of the Middle East or West Asia today find themselves divided into a proliferating number of states with relatively modest (albeit growing) populations. In no small measure the failure to achieve political unity was due to the fact that in the Arab Fertile Crescent, unlike the pattern in Europe or in Ottoman Turkey, there were no established state institutions or unified governing elites who were positioned to rally Arab peoples under one national or dynastic banner. A localized tribal and pastoral culture remained the norm in central

Arabia until the 1930s, while in other Arab lands the control wielded by the Ottoman empire until the end of the nineteenth century effectively precluded the emergence of commonly recognized indigenous leaders.

Today, in arid lands where the principal resource base (oil) is the recent and fortuitous monopoly of a few countries, monarchy continues to function as a legitimate form of government. In Muslim Saudi Arabia, Jordan, Kuwait, Qatar, Bahrain, Oman and United Arab Emirates, political allegiance is directed mainly towards a ruling family and not to any abstract notion of national identity. Efforts among Arab states at regional cooperation have been many during the course of the twentieth century, and sometimes these exertions, as in the case of the 1973 OPEC oil embargo, have been to dramatic effect, but in general the greater goal of modern Arab nationalists – the creation of a politically unified Arab state guided by Islamic principles – has miscarried in the face of age-old enmities. During the past half-century the Muslim world in general, and the Arab world in particular, has been under enormous pressure to change its political and religious culture in the face of Western modernization and the advent of the democratic age. In many of these countries, great economic change has occurred, and this has been most profound in those states where oil revenues have produced a windfall for the regimes in power. Rising material expectations have in some countries impelled greater demands for social change. But the development of oil resources has not advanced the prospect of an all-Arab or all-Muslim polity. Rather the newly acquired wealth has served to further differences between the Islamic states, creating a wide spectrum of regimes whose interests do not always coincide.

Since the end of the First World War a pattern of centralized state-building, sometimes induced by European priorities and economic penetration, has been operative throughout the Islamic world. This process has often involved conflict over the relationship between the needs of the national state and the claims of Islam as an all-encompassing religious system. The most dramatic conflict occurred in the Turkish republic during the 1920s and 1930s, where the government of Kemal Ataturk struggled mightily to create a Western-style secular society.[37] But while Ataturk founded a republic, elsewhere in the former Ottoman lands a very different pattern was imposed. Into the political vacuum created by the destruction of the Ottoman empire in 1918 stepped the French and the British, forging new states and drawing fresh boundaries without bothering to seek the consent of resident Arab peoples. Thus Arab monarchies of the contemporary Middle East are in the main the off-spring of post-First World War British imperial policy. Ironically, just as monarchy was exiting the stage across much of Europe, it was experiencing a new, albeit induced, birth in lands which for centuries had been under the control of non-Arab Muslims.

WESTERN CREATIONS

The power of the French and British to make and unmake governments in the Fertile Crescent is best illustrated by the case of King Faysal of Syria and, subsequently, Iraq. With the outbreak of the First World War and the decision of Ottoman Turkey to ally itself with the Central Powers (Germany and Austria-Hungary), the prospect of establishing the one-state goal of Arab nationalists appeared brighter than it had been in decades. Forming a pact with the British in 1916, Sharif Husayn of the Hashemite family that ruled Mecca, spearheaded a popular Arab revolt against the Turks. As a direct descendant of the Prophet Muhammad and custodian of the holy places of Islam, Husayn hoped to emerge from the fighting as caliph of the Arab world. In initial discussions with the British, Husayn proposed that the borders of the new caliphate include the Arabian peninsula, Iraq, greater Syria and Palestine. Earlier, in a letter of October 1915, the British High Commissioner in Egypt, Sir Henry MacMahon, implied that the British would indeed recognize an independent Arab state, but there were no specifics offered regarding the geographical sweep of such a prospective state.[38] Two years of intense guerrilla warfare against the Ottomans ensued, and in 1918, after the British captured the Syrian city of Damascus, Husayn's son

Faysal was permitted to establish a new Arab government. British subsidies kept this government afloat for the next year.

Faysal demanded that the British recognize him as the monarch of a sovereign Arab state, but at this point the ulterior motives of the victorious Europeans became apparent. For in the Sykes–Picot agreement of 1916, the British and French had secretly agreed to divide between themselves lands that today include Iraq, Lebanon, Jordan, Syria and Israel. Without consulting the inhabitants of the territories in question, the League of Nations subsequently confirmed this arbitrary carve-up. When France received its League of Nations mandate over Syria, King Faysal was asked to stand down. A general Syrian Congress was called in March 1920 and the elected delegates demanded Syrian independence under Faysal. But the French insisted, sending an ultimatum to the king and forcing his abandonment of the throne.[39] The French then proceeded to divide the short-lived kingdom into two separate states: Syria and Lebanon. The British, for their part, took control over Palestine, Iraq and a fifth, newly created state called Transjordan. All of the territories in question were designated as mandates or trusts by the League of Nations, and the mandatory powers were charged with bringing their respective territories to independence as soon as possible.[40] In their mandate of Palestine, the British allowed the settlement of European Jews, a momentous decision for the history of the twentieth century.

The removal of Faysal from Syria led to considerable civil unrest in the French-controlled mandate. By way of compensation, and in acknowledgement of his assistance during the First World War, the British established a constitutional monarchy in Iraq and installed Faysal as king. With a host of more pressing imperial business to address, the British were looking to maintain security at the lowest possible cost in each of their Middle East mandates, and this very much worked to the advantage of the Iraqi elite. The newly installed king was, by and large, acceptable to the many landowners and townsmen in the valley of the Tigris–Euphrates, although his ten-year reign was marked by heavy reliance upon British support. In 1924 a constitution was agreed by an elected constituent assembly which provided for a prime minister and a cabinet responsible to the legislative chamber of deputies. The monarch, however, retained extensive powers: he could dissolve the chamber and enjoyed the exclusive right to name members of the upper house or senate. The lower house or chamber was elected by universal manhood suffrage and all legislation was initiated by this popular body.[41] Under Faysal this constitutional system worked fairly effectively. Before his death in 1933, the king had secured formal independence for Iraq and the new state was admitted to the League of Nations. Under a treaty arrangement, however, the British reserved for themselves the right to utilize Iraq's military facilities and to be consulted when foreign policy issues were under discussion.

King Faysal died unexpectedly in 1933 and was succeeded by his 21-year-old son Ghazi, a man more interested in fast motor cars than in the details of governance. During the 1930s the Iraqi state was under the effective control of a numerically small and intellectually divided elite composed of army officers, rural landowners and *ulema*. Ghazi died in an accident in 1939, and his four-year-old son Faysal II became king under the regency of Faysal I's brother, Prince Abdullah. Two decades of growing resentment over British interference in Iraqi affairs manifested itself when a pro-German government came to power in a 1941 *coup d'état*.[42] The result was a British invasion which restored the regent to power and brought Iraqi oil supplies to the service of the British war effort. At the close of the conflict the Iraqi monarchy and its conservative government were still closely allied to their protectors in Westminster.

The end came for the monarchy in 1958. During the postwar period few economic reforms were undertaken on behalf of the peasant majority. By 1958 over half of all arable land was owned by just 2500 people while the condition of the common labourer continued to deteriorate. The landlords dominated the parliament and blocked land reform, and while oil revenues allowed the monarchy to extend secular education, the government had failed to satisfy the rising aspirations of the majority of Iraqis. Serious land reform, measures to alleviate rural poverty, autonomy from British interference – none of these issues had been addressed by the crown. In July 1958 a military coup took place and the young King Faysal II, his uncle the crown prince and all but one member of the royal family were murdered.[43] A republic was declared by the military officers who were responsible for the killings, but internal coups by army commanders and leaders of the pan-Arab nationalist Baath Party continued for another decade until a military government was established under Ahmad Hasan al-Bakr. In 1979 Hasan was succeeded by his second-in-command Saddam Hussein. The era of an Iraq dominated by ruthless military strongmen was under way.

A similar move by the British to appease the Hashemite family was made in the mandate of Transjordan, where one of Faysal's brothers Abdullah was installed as ruler over lands which corresponded to no particular historic community. In Transjordan, the Hashimite Prince (Amir) Abdullah skilfully cultivated the support of most tribal leaders. From 1921 on the British provided essential grants to the government of the amir, and in 1929 Abdullah issued a constitution which provided for a legislative council.[44] He continued to rule his domain in an orderly fashion with British support and subsidies until the end of the Second World War. In 1946 a treaty was concluded with Britain whereby the amir assumed the title of king and a new constitution was promulgated. Under its terms a two-chamber parliament was established with the upper house appointed by the monarch. During the 1948 war against Israel, King Abdullah incorporated the West Bank and East Jerusalem into a newly named kingdom of Jordan, but both acquisitions were subsequently lost by his grandson King Hussein during the 1967 Arab–Israeli war. With the 1948 absorption of Palestinian lands, Abdullah had increased the size of the population under his control from 400,000 to almost 1.4 million. All refugees were offered full Jordanian citizenship. But many of these new subjects were Palestinian Arabs who expected the king to take a harder line against the Jewish state. On 20 July 1951, as he entered the al-Aqsa Mosque in Jerusalem, the monarch was murdered by a 17-year-old Palestinian. Abdullah was succeeded by his son Tallal, but he abdicated one year later suffering from mental illness. It was then up to the 17-year-old grandson Hussein to stabilize the monarchy in a time of great crisis. At the time of his death in 1998, King Hussein of Jordan had become the longest-serving monarch in the Arab world.[45]

Developments in Egypt after the First World War were not entirely dissimilar to those unfolding in Iraq and Jordan. Again it was the British who established a constitutional monarchy in an attempt to retain influence over an area deemed vital to British imperial interests. Only in Egypt the ruling family could trace its leadership role back to the early nineteenth century at a time when Ottoman authority was still credible. The Ottomans had first annexed Egypt in 1516–17 and maintained nominal sovereignty over the civilization along the Nile until the end of the First World War. During the nineteenth century, however, as imperial power declined and the sultans concentrated their energies on preserving their European territories, Arab lands were increasingly taken over by local despots. In Egypt, Napoleon Bonaparte's brief occupation (1798–1801) was followed by the rise to power of an Albanian-born army officer named Muhammad Ali (r. 1804–41). Although officially a subject of the sultan in Istanbul and serving only as governor, Muhammad Ali pursued an independent course in Egypt and founded the dynasty that held power until the end of the monarchical system in 1952.[46]

Recognizing that the Ottomans could no longer protect Egypt from foreign aggressors, the sizeable community of religious leaders or *ulema* centred in Cairo threw their support behind Muhammad Ali on condition that he respect their advice on all key policy matters. A programme of Western-style economic development was undertaken by the ruler, but increased interference by Britain during the second half of the nineteenth century slowed this process of economic nationalism. Cotton monoculture replaced efforts at broad-based economic development, and the government fell deeply into debt to foreign creditors. After 1882 the British occupied the country, transforming the successors of Muhammad Ali into little more than mouthpieces for London's imperial policy. With the start of the First World War, the British established a protectorate and ruled the country under martial law.

Post-war nationalists demanded an end to the unilaterally declared protectorate and called for the establishment of an independent Egypt. After major outbreaks of civil unrest and failed efforts to find a compromise arrangement, the British government announced the creation of an independent sovereign state in 1922. Sultan Fuad changed his title to king of Egypt, but as in Iraq the British reserved the right to protect their strategic interests (meaning the Canal) and to defend the country against possible aggression. A liberal constitution modelled on that of Belgium permitted the crown the right to dissolve the bicameral assembly, to veto legislation, and to issue decrees in the absence of parliament. Ministers held their office at the pleasure of the crown, and the monarch was commander of the armed forces. Despite these generous executive powers, Fuad was not satisfied and worked consistently throughout the 1920s to undermine an assembly that was dominated by a popular nationalist party called the Wafd. The king dissolved the assembly on a number of occasions in an effort to create the foundations of a semi-autocracy.[47]

Neither King Fuad nor his son and successor King Farouk (r. 1936–52) were able to secure full independence for Egypt, and this was the one issue around which the Wafd party based its appeal. When the 17-year-old Farouk succeeded his father a new alliance with the British was concluded which permitted Egypt control over its own security forces and prepared the way for League of Nations membership. The new king was cheered in the streets at the conclusion of the treaty, and it appeared as though the monarchy would reap enormous political benefits for years to come. However the treaty allowed the British unrestricted access to Egyptian ports, roads and airports in the event of a European war, and when this clause was invoked in 1940 the old resentments returned to the forefront of Egyptian politics.

While amassing a large fortune for itself over three decades of rule, the monarchy did little to promote the social or economic interests of Egypt's large labouring population. Between 1917 and 1937 the population of the kingdom increased from 12.7 to 15.7 million inhabitants, although the area of land under cultivation remained constant. Improved agricultural techniques boosted overall crop yield, but it is safe to say that the quality of life for most Egyptians deteriorated during this period. In 1948 King Farouk prompted Egypt's participation in the first Arab–Israeli war of 1948, and the poor showing of Egyptian forces undercut the king's claim to leadership in the Arab world.[48] The military in particular was quick to blame the politicians and the crown for the operational debacle. By 1950 the monarchy's primary focus on removing all elements of British interference in the life of the state seemed less than compelling in the face of poor schools, inadequate health facilities, and the continuing concentration of land in the hands of a few. The king's personal life was held up to ridicule by increasing numbers of critics. In July 1952 the regime was peacefully ousted by an army coup whose leaders promised land reform and an end to official corruption in high places. A republic was declared in 1953 and the royal house of Muhammad Ali was dissolved, but by 1956 the army commander Gamal Nasser had transformed the recently created office of president into a military dictatorship.

With the exception of the Hashemite kingdom of Jordan, each of the monarchies created by the British in the 1920s failed to meet the expectations of their respective populations. Each was a constitutional monarchy with varying degrees of power accorded to elected leaders in a national assembly. And each dynasty attempted to seek full independence as soon as the royal office was established. In this respect it is interesting that the Muslim amirs (in Arabic one who commands) who were appointed monarchs in the post-First World War period adopted the Western title 'king' in an effort to claim symbolic equality with European heads of state. It was a decisive shift, for historically the Arabic word for king, *malik*, did not always carry a positive connotation. In the first centuries of Islamic expansion, the caliphate was associated with rulership under God's law while kingship represented arbitrary personal rule devoid of religious sanction. Like the ancient Israelites, the Arabs were a tribal people who preferred chiefs who ruled by consensus. Muslims tended to use the word king to describe the rulers of neighbouring infidels like the Byzantines or the Christian monarchs of Europe. Eschewing the crowning or enthronement ceremony more common in the Western tradition, Muslim rulers relied on the ceremony of the *bay'a* or oath of allegiance to signal the official start of their mandate. Actually symbolizing an agreement or consensus between ruler and ruled whereby both sides agree to fulfil specific obligations, this oath solemnizes what in the Muslim tradition comes closest to the modern Western notion of rights. Each side in the Muslim political association owes certain obligations to the other. The ruler must respect and enforce the Holy Law while the subject is obliged to live in obedience to the just and faithful ruler.[49]

The perceived failure on the part of the dynastic houses in Egypt and Iraq to meet this consensual standard contributed not a little to their destruction at the hands of their opponents. Monarchs who had failed to secure full independence for their Muslim subjects were condemned by nationalists who took the principle of Islamic consensus as the cornerstone of politics. Writing about the coup which ended the monarchy in Egypt in 1952, the country's first president, Muhammad Neguib, insisted that 'We seized power because we could no longer endure the humiliation to which we, along with the rest of the Egyptian people, were being subjected.'[50]

INDIGENOUS MONARCHY

Unlike any of the Arab monarchies discussed above, the modern kingdom of Saudi Arabia developed in a political climate where there was no European presence or interference in the wake of the Ottoman break-up. The kingdom was first proclaimed in 1932 by Abd al-Aziz ibn Saud, and that ruler's male offspring continue to rule in a modern state which today possesses the world's largest known oil reserves. Occupying 80 per cent of the Arabian peninsula, the subject population of the kingdom is estimated at between 8 and 10 million, with an additional 5 million Arabic-speaking foreigners in residence. The homeland of the ruling Al Saud family is the Naja region in central Arabia, one of four major regions in the kingdom and also the area where the eighteenth-century religious reformer Muhammad ibn Abd al-Wahhab (1704–92) lived and taught. The Wahhabi movement provided both the rationale for Saudi political and military leadership during the mid-eighteenth century, and for the special religious contours of society under the Saudi monarchy. In particular, the puritanical Abd al-Wahhab stressed the need for all Muslims to rededicate themselves to a strict monotheism while submitting to the direction of a just ruler, one who in regular consultation with the *ulema* is prepared to enforce God's laws as outlined in the Qur'an. For the Wahhabi of Naja, the fusion of *ulema* and monarchy is the sign of true Islamic government.

Supported by Abd al-Wahhab, a mid-eighteenth-century Naja chieftain by the name of Muhammad ibn Saud (*c.* 1704–65) began a violent campaign of military expansion which under his son Abd al-Aziz (*c.* 1720–1803) and grandson Saud (d. 1814) resulted in the conquest of almost the entire Arabian peninsula. This included the holy city of Mecca, wrested in 1803 from the Hashemites, descendants of Muhammad who were at the time under the control of the Ottomans. A capital was established by the founder of Al Saud (House of Saud) at Dir'iya, north of present-day al-Riyadh, but in 1816 the nascent empire was destroyed by Egyptian forces under Ibrahim Pasha, son of the Egyptian ruler and Ottoman viceroy Muhammad Ali. Throughout the remainder of the nineteenth century, while nation states formed across Western Europe, rival factions within the Saud family engaged in chronic and debilitating internecine warfare, the result being the total breakdown of Saudi authority in Naja. Not until the early twentieth century, as Ottoman power declined throughout the Middle East, were Saud family fortunes restored under the leadership of Abd al-Aziz (1880–1951), a descendant of the earliest rulers of Naja. Combining wars of conquest with a total of twenty political marriages with the daughters of important tribal leaders over the course of his adult life, Abd al-Aziz (also known as Ibn Saud) established the Saudi capital at al-Riyadh, allied with the British against the Ottomans during the First World War, and fought the Hashemite rulers of the Hijaz province for control of Mecca and Medina.

The Hashemite ruler Sharif Husayn had been Britain's closest Arab ally during the First World War, and following the war he had proclaimed himself 'King of the Arabs'. Although the British had rewarded two of his sons with mandate kingdoms after the war, Husayn felt betrayed by decisions reached at the Paris Peace Conference. When the new Republic of Turkey officially abolished the Islamic caliphate in 1924, Sharif Husayn took the provocative step of proclaiming himself 'Prince of the Faithful and Successor to the Prophet'.[51] Interpreting this as a bid for mastery in central Arabia, Abd al-Aziz invaded the Hijaz with a band of fanatical fighting men and forced Husayn to abdicate control over the holy cities and the Hijaz province. By the close of the 1920s the Saudis had succeeded in consolidating their personal authority throughout most of the peninsula. Born in conflict with neighbouring Arabs, the kingdom of Saudi Arabia turned to Wahhabi ideology in an effort to create a sense of shared identity among the ethnically and tribally diverse peoples who came under Saudi control.

During the first 150 years of Saudi royal succession, a large measure of violence characterized the selection of leaders. The twentieth century was witness to a more orderly system, mandated by Abd al-Aziz in 1932. In that year the king commanded that the succession should pass down through his sons (there were 44), and not from son to grandson. In 1992 the Basic Law of Government clarified the process, permitting the king to name his heir apparent and, if he should choose to do so, subsequently disqualify the heir. There are now an estimated 4000 or 5000 princes in direct line of descent within the Saud family, and this includes a large number of grandsons of Abd al-Aziz, one of whom will be designated heir once the current generation of sons reaches the age of infirmity. The family represents the main political constituency of the kingdom, and the monarch must have the collective support of the family in order to rule effectively. Members of the royal family head the major national ministries and serve as provincial governors or amirs. All are appointed by and report directly to the king. If one element of this monopoly of high office has changed since mid-century, it is in the educational level achieved by the highest bureaucrats and ministers. Whereas few of the ministers in the 1950s held university degrees, now the majority hold advanced degrees – often from Western institutions – in their fields of expertise.

Abd al-Aziz claimed to rule in full consultation with the Wahhabi *ulema*, and by virtue of this relationship the monarch insisted that he alone constituted the one figure capable of holding the tribal-based kingdom together. In the Saudi-controlled lands, the Wahhabi legacy is very strong, fostering a social ethos where the government is deemed responsible for the good order of individuals and institutions alike. The stability of the monarchy rests in large measure on the continuing belief that the House of Saud governs in consultation with the *ulema*. These men of intellect and faith assist the monarch to mediate between the eternal truths of Islamic law and the daily issues and problems situated in a particular time and place. Although final political authority rests with the king, Saudi monarchs would be affronted by charges of absolutism, since they view themselves as subject to Islamic law and to promoting the interests of Islam with the advice of religious leaders. These leaders, institutionally organized in what is today a state-funded Council of Senior *ulema*, issue *fatwas* (legal rulings) confirming the coherence of political decisions with the Qur'an. The king acts as a final court of appeal and the source of pardon, but he too is expected to abide by the eternal code. One powerful example of the influence exerted by the issuance of a *fatwa* occurred in 1964 when the religious leadership joined with members of the Al Sauds to force the abdication of King Saud, who had ruled the kingdom since his father's death in 1953. His eleven-year reign had been marred by palace intrigue, corruption and waste, while the mismanagement of enormous oil revenues had left the state almost bankrupt.[52] The *fatwa* was a binding religious legal opinion deposing the reigning monarch and proclaiming Saud's half-brother Faysal the new king of Saudi Arabia. Saud was exiled and died in Greece in 1969.

Prior to 1925 there were no formal political institutions to speak of in the Kingdom. Abd al-Aziz ruled in a highly personal manner, consulting with leading figures in the royal family and select religious leaders. In a very poor kingdom which tottered on the brink of bankruptcy in the 1930s and 1940s, direct personal rule was a workable model of royal authority. However even with the influx of oil revenues since the Second World War, subsequent Saudi kings have steadfastly resisted the development of Western-style legislative bodies at the national level. In the Saudi kingdom all political power rests ultimately with the monarch, who following the ideal of the Wahhabi revival is responsible for protecting the Islamic community and the institutions of the faith. There are no representative assemblies to provide any institutional counterweight to the power of the monarch, nor is there a formal separation of executive, legislative and judicial power. In 1992 King Fahd decreed the establishment of a Consultative Council, but its 60-member delegation, composed of princes, businessmen, university officials and technocrats, although charged with advising the monarch on foreign and domestic matters, is appointed by the king. A virtually similar council structure is in place in the Sultanate of Oman, Qatar, Bahrain and the United Arab Emirates.[53] In the view of King Fahd, the Consultative Council simply continues in a more formal manner the process of consultation which had always taken place on an informal level with leaders of the Islamic business, military and religious communities. After naming the members of the council in March 1992, the monarch went out of his way to announce that 'the democratic system prevailing in the world does not suit us here in this country'. For the king, Islam 'is our social and political law; it is a complete constitution of social and economic laws and a system of government and justice'.[54]

Since the accession to the throne of King Faysal in 1964, the monarchy has faced an enormous challenge in trying to balance the forces of modernization with traditional Islamic religious values. Thanks exclusively to post-Second World War oil revenues, a rapid and continuing social and economic transformation of the kingdom has been underway. Under Kings Faysal (r. 1964–75), Khalid (r. 1975–82) and Fahd (r. 1982–), the quality of material life for most Saudi subjects has improved enormously. Education, housing and employment now rival levels enjoyed in fully industrialized Western democracies. However the priorities of the Wahhabi revival continue to jostle uncomfortably with secularization, and the monarchy will continue to struggle with the unsettling implications of modernization while governing a state which is ruled by Islamic law. In a royal decree issued in March 1992, the crown affirmed that the kingdom 'is a sovereign Arab Islamic state with Islam as its religion; God's book (the Qur'an) and the Sunna (the Traditions, or inspired sayings of Muhammad) are its constitution; Arabic is its language; and Riyadh is its capital'.[55] As the custodians of Islam's holiest sites, and as rulers of an Arab population whose ancestors were the first to embrace the message of Muhammad, Saudi kings must uphold the traditional social teachings of Islam while simultaneously addressing the new social-welfare issues raised by a population which is growing by 3.7 per cent each year.

Whether this deeply traditional and conservative society will continue to maintain personal monarchy as the appropriate model of civil organization in the twenty-first century depends, in the end, on a number of variables. The Saudi monarchy today exercises more control over its subject population than at any time in the past. With enormous income from the world's largest oil production facilities and an ever-expanding range of social services under the control of the national government, together with a modern professional military, the king as sole head of government has at his disposal enormous coercive power. But as the responsibilities of government have expanded over the past 30 years, and as the inevitable bureaucratization of public affairs has increased, the ability of the king personally to oversee each department has diminished. Whether or not the enhanced power of senior bureaucrats will satisfy the needs of an expanding population which is denied any direct voice in government affairs is a matter for consideration, especially if meaningful job creation does not keep pace with one of the highest population growth rates in the world.

It is undeniable that the highly individualistic and rights-oriented social values of the West have no place in contemporary Saudi Arabia. The most important social institution remains the extended family, and bloodlines continue to matter more than abstract notions of modern nationhood.[56] The Saudi monarchy is a relatively recent arrival on the political scene, whereas extended family units trace their history back for many centuries. Forging a sense of national identity that transcends the tribal mentality of bloodlines is an ongoing task for the Saudi state, and it is hindered by the concept of family at the very heart of the monarchical principle. Gender relations provide another potential destabilizing force for the future of the monarchy. Overall Saudi society, and especially the family, has been resistant to change in the face of modernization. Calls for broader participation in the political process have been few; challenges to the monarchy remain largely mute. Whether urbanization, communications, transport and education will undermine the conservative social and religious structure remains an open question.

MUSLIM MONARCHY IN A NON-ARAB CONTEXT

The major oil-producing kingdoms – Saudi Arabia, Kuwait, Bahrain, the United Arab Emirates and Oman – are sometimes referred to as 'rentier states'. In these countries oil revenues, secured without much effort, are claimed by the ruling dynasty and employed in a manner consistent with maintaining the ruling family in power. This has often meant vigorous and diverse social welfare programmes for the benefit of all subjects along with comprehensive building projects focused in urban areas. The small emirate of Bahrain provides a good example of the rentier phenomenon. Controlled by Iranian monarchs from 1602 to 1782, the Arab Al Khalifah family took possession of the islands in 1783. Oil was discovered in the 1920s and two American companies received the concession to develop the resource. The company was turned over to the government in 1974, just as oil prices jumped in the world market, and since that time the amir has overseen a social welfare state that provides to a population of 600,000 free education and medical care, along with subsidized housing in newly built towns. A quasi-protectorate under Britain from the 1880s, Bahrain under Amir Isa (b. 1933) declared independence in 1971. A constituent assembly was organized in 1972, but was dissolved by the amir in 1975 and since that date an appointive Consultative Council has advised the amir and his cabinet. With financial support from the Saudis and military aid from the United States, this tiny kingdom has remained autonomous under the leadership of a hereditary and anti-parliamentary regime.[57]

Another example of the rentier phenomenon can be found in the tiny kingdom of Kuwait. With oil reserves totalling 97 billion barrels (compared to the USA' s 26 billion) in 1990 Kuwait was the focus of an unlikely alliance between the United States and Arab nations Saudi Arabia and Syria. When Iraq's Saddam Hussein invaded Kuwait in 1990 in an effort to add the emirate's oil resources to his own reserves of 100 billion barrels, his forces were expelled and the Kuwaiti royal family was restored to power. There was a call from US authorities that the royal family move to democratize the political process, but little change occurred during the 1990s. In fact only four years before the Iraqi invasion, the emir of Kuwait, Sheikh Jabir al-Ahmad as-Sabah, had suspended the kingdom's national assembly, a body elected by the 63,000 eligible male voters in a land of nearly 1.8 million people.[58] Still the Gulf War allies announced as their key objective in the military operation the restoration of Kuwait's 'legitimate government', a regime which made no promises to forward political pluralism should it be restored to power by the forces of the democratic West.

A key challenge to the rentier monarchies, indeed to all monarchies in the Muslim Middle East, stems from the growth of fundamentalist Islam or 'Islamism'. Since the successful Iranian revolution of 1979, fundamentalists have been calling for the establishment of regimes dedicated to the enforcement of *shari'a* and restructuring society and state according to an idealized image of the early faith. Working out of mosques, religious societies, universities and charitable institutions, Muslim radicals view the oil-rich monarchies of Saudi Arabia and Kuwait, for example, as altogether too sympathetic to Western interests in particular and to a broader pattern of Western materialism in general.[59] There is even a modicum of fear that should genuine political participation be permitted in these monarchies, democratic processes themselves would facilitate the forces of Islamic fundamentalism. Radical Islamicists would secure access to power only to create anti-democratic theocratic regimes. The kingdom of Iran experienced just such a denouement in the 1970s.[60]

Since the establishment of the Safavid dynasty in 1501, Iran has been inextricably linked to Shi'a Islam, and under the Safavid monarchs the influence of the community of religious scholars, the *ulema*, began to shape all aspects of Iranian culture. Safavid rule ended in the early eighteenth century, and from the 1780s until 1925 Iran was ruled by the autocratic Qajar dynasty, but in large measure their control never extended to the countryside in an effective manner. During the second half of the nineteenth century Nasi al-Din Shah (1848–96) sold off substantial economic concessions to Western and Russian interests. Banking, transport and commercial rights were granted to foreigners, giving rise to a clergy-led movement calling for the adoption of a formal constitution limiting the power of the shahs. By the start of the First World War, the shahs were being constantly challenged by tribal chiefs, Shi'a clergymen, reform-minded bureaucrats, and merchants who resented concessions to foreign producers.[61]

It was in these circumstances that a military leader trained in the Russia Cossack Brigade, Reza Khan, seized political power from the Qajar dynasty in 1921 and declared himself shah in 1926. Over the next twenty years a government-sponsored programme of westernization, similar in style to that carried out under Ataturk in Turkey, began the process of transforming a traditional Islamic society into a modern state. Secular education and law reform were introduced, the adoption of Western-style dress was ordered, and the veil was outlawed for women. The Shi'a *ulema* were increasingly marginalized by the shah, who spent large sums on building a modern army, but no effort was made to develop representative institutions of government. Opponents of the regime were routinely exiled, jailed, tortured or executed. Intent on westernizing his country on the economic front, the shah refused to concede even a modicum of the political liberties associated with Western states.[62]

When the monarch, who deeply resented British and Russian interference in his kingdom's affairs, proclaimed Iran's neutrality in the Second World War, British and Soviet troops invaded in 1941 and forced the abdication of Reza Khan in favour of his son, Muhammad Reza Pahlavi. Under the new monarch a parliamentary system emerged and political parties were allowed to compete in free elections. Iran's oil resources (potential reserves of 93 billion barrels) were developed by the British after the war, but in 1951 when Prime Minister Muhammad Musaddeq nationalized the oil industry, British and American intelligence conspired with the shah's army to overthrow the prime minister. This action placed the monarchy in a very poor light from the point of view of Iranian nationalists. The shah now began to govern as an absolute ruler. He suspended the parliament and refused to call new elections. Corruption within the government, together with political repression in the face of economic hardship during the 1970s, led to a resurgence of Islamic fundamentalism. The fundamentalists argued that the monarchy had become nothing more than a tool of Western imperial interests, and that the whole course of Iranian economic development and concomitant secularization were antithetical to the Islamic Shi'a tradition.[63]

An abortive revolt against the monarch had taken place in 1963 under the leadership of the religious leader Ayatollah Khomeini, and from his exile in Iraq the Ayatollah had kept up a campaign of opposition to the absolute monarchy. The disparity between the enormous sums spent by the regime on military modernization and the continuing destitution of the peasant majority contributed to the growing sense of popular opposition to the regime. In 1977 critics of the government organized a series of protests. Returning to Tehran in 1979 and leading millions of subjects who had become disillusioned with the shah's repressive system, the ailing monarch was forced into exile and an Islamic theocratic republic was declared. Islamic law was restored, the *ulema* took control of policy-making, and women were ordered to return to draping themselves in the chador. According to Khomeini, the implementation of Islamic law in all departments of life and the right of the clergy to formulate political policy represented the core goals of the revolution. In March 1979 a national plebiscite was held and the vote was in favour of abolishing the monarchy in favour of establishing a theocratic republic. While a new constitution provided for a parliament and a president of the republic, all effective political power remained in the hands of Khomeini and his clerical supporters. War with Iraq during the 1980s, while costing the lives of perhaps 1 million Iranians, solidified the control wielded by the Khomeini-led clerical elite. Thus the autocracy and intolerance of the Iranian monarchy had been replaced in the space of one year by a clerical regime every bit as powerful as its predecessor.

The success of the Islamic revolution in Iran may suggest that movement away from monarchies in certain Muslim countries does not automatically mean that liberal and pluralist democracy is the preferred alternative. And the staying power of brutal one-party states in places like Iraq, Iran and Syria indicate that the democratic alternative is anything but vital in the Muslim world today. Where monarchy does survive, oil wealth and its effective utilization within society for the educational and material improvement of the subject population has allowed the crown to remain in place and exercise significant political power. Whether the institution can survive in lieu of this exceptional source of wealth is, at the start of a new century, very much an open question.

7 Queen Elizabeth I and Charles, Prince of Wales after his investiture at Caernarfon Castle, 1969.

SEVEN

Monarchy and the State in the Twenty–First Century

Modern governments around the world today exercise coercive, regulatory and directive authority over their citizens or subjects to a degree scarcely imagined by the most absolute of early modern divine right monarchs. Two world wars, unprecedented in their scope and sheer destructive impact, necessitated the organization of each nation's resources and productive capacities in a unified manner, and this task was most effectively undertaken by centralized governments. Together with the need to provide for the nation's defence in an age of increased, and increasingly expensive, military conflict, national governments also assumed a wide array of domestic responsibilities which prior to the twentieth century were most often thought to be within the exclusive purview of individual and community. General health, education, police and related social services increasingly came under the regulatory or direct management of central state authority. The economic well-being of the population as a whole, once largely the affair of the family and the village, became after the First World War the bond and duty of politicians and the official bureaucracy. All of this has led to an unparalleled concentration of power, for good or ill, in the hands of the leaders of the nation state. When coupled with the continuing appeal of a self-constructed nationalism, the aggrandizement of state power stands as the most profound development in civil society over the past 500 years.

What role, if any, has monarchy to play in this type of radically transformed political environment? As we have seen, the principal alteration in the institution of monarchy over the last millennium has involved desacralization, the abandonment of religious sanctions for rule by one and in its place the appropriation of nationalist and broader cultural warrants. In the aftermath of the English, American and French Revolutions, Western monarchs found their strongest source of legitimacy in the rhetoric of incipient nationalism and cultural singularity. By associating themselves with the traditional habits of thought and collective aspirations of a people distinguished by language and common experience, European monarchs and their apologists skilfully refurbished the office of the hereditary executive in a manner designed to appeal to an increasingly democratic polity. During the course of the nineteenth century and into the second decade of the twentieth, crowned heads of state enjoyed renewed popularity even as political rights were slowly extended to an ever-widening circle of the male population. The calamity of total war in a modern, mechanized environment, together with the incapacity of Europe's most powerful monarchs to arrest the violence, hardship and loss of life during the Great War, signalled the inglorious end of monarchy in Germany, Russia and Austria-Hungary. And in those Western states where they did retain their crowns, monarchs had ceded substantive political power to elected officials long before the outbreak of war in 1914. Royalty in the twentieth-century West continued to serve as a symbol or focus of historic national identity, but it was manifestly shorn of the more bellicose associations common during the preceding age of European imperialism.

Elsewhere around the globe we can discern the same general trend away from sacred status as the varied forces of modernization, secularization and democratization made their impress on subject peoples. Throughout Latin America (with the one exception of Brazil), monarchy fell victim in the early nineteenth century to the powerful appeal of republican theory and its apparently successful practice in the United States. The emphatic rejection of 300 years of Spanish royal hegemony from Mexico in the north to Chile in the south did not, in the end, translate into the successful emergence of stable and prosperous republics, and the rapid ascension to power of military strongmen throughout the continent highlighted the enormity of the challenge facing peoples who had no previous experience of self-government. A similar pattern unfolded in post-colonial Black Africa. Beginning in the early 1960s independent republics were established with much optimism and confidence in former British and French colonies, but the recent history of many of these nations (there are now over 50 sovereign African states) has been anything but propitious. The decades of European colonialism had done little to advance the educational and economic status of the majority population, and the Western-trained elites who inherited political power were not able to meet the high expectations of multicultural and multilingual citizen populations for an improved quality of life after independence. The emergence of intolerant military strongmen in the wake of civil wars, ethnic conflicts and political assassinations all contributed to a situation where the leaders of anti-democratic regimes came to be viewed by some Africanists 'as the inheritors of the mantle of pre-colonial African kingship'.[1]

In East Asia, China's imperial system continued along its seemingly immutable path, time-tested and self-referential, until at last the incursions of avaricious and technologically advanced Western powers induced unwanted change at every level of Chinese society. And at this crucial juncture in a long and distinguished history the monarchy failed to adapt, opting instead for a reaffirmation of the ancient, and deeply conservative Confucian ideal. Centuries of relative isolation and economic self-sufficiency, while of enormous advantage in securing political unity and order over a large and divergent land mass, was of minimal value in contesting the encroachment of Western trade, Western ideas and Western religious forms, especially when these were interjected within the context of superior military force. China's imperial tradition, the office and functions of the emperor, the supportive role of the official bureaucracy, all conspired to hamper the effectiveness of central government during the pivotal nineteenth century.

By 1900, the Qing dynasty appeared incapable of providing the type of moral leadership which had always been associated with the Mandate of Heaven. Unfortunately the adoption of the republican alternative in China, as earlier in Latin America, was stillborn, with failed coalitions and military leaders vainly attempting to provide the world's most populous nation with a viable and vigorous alternative to the imperial norm. Eventually a new mandate was constructed, albeit in a fashion sharply devoid of transcendental significance, by the ragged peasant armies of Mao Tse-ung in 1949. Upwards of two thousand years of rule by one in China constituted poor preparation for a pluralist alternative, and in this respect Mao and his successors have built their own intolerant regime on rather solid cultural foundations. In the estimate of one recent observer, the success and consolidation of the 1949 revolution could not have been achieved 'without conscious direction from a state inheriting all the mysterious prestige of the traditional bearers of the Mandate of Heaven'.[2] Whether the new regime can negotiate the pressures of the Western paradigm more effectively than its imperial predecessor is, at this point, an unanswered question.

J. M. Roberts has recently observed that, excepting Europe, there are now more dictators and authoritarian regimes in the world than there were in 1939.[3] Whether or not one agrees with this claim, current talk in the West about the spread of democracy and constitutional, responsible government may need qualification. The disturbing fact remains that in many post-colonial states the authoritarian route is one which apologists insist is best fitted to prevent the sorts of social fragmentation inimical to sustained economic development. The absence of personal freedoms and constitutional rights, the quick recourse to coercive measures when resistance to political authoritarianism emerges, the integrity of the leadership principle as a prerequisite to material improvement for all – these characteristics of so many modern regimes suggest that some of the less than generous intellectual assumptions which undergirded the institution of monarchy around the world for centuries are with us still. Obviously modern authoritarian regimes avoid making leadership claims based on supernatural sanction and instead anchor their moral authority to govern on the basis of their ability to deliver a higher standard of living, to enhance national prestige, or to advance a broad religio-cultural agenda. But the assumption, implicit in modern authoritarian and dictatorial politics, that one individual or elite group is best positioned to discern, define and advance the collective aspirations of a constructed national identity and nation-state idea, is not altogether alien to one component of an earlier monarchical temperament. But it is a component that has been rejected by modern monarchy – and this fact is central to our understanding of the institution in democratic culture.

In the year 1000, all global societies were by modern Western standards extraordinarily poor and ignorant. Their hierarchical social structures, their religious explanations of life, their unfamiliarity with the prospect of a world that might be other than it was, placed the overwhelming majority of women and men in physical conditions where the idea of natural superiors or hierarchies of dominance was anything but alien or peculiar. This very traditional, and deeply undemocratic, assumption respecting human nature has been abandoned by the majority of the world's 27 remaining monarchies. With perhaps the exception of a few Arab kingdoms, the existence of the royal office no longer carries with it the connotation that the natural order of humanity is one of hierarchy and inequality. Maintenance of the royal family and the largely ceremonial functions associated with the crown are today predicated on the widespread assumption that non-elected leaders carry on their duties in the service of a sovereign people, all of whom enjoy equal political rights. Like their republican counterparts, most monarchs are now held to standards of utility which would have been unthinkable prior to the mid-nineteenth century. Even in Muslim monarchies the utilitarian standard is in evidence. As we have seen, the stability and credibility of some of these royal dynasties is closely tied to the fortuitous concentration of oil resources, together with the dedication of oil revenues to domestic economic development.

The historically significant is more often than not associated with change, with deliberate human alteration, both in the short and long term, of the environment in which people live. That environment includes everything from the social context to material factors to the realm of ideas. Over the past 200 years the brisk pace of significant change in this broadly defined setting has presented an enormous challenge to those who think about the past and its meaning for the present generation. As the mass of factual data accelerates and imposes itself on us, we find that searching for moments of alteration in the human experience helps us to organize the unkempt source materials. Of less concern to historians, and to the public in general, are the structures of continuity and patterns of coherence in the human experience, for in these we are less apt to locate the elements of dynamism and innovation which lay at the core of the modern experience, particularly within the Western experience.

Our examination of the institution of royal office over the past millennium presents us with a robust archetype of institutional continuity amidst fundamental social and economic change. While the overwhelming majority of states around the globe have foregone the institution in favour of models of governance claiming greater affiliation with the will of the common people, those countries which retain the royal office continue to uncover worthwhile and quite practical reasons for supporting the crown. From instrument of restored democracy in Spain to impartial arbiter between military and democratic forces in Thailand, monarchy has proved itself to be, in a handful of modern societies at least, both relevant and resilient.

The power to advise and to warn may not strike us as especially formidable at the opening of the twenty-first century, but quite possibly it is a salutary force, a model of public-mindedness in a world where the promise of democracy is too often associated exclusively with the advancement of individual, party, and narrowly national claims. Much diminished and greatly transformed though it may be the world over, monarchy continues to remind us of values beyond the primacy of the particular and the material. At the very least, the institution's persistence is a reliable illustration of humanity's aptitude for intellectual transformation, for redefinition and adjustment in the face of sweeping change. Perhaps the survival of rule by one, even in the face of its many twentieth-century perversions, allows us to better critique our own commitment to a model of civil society where fundamental human equality is the ruling assumption. Of course most extant monarchs the world over accept that assumption, but their arbitrarily elevated status, itself the intellectual offspring of an earlier world-view, allows us to keep at the forefront of our thoughts and action the exceptional novelty – and fragility – of the democratic alternative.

STUARTS

*) JAMES I (Bible Man)

     ↓

* CHARLES I (Removed by Parliament)   Beheaded

OLIVER CROMWELL, LORD PROTECTOR, parliament dude

RESTORATION

* CHARLES II (back from France Exile)

* JAMES II (brother, catholic dude)

JAMES II REMOVED BY PARLIAMENT

* WILLIAM & MARY (replaced James II)

GLORIOUS REVOLUTION OF 1688

* ANNE (last of the line)

The Tudors came before the Stuarts

References

INTRODUCTION: THE IDEA OF MONARCHY

1 Dante, *Monarchia*, ed. and trans. Prue Shaw (Cambridge, 1995), p. 19.
2 On the near universality of democratic models as the standard for legitimate political authority today, see John Dunn, ed., *Democracy: The Unfinished Journey* (Oxford, 1992), pp. 239–66.
3 Thomas Paine, *The Life and Works of Thomas Paine*, ed. William M. Van der Weyde (New York, 1925), vol. I, p. 275.
4 Aristotle, *The Complete Works of Aristotle*, ed. Jonathan Barnes (Princeton, NJ, 1984), vol. II, p. 2041.
5 John Locke, *Two Treatises of Government*, ed. Peter Laslett (Cambridge, 1967), Book 1, Section 105.
6 *The Adams-Jefferson Letters*, ed. Lester J. Cappon (Chapel Hill, NC, 1959), vol. II, p. 401.
7 See A. M. Hocart, *Kings and Councillors: An Essay in the Comparative Anatomy of Human Society* (Chicago, 1970), originally published 1936. For an interesting discussion of imaging God as a king see Daniel D. Williams, 'Deity, Monarchy, and Metaphysics: Whitehead's Critique of the Theological Tradition', in *The Relevance of Whitehead*, ed. Ivor LeClerc (London, 1961), pp. 353–72.
8 I am indebted to Reinhard Bendix, *Kings or People: Power and the Mandate to Rule* (Berkeley, CA, 1979), p. 8, for this reference to Rousseau.
9 On the traditional view of God as King, see Walter Lippmann's reflections in *A Preface to Morals* (New York, 1935), pp. 22–4. More generally, see Jeffrey W. Merrick, *The Desacralization of the French Monarchy in the Eighteenth Century* (Baton Rouge, LA, 1990), chapter 1, and Harold Nicolson, *Kings, Courts and Monarchies* (New York, 1962), pp. 188–206.
10 Marc Bloch, *The Royal Touch*, trans. J. E. Anderson (London, 1973).
11 Colin Morris, *The Papal Monarchy* (Oxford, 1989), pp. 17–18.
12 Jeremy Black, *Convergence or Divergence? Britain and the Continent* (New York, 1994), p. 54.
13 For a good discussion of the place of the hereditary principle in its early modern English context, see Howard Nenner, *The Right to be King* (Chapel Hill, NC, 1995).
14 Bernard Guenee, *States and Rulers in Later Medieval Europe*, trans. Juliet Vale (Oxford, 1985), p. 67.
15 Antony Black, *Political Thought in Europe, 1250–1450* (Cambridge, 1992), p. 136. See also Merrick, *Desacralization*, pp. 1–26.

16 John Stuart Mill, *On Liberty* (Harmondsworth, 1968), p. 59.

17 Guenee, *States and Rulers*, p. 73.

18 Kenneth Minogue, *Politics: A Very Short Introduction* (Oxford, 1995), pp. 2–3.

ONE · ASIAN ARCHETYPES: CHINESE ABSOLUTISM AND
JAPANESE SYMBOLISM

1 John King Fairbank, *China: A New History* (Cambridge, MA, 1992), XVI.

2 Richard J. Smith, *China's Cultural Heritage: The Qing Dynasty, 1644–1912*, 2nd edn (Boulder, CO, 1994), p. 27.

3 Michael Loewe, *The Pride that was China* (New York, 1990), p. 123.

4 Smith, *China's Cultural Heritage*, p. 29.

5 Quoting Michael Loewe, *The Cambridge History of China* (Cambridge, 1986), vol. 1, p. 14. See also Loewe, *Imperial China: The Historical Background to the Modern Age* (New York, 1966), p. 60.

6 Jack L. Dull, 'The Evolution of Government in China', in Paul S. Ropp, ed., *Heritage of China: Contemporary Perspectives on Chinese Civilization* (Berkeley, CA, 1990), p. 61.

7 Fairbank, *China: A New History*, p. 18; June Grasso and Michael Kort, *Modernization and Revolution in China* (New York, 1991), pp. 12–13.

8 The Qin Emperor (221–206 BCE) abolished primogeniture and instituted a system of freehold farming.

9 Grasso and Kort, *Modernization and Revolution*, p. 3.

10 Lucian W. Pye, *China: An Introduction* (New York, 1991), p. 58; Loewe, *Imperial China*, p. 77. For commentary on the moral leadership of the Han dynasty emperors, see William Theodore de Bary, ed., *Sources of the Chinese Tradition* (New York, 1960), vol. 1, pp. 160–5.

11 William H. McNeill, *A World History* (Oxford, 1999), pp. 107, 109. On the ritual duties of the emperor, see Evelyn S. Rawski, *The Last Emperors: A Social History of Qing Imperial Institutions* (Berkeley, CA, 1998), pp. 200–3.

12 Loewe, *Pride that was China*, p. 119.

13 Fairbank, *China: A New History* p. 69. On the office of censor in Chinese imperial history, see Charles O. Hucker, *The Censorial System of Ming China* (Stanford, CA, 1966).

14 Quoting Etienne Balazs, *Chinese Civilization and Bureaucracy: Variations on a Theme* (New Haven, 1964), p. 6.

15 E. A. Kracke, Jr., 'The Chinese and the Art of Government', in Raymond Dawson, ed., *The Legacy of China* (Boston, 1990), p. 333.

16 W. J. F. Jenner, *The Tyranny of History: The Roots of China's Crisis* (Harmondsworth, 1992), p. 49.

17 Charles O. Hucker, *China's Imperial Past* (Stanford, 1975), pp. 12–13. Some insight into peasant life under the Han is provided by Michael Loewe, *Everyday Life in Early Imperial China* (New York, 1968), pp. 163–79. For a later period see Susan Naquin and Evelyn S. Rawski, *Chinese Society in the Eighteenth Century* (New Haven, 1987).

18 *Ibid.*, pp. 310–11. See also Etienne Balazs, 'Imperial China: The Han Dynasty', in Molly Joel Coye, Jon Livingston and Jean Highland, *China:*

Yesterday and Today (New York, 1984), p. 27.

19 Fairbank, *China: A New History*, p. 48.

20 J. M. Roberts, *History of the World* (Oxford, 1993), pp. 442, 445.

21 Dull, 'The Evolution of Government in China', refers to the same period as the era of 'gentry government'.

22 Charles O. Hucker, *China to 1850: A Short History* (Stanford, 1978), p. 103.

23 Quoting Immanuel C. Y. Hsu, *The Rise of Modern China*, 4th edn (New York, 1990), p. 10.

24 Grasso and Kort, *Modernization and Revolution*, p. 16.

25 Robert M. Somers, 'The End of the T'ang', in *Cambridge History of China*, vol. III, pp. 682–700, discusses the problems facing T'ang society. See also Hucker, *Imperial Past*, pp. 269–70.

26 Kracke, 'Chinese Art of Government', p. 314.

27 Hucker, *China's Imperial Past*, pp. 303–4.

28 Dull, 'The Evolution of Government in China', pp.72–3.

29 Hucker, *China's Imperial Past*, p. 304; Albert Chan, *The Glory and Fall of the Ming Dynasty* (Norman, OK, 1982), pp. 14–15, discusses the arbitrary behaviour of the first Ming emperor toward errant officials.

30 Jenner, *The Tyranny of History*, p. 41.

31 Hucker, *China: A Short History*, p. 107. Also Hucker, *A Dictionary of Official Titles in Imperial China* (Stanford, 1985), p. 40.

32 Hucker, *China's Imperial Past*, p. 323.

33 Lucian Pye, *China: An Introduction*, 4th edn (New York, 1991), p. 64. The first Ming emperor, Hongwu, had 26 sons. On the role of royal offspring see Edward L. Dreyer, *Early Ming China: A Political History* (Stanford, CA, 1982), pp. 148–56.

34 Dull, 'The Evolution of Government in China', pp.75, 85.

35 Kracke, Jr., 'The Chinese and the Art of Government', pp. 313–14.

36 Ray Huang, *China: A Macrohistory* (Armonk, NY, 1988), pp.155–6. Louise Levathes, *When China Ruled the Seas* (New York, 1994). On Chinese attitudes toward their Southeast Asian neighbours during the era of Ming trade, see Wang Gungwu, 'Early Ming Relations with Southeast Asia', in John Fairbank, ed., *The Chinese World Order: Traditional China's Foreign Relations* (Cambridge, MA, 1968), pp. 34–62.

37 Paul Kennedy, *The Rise and Fall of the Great Powers* (New York, 1987), p. 6.

38 S. A. M. Adshead, *China in World History* (New York, 1988), p. 110.

39 William H. McNeill, *The Rise of the West* (Chicago, 1963), p. 531.

40 Balazs, *Chinese Civilization*, p. 11.

41 Timothy Brook, *The Confusions of Pleasure: Commerce and Culture in Ming China* (Berkeley, CA, 1998), offers the most recent treatment of commercial culture in traditional China. Cf. McNeill, *Rise of the West*, p. 529; Balazs, 'Imperial China', p. 153.

42 Kennedy, *Great Powers*, p. 9. Recruitment into and promotion within the civil service during the Ming period is detailed by Charles Hucker, 'Ming Government', in *Cambridge History of China*, vol. VIII, pp. 30–41.

43 Hucker, *Imperial Past*, pp. 283–7. Mongol government is described by David M. Farquhar, 'Structure and Function in Yuan Imperial

Government', in John D. Langlois, Jr., *China Under Mongol Rule* (Princeton, 1981), pp. 25–55.

44 Quoting Hucker, *Imperial Past*, p. 287.

45 John A. Harrison, *The Chinese Empire* (New York, 1972), pp. 313–16. Sixteen emperors successively ruled China during the Ming period (1368–1644). All were descendants of the first Ming emperor.

46 John D. Langlois, 'The Hung-wu Reign', in *Cambridge History of China*, vol. VII, pp. 149–69; Hucker, *Imperial Past*, p. 291; Chan, *Glory and Fall*, pp. 16–17.

47 Harrison, *Chinese Empire*, p. 317. See also Jonathan Spence, *The Search for Modern China* (New York, 1990), chapter 1, for a good description of the breakdown of Ming authority.

48 Story in Hucker, *Imperial Past*, p. 306.

49 *Ibid.*, p. 293.

50 Harrison, *Chinese Empire*, p. 322.

51 Hucker, *Imperial Past*, p. 293. James Bunyon Parsons, *Peasant Rebellions of the Late Ming Dynasty* (Ann Arbor, MI, 1970), provides detail on the peasant problem. A good survey of the Qing period is Richard J. Smith, *China's Cultural Heritage: The Qing Dynasty, 1644–1912* (Boulder, CO, 1994).

52 Smith, *China's Cultural Heritage*, pp. 44–5. Qing court life and protocol is described by Rawski, *The Last Emperors*, pp. 17–55.

53 The best survey of the reign in the emperor's own words, is provided by Jonathan Spence, *Emperor of China: Self-Portrait of K'ang-hsi* (New York, 1974). See also Lawrence D. Kessler, *K'ang-Hsi and the Consolidation of Ch'ing Rule, 1661–1684* (Chicago, 1976).

54 Smith, *China's Cultural Heritage*, p. 47; Rawski, *Last Emperors*, pp. 24–34.

55 Quoted in Harrison, *Chinese Empire*, p. 327.

56 Louis J. Gallagher, S.J., trans., *China in the Sixteenth Century: The Journals of Matteo Ricci, 1583–1610* (New York, 1943), p. 43.

57 Mark Mancall, *China at the Center: 300 Years of Foreign Policy* (New York, 1984), pp. 20–4.

58 Voltaire, *Ancient and Modern History*, in *The Works of Voltaire* (New York, 1901), vol. XV, p. 146.

59 Emperor Ch'ien-lung to George III in Philip F. Riley, ed., *The Global Experience: Readings in World History since 1500* (Englewood Cliffs, NJ, 1992), vol. II, p. 82. Macartney's journal is edited by John Cranmer-Byng, *An Embassy to China* (Hamden, CT, 1963).

60 Smith, *China's Cultural Heritage*, p. 279. W. C. Costin, *Great Britain and China, 1833–1860* (Oxford, 1968), treats foreign relations during a critical era.

61 Jack Gray, *Rebellions and Revolutions: China from the 1800s to the 1980s* (Oxford, 1990), pp. 52–72; Roberts, *History of the World*, p. 804. See Vincent Y. C. Shih, *The Taiping Ideology* (Seattle, WA, 1972) for the intellectual background.

62 Quoting Smith, *China's Cultural Heritage*, p. 280.

63 Fairbank, *China: A New History*, p. 229; Gray, *Rebellions and Revolutions*, pp. 126–51.

64 Mikiso Hane, *Premodern Japan* (Boulder, CO, 1991), offers a good survey

of the period before the nineteenth-century Meiji Restoration. See also Conrad Totman, *Early Modern Japan* (Berkeley, CA, 1993); Totman, *Japan Before Perry* (Berkeley, CA, 1981).

65 Hane, *Premodern Japan*, pp. 9–10, 16–17.

66 Totman, *Japan Before Perry*, pp. 24–5.

67 Jean-Pierre Lehmann, *The Roots of Modern Japan* (New York, 1982), p. 15.

68 John Whitney Hall, 'A Monarch for Modern Japan', in Robert E. Ward, ed., *Political Development in Modern Japan* (Princeton, NJ, 1968), p. 21.

69 Lehmann, *Roots of Modern Japan*, p. 14.

70 Edwin O. Reischauer, *Japan: The Story of a Nation* (New York, 1970), p. 43.

71 Reinhard Bendix, *Kings or People: Power and the Mandate to Rule* (Berkeley, CA, 1979), p. 454; Lehmann, *Roots of Modern Japan*, p. 19.

72 Lehmann, *Roots of Modern Japan*, p. 31.

73 Quoting Louis G. Perez, *The History of Japan* (Westport, CT, 1998), p. 71.

74 Lehmann, p. 48.

75 Bendix, *Kings or People*, p. 436.

76 W. G. Beasley, 'Meiji political institutions', in Marius B. Jansen, ed., *The Cambridge History of Japan*, vol. v, pp. 618, 621. See also George M. Wilson, *Patriots and Redeemers in Japan* (Chicago, 1992) and W. G. Beasley, *The Meiji Restoration* (Stanford, CA, 1972), especially pp. 117–40.

77 Jerrold M. Packard, *Sons of Heaven: A Portrait of the Japanese Monarchy* (New York, 1987), pp. 198–9.

78 W. G. Beasley, *The Rise of Modern Japan* (New York, 1995), pp. 61–5; Roberts, *History of the World*, p. 812.

79 Lehmann, *Roots of Modern Japan*, p. 155.

80 Ito Hirobumi, 'Commentaries on Constitutional Provisions Relating to the Emperor's Position', in David J. Lu, ed., *Japan: A Documentary History* (New York, 1997), vol. II, p. 340.

81 *Ibid.*

82 'Rescript on Education', in Lu, ed., *Japan*, p. 344.

83 Hall, 'Monarch for Modern Japan', p. 52.

84 Perez, *History of Japan*, p. 135.

85 Beasley, *Rise of Modern Japan*, p. 186.

86 Quoting Edward J. Drea, *In the Service of the Emperor: Essays on the Imperial Japanese Army* (Lincoln, NB, 1998), p. 175.

87 MacArthur to Eisenhower, in Lu., *Japan*, p. 468.

88 Hall, 'Monarch for Modern Japan', p. 29.

89 Haruhiro Fukui, 'Postwar Politics, 1945–1973', in Peter Duus, ed., *Cambridge History of Japan*, vol. VI, p. 177.

TWO · MONARCHY WITHOUT MANUSCRIPTS: SUB-SAHARAN AFRICA AND THE AMERICAS

1 Quoting Robin Hallett, *Africa to 1875* (Ann Arbor, MI, 1970), p. 28. Useful surveys of Africa include Roland Oliver and J. D. Fage, *A Short History of Africa* (Harmondsworth, 1985) and Paul Bohannan and Philip Curtin, *Africa and Africans* (Prospect Heights, IL, 1988).

2 John Iliffe, *Africans: The History of a Continent* (Cambridge, 1995), p. 70.

See also Robert W. July, *A History of the African People* (Prospect Heights, IL., 1992), pp. 42–7.

3 M. El Fasi and I. Hrbek, 'Stages in the Development of Islam and its Dissemination in Africa', in M. El Fasi, ed., *Unesco General History of Africa* (Berkeley, CA, 1988), vol. III, pp. 67–91.

4 Roland Oliver, *The African Experience* (New York, 1996), p. 145. Chapter 12 of Oliver's book, entitled 'Pomp and Power', provides a wealth of information on the culture of African monarchy.

5 Philip Curtin, Steven Feierman, Leonard Thompson and Jan Vansina, *African History* (Boston, 1978), pp. 33–5, provide an overview of differing interpretations respecting the rise of African states.

6 Oliver, *African Experience*, p. 146.

7 *Ibid.*, p. 148.

8 Basil Davidson, *The Africans: An Entry to Cultural History* (London, 1969), pp. 190–1; Oliver and Fage, *Short History*, p. 45.

9 Laurence Cockcroft, *Africa's Way: A Journey from the Past* (London, 1990), pp. 24–5.

10 John Mbiti, *African Religions and Philosophy* (New York, 1969), p. 109; Cockcroft, *Africa's Way*, p. 35.

11 Nehemia Levtzion, 'The Shara and the Sudan from the Arab Conquest of the Magrib to the Rise of the Almoravids', in J. D. Fage, ed., *The Cambridge History of Africa* (Cambridge, 1978), vol. II, pp. 637–84.

12 July, *History of the African People*, pp. 58–9.

13 Iliffe, *Africans*, p. 52.

14 *Ibid.*, p. 149.

15 J. D. Fage, *A History of Africa* 3rd edn (New York, 1996), p. 56.

16 Harry A. Gailey, Jr., *History of Africa from Earliest Times to 1800* (New York, 1970), vol. I, p. 61.

17 Curtin *et al.*, *African History*, p. 88.

18 Al Omari, 'Mali in the Fourteenth Century', in Basil Davidson, ed., *The African Past: Chronicles from Antiquity to Modern Times* (Boston, 1964), p. 77.

19 Nehemia Levtzion, 'The Western Maghrib and Sudan', in *Cambridge History of Africa*, vol. III, pp. 376–81, contains a good analysis of Mansa Musa's tenure as king.

20 Quoting Iliffe, *Africans*, p. 53.

21 Crockcroft, *Africa's Way*, p. 41.

22 Iliffe, *Africans*, p. 72.

23 Fage, *History of Africa*, p. 130; Roland Oliver, *The African Experience* (New York, 1996), pp. 110–12.

24 Quoting Fage, *History of Africa*, p. 132.

25 Iliffe, *Africans*, p. 80.

26 Fage, *History of Africa*, p. 138.

27 Quoting Bohannan and Curtin, *Africa and Africans*, p. 286. On the Muslim role in the African slave trade, see John H. Hanson, 'Islam and African Societies', in Phyllis M. Martin and Patrick O'Meara, eds, *Africa* (Bloomington, IN, 1995), pp. 105–7.

28 Iliffe, *Africans*, p. 73.

29 *Ibid.*, p. 592.

30 *Ibid.*, p. 76.
31 Afonso quoted in Davidson, ed., *The African Past*, p. 192.
32 Robert O. Collins, *African History* (New York, 1971), p. 350.
33 Iliffe, *Africans*, p. 149. On the Portuguese role in Congo, see John Biggs-Davidson, *Africa: Hope Deferred* (London, 1972), pp. 32–4; Oliver and Fage, *Short History*, pp. 128–30.
34 Oliver, *African Experience*, p. 155.
35 Cockcroft, *Africa's Way*, pp. 50–1.
36 Quoting Bill Freund, *The Making of Contemporary Africa* (Boulder, CO, 1998), p. 21.
37 Quoting Oliver, *African Experience*, p. 158.
38 A solid overview is provided by Alvir M. Josephy, Jr., *The Indian Heritage of America* (New York, 1973).
39 William H. McNeill, *A World History* (Oxford, 1999) p. 278.
40 John A. Crow, *The Epic of Latin America*, 3rd edn (Berkeley, CA, 1980), pp. 45–8.
41 Miguel Leon-Portilla, 'Mesoamerica before 1519', in Leslie Bethell, ed., *The Cambridge History of Latin America* (Cambridge, 1984), vol. I, p. 17.
42 On Aztec civilization in general see Michael E. Smith, *The Aztecs* (Cambridge, MA, 1996); Nigel Davies, *The Aztec Empire: the Toltec Resurgence* (Norman, OK, 1987); and Susan Gillespie, *The Aztec Kings: The Construction of Rulership in Mexica History* (Tucson, AZ, 1989).
43 Hernan Cortes, *Letters from Mexico*, trans. and ed. Anthony Pagden (New Haven, CT, 1986), p. 109.
44 Crow, *Epic of Latin America*, p. 50.
45 Peter N. Stearns *et al.*, *World Civilizations: The Global Experience* (New York, 1996), vol. I, p. 385.
46 John Murra, 'Andean Societies before 1532', in *The Cambridge History of Latin America* (Cambridge, 1984), vol. I, p. 77.
47 J. H. Elliot, 'The Spanish Conquest and Settlement of America', in *The Cambridge History of Latin America* (Cambridge, 1984), vol. I, p. 185.
48 Mark A. Burkholder and Lyman L. Johnson, *Colonial Latin America*, 3rd edn (Oxford, 1998), pp. 42–50.
49 Peter Bakewell, *A History of Latin America* (Oxford, 1997), pp. 96–100, discusses the variables during these decades.
50 Alfred W. Crosby, *Germs, Seeds and Animals* (Armonk, NY, 1994), chap. 1. William H. McNeill, *Plagues and Peoples* (New York, 1997), provides a compelling account of the epidemiological disaster.
51 Quoted in J. M. Roberts, *History of the World* (Oxford, 1993) p. 503.
52 Cortes in Pagden, ed., *Letters*, p. 48. See also J.H. Elliot, 'Spain and America in the Sixteenth and Seventeenth Centuries, in *The Cambridge History of Latin America* (Cambridge, 1984), vol. I, p. 297.
53 Bakewell, *History of Latin America*, p. 130.
54 Elliot, 'Spain and America', p. 294.
55 Bakewell, *History of Latin America*, p. 125.
56 Elliot, 'Spain and America', p. 292.
57 Bernard Bailyn *et al.*, *The Great Republic: A History of the American People* (Lexington, MA, 1977), vol. I, p. 17.

58 Elliot, 'The Spanish Conquest and Settlement', p. 193.
59 *Ibid.*, pp. 194–5.
60 Bakewell, *History of Latin America*, p. 130.
61 Crow, *Epic of Latin America*, pp. 416–18.
62 Burkholder and Johnson, *Colonial Latin America*, p. 315.
63 Bakewell, *History of Latin America*, p. 387.
64 De Macedo quoted in E. Bradford Burns, *A History of Brazil*, 3rd edn (New York, 1993), pp. 115–16.
65 Thomas E. Skidmore and Peter H. Smith, *Modern Latin America*, 4th edn (New York, 1997), p. 34.
66 Bakewell, *History of Latin America*, p. 443.
67 Burkholder and Johnson, *Colonial Latin America*, p. 327.
68 Peter Winn, *Americas: The Changing Face of Latin America and the Caribbean* (Berkeley, CA, 1995), pp. 79–81. See also David Bushnell and Neill Macaulay, *The Emergence of Latin America in the Nineteenth Century* (New York, 1988), pp. 146–52.
69 Skidmore and Smith, *Modern Latin America*, p. 149.
70 *Ibid.*, p. 153.
71 *Ibid.*, p. 155.

THREE · THEOCRATIC MONARCHY: BYZANTIUM AND THE ISLAMIC LANDS

1 Peter N. Stearns *et al.*, *World Civilizations: The Global Experience* (New York, 1996), vol. 1, p. 333. The best recent survey is Warren Treadgold, *A History of the Byzantine State and Society* (Stanford, CA, 1997).
2 Michael McCormick, 'Emperors', in Guglielmo Cavallo, ed., *The Byzantines* (Chicago, 1997), p. 230; see also D. A. Miller, *The Byzantine Tradition* (New York, 1966), p. 2.
3 Richard Southern, *Western Society and the Church in the Middle Ages* (Harmondsworth, 1986), pp. 56–67.
4 René Guerdan, *Byzantium* (New York, 1962), p. 17. See also Mark Whittow, *The Making of Byzantium, 600–1025* (Berkeley, CA, 1996), pp. 135–6, for the Byzantine view of God's power.
5 Eusebius discussed in J. H. Burns, ed., *The Cambridge History of Medieval Political Thought* (Cambridge, 1988), p. 52.(All future references will be abbreviated *CHMPT*).
6 Miller, *Byzantine Tradition*, pp. 28–31; Steven Runciman, *Byzantine Civilization* (New York, 1965), pp. 52–4.
7 'Medieval Political Theory' in Burns, ed., *CHMPT*, p. 63.
8 McCormick, 'Emperors', p. 251.
9 Cavallo, ed., *The Byzantines*, pp. 2–3.
10 A. A. Vasiliev, *History of the Byzantine Empire* (Madison, WI, 1961), vol. II, pp. 469–70. On appointments and dismissals, see John Meyendorff, 'Byzantine Church', in Joseph Strayer, ed., *Dictionary of the Middle Ages* (New York, 1983), vol. II, p. 459.
11 Patriarch Antony IV to Basil I, grand prince of Moscow, quoted in André Guillou, 'Functionaries', in Cavallo, ed., *The Byzantines*, p. 210.

12 Guillou, 'Functionaries', p. 197. Donald M. Nicol, *Byzantium and Venice* (Cambridge, 1988), explores relations between two economic powerhouses.

13 John L. Esposito, *Islam: The Straight Path* (New York, 1991), pp. 3–33; Emory C. Bogle, *Islam: Origin and Belief* (Austin, TX, 1998), pp. 1–25, offer useful introductions.

14 Bernard Lewis, *Islam in History* (Chicago, 1993), pp. 261–2.

15 Patricia Crone, *God's Caliph: Religious Authority in the First Centuries of Islam* (Cambridge, 1986), argues that the early caliphs combined political and religious authority.

16 Abu Bakr quoted in Akbar S. Ahmed, *Discovering Islam: Making Sense of Muslim History and Society* (New York, 1988), p. 33.

17 Bogle, *Islam: Origin and Belief*, p. 48.

18 Esposito, *Islam: The Straight Path*, p. 53.

19 Quoted in John Mckay *et al.*, *A History of World Societies* (Boston, 1992), vol. II, p. 899.

20 Jiu-Hwa Upshur *et al.*, *World History* (St Paul, MN, 1995), p. 379.

21 For the best overview of early developments, see Bernard Lewis, *Istanbul and the Civilization of the Ottoman Empire* (Norman, OK, 1963) pp. 10–27.

22 Fernand Braudel, *The Mediterranean World in the Age of Philip II* (New York, 1972), vol. II, p. 665.

23 Richard Greaves *et al.*, *Civilizations of the World* (New York, 1997), p. 525; Constance Head, *Imperial Twilight* (Chicago, 1977), pp. 155–63.

24 Giacomo de' Trapezuntios quoted in P. M. Holt, Ann K. S. Lambton and Bernard Lewis, eds, *The Cambridge History of Islam* (Cambridge, 1970), vol. IA, pp. 296–7. The chapters on the rise of the Ottoman empire were contributed by Halil Inalcik and all subsequent references will be to Inalcik, *CHI*.

25 Inalcik, *CHI*, pp. 306–7.

26 Paul Coles, *The Ottoman Impact on Europe* (New York, 1968), p. 34.

27 Greaves *et al.*, *Civilizations*, p. 523.

28 Lewis, *Istanbul and the Civilization of the Ottoman Empire*, p. 48.

29 Inalcik, *CHI*, pp. 297–8; Marshall G. S. Hodgson, *The Venture of Islam* (Chicago, 1974), vol. III, pp. 99–101.

30 Braudel, *Mediterranean World*, vol. I, p. 410.

31 Lewis, *Istanbul and the Civilization of the Ottoman Empire*, p. 40. Wayne Vucinich, *The Ottoman Empire: Its Record and Legacy* (Huntington, NY, 1979), p. 15, says that Murad I (1359–89) was the first to adopt the title of sultan.

32 Vucinich, p. 26. Roger Bigelow Merrimoan, *Suleiman the Magnificent, 1520–1566* (New York, 1966), chap. 7, provides a good overview of the caliph's power in the mid-sixteenth century.

33 Inalcik, *CHI*, pp. 320–2.

34 Vucinich, *Ottoman Empire*, p. 26. For the structure of government in the fourteenth century, see Stanford Shaw, *History of the Ottoman Empire and Modern Turkey* (Cambridge, 1976), vol. I, pp. 22–7.

35 Vucinich, *Ottoman Empire*, p. 24; Hodgson, *Venture of Islam*, p. 102; Albert Howe Lybyer, *The Government of the Ottoman Empire in the Time of*

    Suleiman (New York, 1966), pp. 91–3.
36 Inalcik, *CHI*, p. 301.
37 Coles, *Ottoman Impact*, p. 58.
38 Halil Inalcik, *The Ottoman Empire: The Classical Age, 1300–1600* (New York, 1973), p. 46.
39 Coles, *Ottoman Impact*, pp. 46–7; Inalcik, *CHI*, pp. 342–53.
40 Coles, *Ottoman Impact*, p. 70.
41 *Ibid.*, p. 34.
42 *Ibid.*
43 Vucinich, *Ottoman Empire*, p. 24; Ira M. Lapidus, *A History of Islamic Societies* (Cambridge, 1988), pp. 333–4.
44 Shaw, *Ottoman Empire and Modern Turkey*, p. 170.
45 Inalcik, *Ottoman Empire*, pp. 42, 45.
46 Inalcik, *CHI*, pp. 344, 350.
47 William McNeill, *A World History* (Oxford, 1999), p. 341.
48 William H. McNeill, *A History of the Human Community* (New York, 1997), vol. II, p. 417.
49 Shaw, *Ottoman Empire and Modern Turkey*, p. 150.
50 Coles, *Ottoman Impact*, p. 66.
51 Ranbir Vohra, *The Making of India: A Historical Survey* (New York, 1997), pp. 12–13.
52 T. Walter Wallbank, *A Short History of India and Pakistan* (New York, 1965), p. 48.
53 H. A. R. Gibb, ed. and trans., *Ibn Battuta: Travels in Asia and Africa, 1325–1354* (New York, 1969), p. 194.
54 J. M. Roberts, *History of the World* (Oxford, 1993), p. 418. The early Muslim kingdoms are discussed in detail by D. P. Singhal, *India and World Civilization* (Lansing, MI, 1969), vol. II, chapter 4.
55 Vohra, *Making of India*, p. 37
56 John F. Richards, *The Mughal Empire* (Cambridge, 1993), p. 3.
57 Mughal was the Persian word for Mongol.
58 L. King, ed., *Memoirs of Babur*, 2 vols, trans. J. Leyden and W. Erskine (Oxford, 1921).
59 W. H. Moreland and Atul Chandra Chatterjee, *A Short History of India* (London, 1962), pp. 204–9; Percival Spear, *A History of India: From the Sixteenth Century to the Twentieth Century* (London, 1990), pp. 23–5.
60 Richards, *Mughal Empire*, p. 12; Spear, *History of India*, p. 31.
61 Moreland and Chatterjee, *Short History*, p. 215.
62 Richards, *Mughal Empire*, p. 40.
63 Burton Stein, *A History of India* (Oxford, 1998), p. 172. See also Ram Prasad Tripathi, 'The Turko-Mongol Theory of Kingship', in Muzaffar Alam and Sanjay Subrahmanyam, eds, *The Mughal State, 1526–1750* (Oxford, 1998), pp. 115–25.
64 Hermann Kulke and Dietmar Rothermund, *A History of India* (London, 1998), p.190; Aziz Ahmad, *Studies in Islamic Culture in the Indian Environment* (Oxford, 1964), pp. 167–81; Richards, *Mughal Empire*, p. 40.
65 Quoted in Stein, *History of India*, p. 173.
66 Richards, *Mughal Empire*, p. 49. According to Catherine B. Asher,

Architecture of Mughal India (Cambridge, 1992), p. 39: 'artistic production on both an imperial and sub-imperial level was closely linked to notions of state polity, religion and kingship'.

67 Spear, *History of India*, pp. 36–7.
68 Richards, *Mughal Empire*, p. 15.
69 *Ibid.*, p. 75; Stein, *History of India*, p. 169.
70 Spear, *History of India*, p. 44.
71 Akbar's encouragement of non-Muslims is discussed by S. M. Ikram, *Muslim Civilization in India* (New York, 1964), pp. 148–9.
72 Irfan Habib, 'India during the Mughal Period', in S. N. Sridhar, ed., *Ananya: A Portrait of India* (New York, 1997), chap. 4; Richards, *Mughal Empire*, p. 282.
73 Richards, *Mughal Empire*, p. 79.
74 *Ibid.*, pp. 63, 75.
75 Philip Lee Ralph, *World Civilizations* (New York, 1991), vol. I, p. 761.
76 *Ibid.*, p. 767.
77 Spear, *History of India*, p. 41.
78 *Ibid.*, p. 43.
79 John Keay, *The Honourable Company: A History of the English East India Company* (New York, 1991) and Geoffrey Moorhouse, *India Britannica* (New York, 1983) discuss the early contacts; Richards, *Mughal Empire*, pp. 288–9.
80 *Ibid.*, pp. 45, 56.
81 Roberts, *History of the World*, p. 426. This view is confirmed by Singhal, *India and World Civilization*, p. 198.
82 Richards, *Mughal Empire*, pp. 94–5.
83 Stein, *History of India*, p. 185.
84 Richards, *Mughal Empire*, p. 295.
85 Quoted in Vohra, *Making of India*, p. 47.
86 *Ibid.*, p. 44; Ikram, *Muslim Civilization*, pp. 254–5; Penderel Moon, *The British Conquest and Dominion of India* (London, 1989), p. 11; C. A. Bayly, *Indian Society and the Making of the British Empire* (Cambridge, 1988), pp. 7–13.
87 Paul Kennedy, *The Rise and Fall of the Great Powers* (New York, 1987), pp. 11–12.

FOUR · THE EUROPEAN ANOMALY, 1000–1500

1 Antony Black, *Political Thought in Europe, 1250–1450*, (Cambridge, 1992), p. 137.
2 D. E. Luscombe, 'The Formation of Political Thought in the West', in J.H. Burns, ed., *Cambridge History of Medieval Political Thought* (Cambridge, 1988), p. 163.
3 Reinhard Bendix, *Kings or People: Power and the Mandate to Rule* (Berkeley, CA, 1979), p. 25.
4 *Ibid.*, p. 22. See also Henry A. Meyers, *Medieval Kingship* (Chicago, 1982), pp. 3–4.
5 Bendix, pp. 218–22.

6 Brian Tierney, *Religion, Law and the Growth of Constitutional Thought,
1150–1650* (Cambridge, 1982), pp. 8–9.

7 Susan Reynolds, *Kingdoms and Communities in Western Europe, 900–1300*
(Oxford, 1984), p. 216.

8 Jeremy Black, *Convergence or Divergence? Britain and the Continent* (New
York, 1994), p. 22.

9 Black, *Political Thought*, p. 139.

10 Thomas Aquinas, *On Kingship* (Toronto, 1949), p. 180.

11 Black, *Political Thought*, p. 139.

12 Meyers, *Medieval Kingship*, pp. 16–17.

13 *Ibid.*, pp. 47–8. On Augustine's view of history and the role of civil
authority, see Alan Richardson, *History Sacred and Profane* (Philadelphia,
1964), pp. 55–64.

14 Augustine, *The City of God*, in Whitney J. Oates, ed., *Basic Writings of St
Augustine* (New York, 1948), vol. II, p. 493.

15 Neil B. McLynn, *Ambrose of Milan* (Berkeley, 1994), pp. 315–30.

16 Ambrose quoted in Brian Tierney, ed., *The Crisis of Church and State,
1050–1300* (Englewood Cliffs, NJ, 1964), p. 9.

17 Pope Gelasius in Tierney, ed., *Crisis*, p. 13. For context, see Geoffrey
Barraclough, *The Medieval Papacy* (New York, 1968), pp. 28–9, and
Walter Ullmann, *The Growth of Papal Government in the Middle Ages*
(London, 1965), pp. 14–31.

18 R. W. Southern, *Western Society and the Church in the Middle Ages*
(Harmondsworth, 1986), pp. 24–5; Ullmann, *Papal Government*, pp. 3–10.

19 Pierre Riche, *The Carolingians*, trans. Michael Idomir Allen
(Philadelphia, 1993), pp. 120–3, and Roger Collins, *Charlemagne*
(Toronto, 1998), pp. 141–59, discuss the significance of the coronation.

20 John Morrall, *Political Thought in Medieval Times* (London, 1958), p. 24;
Southern, *Western Society and the Church*, p. 31.

21 Luscombe, 'Formation of Political Thought' in *CHMPT*, p. 166.

22 Maurice Keen, *The Pelican History of Medieval Europe* (Harmondsworth,
1969), p. 67.

23 Alcuin quoted in Southern, *Western Society and the Church*, p. 32.

24 Black, *Political Thought*, p. 43. The best recent study is Colin Morris, *The
Papal Monarchy* (Oxford, 1989).

25 Quoted in Keen, *History of Medieval Europe*, p. 68.

26 Tierney, ed., *Crisis of Church and State*, p. 42.

27 'Deposition of Henry by Gregory', in *ibid.*, p. 61; Margaret Deanesly, *A
History of the Medieval Church, 590–1500* (London, 1994), pp. 100–1.

28 John A. F. Thomson, *The Western Church in the Middle Ages* (London,
1998), pp. 63–4; R. van Caenegem, 'Government, Law and Society', in
Burns, ed., *CHMPT*, pp. 174, 187.

29 Edward Peters, *Europe and the Middle Ages* (New York, 1997), pp. 198–9;
Brian Tierney, *Western Europe in the Middle Ages, 300–1450* (New York,
1970), p. 266.

30 Luscombe, 'The Formation of Political Thought in the West', in Burns,
ed., *CHMPT*, pp. 159–61; also van Caenegem, 'Government, Law and
Society', in *ibid.*, p. 176.

31 Black, *Convergence or Divergence?*, pp. 25–6.
32 On Anglo-Saxon government, see Frank Stenton, *Anglo-Saxon England* (Oxford, 1992), pp. 236–8, and Alfred P. Smyth, *King Alfred the Great* (Oxford, 1995), esp. chapter 16.
33 Stenton, *Anglo-Saxon England*, p. 368.
34 Elizabeth M. Hallam, *Capetian France, 987–1328* (London, 1983), pp. 114–19; Tierney, *Western Europe in Middle Ages*, p. 266.
35 Robert Fawtier, *The Capetian Kings of France* trans., Lionel Butler and R. J. Adam (New York, 1960), pp. 85–6; Peters, p. 291.
36 Maurice Keen, *Medieval Europe* (New York, 1968), p. 110; R. H. C. Davis, *A History of Medieval Europe* (London, 1991), p. 299.
37 Keen, *Medieval Europe*, pp. 197–8.
38 On the reign of Louis VIII, see William Chester Jones, 'The Capetians from the Death of Philip II to Philip IV', in David Abulafia, ed., *The New Cambridge Medieval History* (Cambridge, 1999), vol. v, pp. 279–89.
39 Tierney, *Religion, Law and Constitutional Thought*, p. 10.
40 Kenneth Pennington, 'Law, Legislative Authority and Theories of Government, 1150–1300', in Burns, ed., *CHMPT*, p. 426.
41 *Ibid.*, pp. 182–3. See also Barraclough, *Medieval Papacy*, pp. 77–93, for coverage of the investiture struggle.
42 On the early development of canon law see I. S. Robinson, 'Church and Papacy', in Burns, ed., *CHMPT*, pp. 266–77; Bernard Guenee, *States and Rulers in Later Medieval Europe*, trans. Juliet Vale (Oxford, 1985), pp. 81–2; Joseph H. Lynch, *The Medieval Church: A Brief History* (London, 1992), pp. 169–71; and Thomson, *Western Church*, pp. 143–4.
43 Tierney, *Religion, Law and Constitutional Thought*, p. 17.
44 Pennington 'Law, Legislative Authority and Theories of Government' in Burns,ed.,*CHMPT*, pp. 430–1, 437.
45 W. L. Warren, *Henry II* (Berkeley, 1973), chapters 6–10, provides the best overview of the king's government. See also Richard Mortimer, *Angevin England, 1154–1258* (Oxford, 1994), pp. 51–63; Guenee, *States and Rulers*, p. 172.
46 Black, *Political Thought*, p. 163.
47 Tierney, *Western Europe*, p. 324; Black, *Political Thought*, p. 165.
48 Black, *Political Thought*, p. 166. See also Guenee, *States and Rulers*, p. 174.
49 Michael Prestwich, *Edward I* (Berkeley, CA, 1988), esp. chap. 17, and Alfred L. Brown, *The Governance of Late Medieval England, 1272–1461* (Stanford, 1989), pp. 156–68.
50 Joseph Strayer, *On the Medieval Origins of the Modern State* (Princeton, 1970), p. 45.
51 Hallam, *Capetian France*, pp. 278–83; Thomson, *Western Church*, pp. 167–8.
52 Oliver Davies, *God Within: The Mystical Tradition of Northern Europe* (New York, 1988), chap. 2, offers a good introduction to Eckhart.
53 David Nicholas, *The Evolution of the Medieval World* (London, 1992), pp. 471–7; Eamon Duffy, *Saints and Sinners: A History of the Popes* (New Haven, 1997), pp. 123–31.
54 John of Paris, 'Potestate et Papali', in Brian Tierney, ed., *The Middle Ages:*

Sources of Medieval History (New York, 1999), p. 291. See also Marsilius of
Padua, *Defensor Pacis*, trans. Alan Gewirth (Toronto, 1986).
55 A. MacKay, *Spain in the Middle Ages* (London, 1977), esp. chap.7, and
J. N. Hilgarth, *The Spanish Kingdoms, 1250–1516* (Oxford, 1978), chap. 4.

FIVE · MONARCHY AND EUROPEAN HEGEMONY, 1500–1914

1 Recent discussions of the West's rise to global dominance include David
Landes, *The Wealth and Poverty of Nations* (New York, 1998), and André
Gunder Frank, *Reorient: Global Economy in the Asian Age* (Berkeley, 1998).

2 Landes, *Wealth and Poverty*, pp. 45–59, argues that European
inventiveness was a key characteristic of the period 1000–1500.

3 Jeremy Black, *Why Wars Happen* (New York, 1998), pp. 47–8.

4 Good examples of the rise of nationalist sentiment combined with a
defence of a national Church can be found in the speeches of Queen
Elizabeth I. See George P. Rice, Jr., ed., *The Public Speaking of Queen
Elizabeth* (New York, 1966).

5 W. M. Spellman, *European Political Thought, 1600–1700* (London, 1998),
p. 15.

6 Philippe Duplessis Mornay, *Vindiciae contra tyrannos*, in Julian H.
Franklin, ed., *Constitutionalism and Resistance in the Sixteenth Century*
(New York, 1960), p. 297

7 Paul Kennedy, *Rise and Fall of the Great Powers* (New York, 1987), p. 13.

8 *Ibid.*, p. xvii.

9 Steven Saunders Webb, *The Governors General* (Chapel Hill, 1979) and
1676: The End of American Independence (New York, 1984), analyse the
military component of English settlement.

10 Quoted in A. F. Upton, 'Sweden', in John Miller, ed., *Absolutism in
Seventeenth-Century Europe* (London, 1990), p. 116.

11 Jean Bodin, *The Six Books of a Commonweal*, trans. Richard Knolles
(London, 1606), ed. K. D. McRae (Cambridge, MA, 1962), p. 84.

12 James I, *The Trew Law of Free Monarchy*, in J. McIlwain, ed., *The Political
Works of James I* (New York, 1965), p. 62.

13 Antony Alcock, *A Short History of Europe* (New York, 1998), p. 145.

14 Nanerl Keohane, *Philosophy and the State in France: The Renaissance to the
Enlightenment* (Princeton, NJ, 1980), p. 3.

15 Spellman, *European Political Thought*, pp. 42–3. See also Kenneth
Pennington, *Europe in the Seventeenth Century* (London, 1989),
pp. 383–4, and more generally, Henry Kamen, *Golden Age Spain* (Atlantic
Highlands, NJ, 1988).

16 Roland N. Stromberg, *European Intellectual History since 1789*
(Englewood Cliffs, NJ, 1994), p. 15.

17 Quotes from *The Times*, *Spectator* and Bagehot contained in David
Cannadine and Simon Price, eds, *Rituals of Royalty: Power and Ceremonial
in Traditional Societies* (Cambridge, 1987), pp. 208, 213.

18 Alexander III quoted in J. M. Roberts, *Europe, 1880–1945* (New York,
1989), p. 67.

19 M. S. Anderson, *The Ascendancy of Europe, 1815–1914* (London, 1985), p. 63.

20 *Ibid.*, p. 65.
21 J. S. Mill, *Representative Government* quoted in Anderson, p. 209. On the role of nationalism in the nineteenth century, see Norman Rich, *The Age of Nationalism and Reform, 1850–1890* (New York, 1977).
22 Leopold von Ranke quoted in Anderson, *Ascendancy*, p. 210.
23 Peter Jones, *The 1848 Revolutions* (London, 1991), provides a good overview. Cf. Anderson, *Ascendancy*, pp. 85–7.
24 J. M. Roberts, *History of the World* (Oxford, 1993), p. 738.
25 Anderson, *Ascendancy*, p. 98.
26 Denis Mack Smith, *Italy and its Monarchy* (New Haven, CT, 1989), p. 4.
27 Bismarck, *The Memoirs*, trans A. J. Butler, 2 vols, (New York 1966), 1: 17.
28 Felix Gilbert, *The End of the European Era, 1890 to the Present* (New York, 1970), p. 64.
29 Anderson, *Ascendancy*, pp. 113–14.
30 Gilbert, *End of the European Era*, p. 7.
31 William R. Keylor, *The Twentieth-Century World: An International History*, 3rd edn (New York, 1996), p. 44.
32 Gordon Craig, *Germany: 1866–1945* (Oxford, 1978), esp. pp. 49–53.
33 Keylor, *Twentieth Century World*, p. 45.
34 William quoted in *Germany*, p. 267. See also Thomas A. Kohut, *William II and the Germans* (New York, 1991).
35 John C. G. Rohl, *The Kaiser and his Court: Wilhelm II and the Government of Germany* (Cambridge, 1994), p. 11.
36 Laurence Lafore, *The Long Fuse: An Interpretation of the Origins of World War I* (New York, 1971), pp. 56, 59.
37 Roberts, *Europe 1880–1945*, p. 202.
38 Lafore, *The Long Fuse*, p. 73.
39 Roberts, *Europe 1880–1945*, p. 208.
40 Richard Wortman, 'Moscow and Petersburg: the Problem of Political Center in Tsarist Russia, 1881–1913', in Sean Wilentz, ed., *Rights of Power: Symbolism, Ritual and Politics since the Middle Ages* (Philadelphia, 1985).
41 Roberts, *Europe 1880–1945*, p. 189. Marc Ferro, *Nicholas II : Last of the Tsars* (New York, 1993), is a readable biography.

SIX · ENDINGS AND REMNANTS: MONARCHY IN THE
TWENTIETH CENTURY

1 Heinz Gollwitzer, *Europe in the Age of Imperialism, 1880–1914* (New York, 1969), provides a useful introduction. More recently, see John Lowe, *The Great Powers, Imperialism and the German Problem* (London, 1994).
2 J. M. Roberts, *Europe 1880–1945* (London, 1989), pp. 19, 22.
3 Jeremy Black, *War and the World: Military Power and the Fate of Continents* (New Haven, 1998), p. 232.
4 Antony Alcock, *A Short History of Europe* (New York, 1998) pp. 204–5. Benjamin J. Cohen, *The Question of Imperialism* (New York, 1973), chap. 2, discusses the political and economic motivations behind late nineteenth-

century European expansion.

5 Terence Ranger, 'The Invention of Tradition in Colonial Africa', in Eric Hobsbawm and Terence Ranger, eds, *The Invention of Tradition* (Cambridge, 1984), p. 212.

6 J. M. Roberts, *A History of the World* (Oxford, 1993) pp. 818–19.

7 Bernard S. Cohn, 'Representing Authority in Victorian India', in Hobsbawm and Ranger, eds, *The Invention of Tradition*, pp. 165–7.

8 Arno J. Mayer, *The Persistence of the Old Regime: Europe to the Great War* (London, 1981), p. 4; Roberts, *Europe 1880–1945*, p. 59.

9 Roberts, *Europe 1880–1945*, p. 131; Mayer, *Persistence*, pp. 10, 13.

10 R. D. Anderson, *France, 1870–1914* (London, 1977), pp. 100–18, and Theodore Zeldin, *France, 1848–1945* (Oxford, 1973), vol. I, pp. 587–9, discuss the political instability of the era.

11 Spencer M. Di Scala and Salvo Mastellone, *European Political Thought, 1815–1989* (Boulder, CO, 1998), pp. 138–9.

12 Felix Gilbert, *The End of the European Era, 1890 to the Present* (New York, 1970), p. 50.

13 Heinrich von Treitschke, *Politics* ed., and trans., Hans Kohn (New York, 1963), esp. pp. 172–80.

14 Gilbert, *End of the European Era*, pp. 3–5.

15 On this subject see David Cannadine and Simon Price, eds, *Rituals of Royalty: Power and Ceremonial in Traditional Societies* (Cambridge, 1987) p. 15.

16 Mayer, *Persistence*, p. 137.

17 David E. Barclay, 'Ritual, Ceremonial and the Invention of the Monarchial Tradition in Nineteenth-Century Prussia', in Heinz Duchhardt, Richard Jackson and David Sturdy, eds, *European Monarchy* (Stuttgart, 1992), pp. 207–20.

18 William II quoted in Laurence Lafore, *The Long Fuse: An Interpretation of the Origins of World War I* (New York, 1971), pp. 187, 213.

19 Michael Howard, 'Europe on the Eve of the First World War', in R. J. W. Evans and Hartmut Pogge von Strandmann, eds, *The Coming of the First World War* (Oxford, 1990), pp. 1–18; James Joll, 'The Mood of 1914', in Holger H. Herwig, ed., *The Outbreak of World War I* (Lexington, MA, 1991), pp. 13–18.

20 Gilbert, *End of the European Era*, p. 5.

21 Nicholas II, *The Complete Wartime Correspondence of Tsar Nicholas II and the Empress Alexandra*, ed. Joseph T. Fuhrmann (Westport, CT, 1999), p. 25.

22 Bergson quoted in Roland N. Stromberg, *European Intellectual History since 1789*, (Englewood Cliffs, NJ, 1994), p. 190.

23 Quoted in John C. G. Rohl, *The Kaiser and His Court: Wilhelm II and the Government of Germany* (Cambridge, 1994), p. 9.

24 Wolfgang J. Mommsen, *Imperial Germany, 1867–1918* (New York, 1990), p. 99.

25 Rolland quoted in Stromberg, *European Intellectual History*, p. 189.

26 Spencer C. Tucker, *The Great War, 1914–18* (Bloomington, IN, 1998), pp. 25–6; Roberts, *Europe 1880–1945*, p. 282.

27 William R. Keylor, *The Twentieth-Century World: An International History*, 3rd edn (New York, 1996), p. 57. Keith Robbins, *The First World War*

(Oxford, 1984), pp. 150–64, offers a succinct treatment of the experiences of combatants.

28 Marc Ferro, *Nicholas II: Last of the Tsars*, trans. Brian Pearce (New York, 1993), p. 204.

29 Karl R. Stadler, *Austria* (New York, 1971), p. 51.

30 F. R. Bridge, *The Hapsburg Monarchy among the Great Powers, 1815–1918* (Oxford, 1990), p. 347. See also Z. A. B. Zeman, *The Break-up of the Hapsburg Empire, 1914–1918* (London, 1961), pp. 109–10.

31 Emperor Karl quoted in Bridge, *Hapsburg Monarchy*, p. 361.

32 *Ibid.*, p. 367. On the diplomacy of the final year of the war, see David Stevenson, *The First World War and International Politics* (Oxford, 1988), pp. 183–221.

33 Attribution to the Prophet Muhammad in Bernard Lewis, *The Political Language of Islam* (Chicago, 1988), p. 43.

34 Nissim Rejwan, *Arabs Face the Modern World: Religious, Cultural and Political Responses to the West* (Gainesville, FL, 1998), pp. 193, 206.

35 Lewis, *Political Language*, pp. 29, 31.

36 *Ibid.*, pp. 46–7, 50.

37 William L. Cleveland, *A History of the Modern Middle East* (Boulder, CO, 1994), pp. 167–72, discusses the reforms of Ataturk.

38 *Ibid.*, p. 149.

39 Ira M. Lapidus, *A History of Islamic Societies* (Cambridge, 1988), p. 642.

40 Sydney Nettleton Fisher and William Ochsenwald, *The Middle East: A History* (New York, 1997), vol. II, p. 442.

41 Peter Mansfield, *A History of the Middle East* (Harmondsworth, 1991), p. 196. See also L. Carl Brown, *International Politics and the Middle East* (Princeton, 1984), pp. 117–22.

42 Reeva Simon, *Iraq Between the Two World Wars* (New York, 1986), covers British involvement in Iraq, with a focus on the military elite who took effective power by the late 1930s.

43 Samira Haj, *The Making of Iraq, 1900–1963* (Albany, NY, 1997), pp. 111–39; Mansfield, *History of the Middle East*, p. 262; Fisher and Ochsenwald, *The Middle East*, vol. II, p. 609.

44 Fisher and Ochsenwald, *The Middle East*, vol. II, p. 459. On King Abdullah, see Mary C. Wilson, *King Abdullah, Britain and the Making of Jordon* (Cambridge, 1990).

45 Mansfield, *History of the Middle East*, pp. 239–40; Fisher and Ochsenwald, *The Middle East*, vol. II, pp. 681–2; Wilson, *King Abdullah*, pp. 207–8. On recent developments see Kamal Salibi, *The Modern History of Jordan* (London, 1998).

46 Arthur Goldschmidt, Jr., *Modern Egypt: The Formation of a Nation-State* (Boulder, CO, 1988), pp. 13–22.

47 Selma Botman, 'The Liberal Age, 1923–1952', in M. W. Daly, ed., *The Cambridge History of Egypt* (Cambridge, 1998), vol. II, pp. 285–6; Mansfield, *History of the Middle East*, pp. 179, 192.

48 Fisher and Ochsenwald, *The Middle East*, vol. II, pp. 431, 540.

49 Lewis, *Political Language*, pp. 55, 58, 69.

50 Nagib and Sadat quoted in William R. Polk, *The Arab World Today*

(Cambridge, 1991), p. 306.

51 Mansfield, *History of the Middle East*, p. 185; Cleveland, *Modern Middle East*, pp. 215–18.

52 David D. Long, *The Kingdom of Saudi Arabia* (Gainesville, FL, 1997), p. 34–5.

53 Rejwan, *Arabs Face the Modern World*, p. 202.

54 King Fahd quoted in *ibid.*, p. 204.

55 Long, *Kingdom*, p. 40.

56 *Ibid.*, p. 16; Cleveland, *Modern Middle East*, pp. 386–7.

57 Fisher and Ochsenwald, *The Middle East*, vol. II, pp. 646–8.

58 Rejwan, *Arabs Face the Modern World*, p. 209.

59 *Ibid.*, p.203. For a discussion of Islamism in the contemporary world, see Ibrahim A. Karawan, *The Islamist Impasse* (Oxford, 1997).

60 Karawan, *Islamic Impasse*, p. 30.

61 Mansfield, *History of the Middle East*, pp. 136–48.

62 For a sympathetic account of the first Pahlavi monarch, see L. P. Elwell-Sutton, 'Reza Shah the Great' in George Lenczowski, ed., *Iran Under the Pahlavis* (Stanford, CA, 1978), pp. 1–50.

63 On the collapse of the regime see Jahangir Amuzegar, *The Dynamics of the Iranian Revolution* (Albany, NY, 1991).

SEVEN · MONARCHY AND THE STATE IN THE TWENTY-FIRST CENTURY

1. J. M. Roberts, *History of the World* (Oxford, 1993), pp. 1029–30.

2. *Ibid.*, p. 843.

3. *Ibid.*, p. 827.

Bibliography

Adshead, S. A. M.,*China in World History* (New York, 1988)

Ahmad, A., *Studies in Islamic Culture in the Indian Environment* (Oxford, 1964)

Ahmed, A. S., *Discovering Islam: Making Sense of Muslim History and Society* (New York, 1988)

Alcock, A., *A Short History of Europe* (New York, 1998)

Amuzegar, J., *The Dynamics of the Iranian Revolution* (Albany, NY, 1991)

Anderson, M. S., *The Ascendancy of Europe, 1815–1914* (London, 1985)

Anderson, R. D., *France, 1870–1914* (London, 1977)

Aristotle, *The Complete Works of Aristotle*, ed. Jonathan Barnes (Princeton, NJ, 1984), vol. II

Asher, C. B., *Architecture of Mughal India* (Cambridge, 1992)

Augustine, *The City of God*, in *Basic Writings of St. Augustine*, ed. W. J. Oates (New York, 1948), vol. II

Bailyn, B. *et al.*, *The Great Republic: A History of the American People* (Lexington, MA, 1977), vol. I

Bakewell, P., *A History of Latin America* (Oxford, 1997)

Balazs, E., *Chinese Civilization and Bureaucracy: Variations on a Theme* (New Haven, 1964)

—, 'Imperial China: The Han Dynasty', in M. J. Coye, J. Livingston and J. Highland, *China: Yesterday and Today* (New York, 1984)

Barclay, D. E., 'Ritual, Ceremonial and the Invention of the Monarchial Tradition in Nineteenth-Century Prussia', in *European Monarchy*, ed. H. Duchhardt, R. Jackson and D. Sturdy (Stuttgart, 1992), pp. 207–20

Barraclough, G., *The Medieval Papacy* (New York, 1968)

Bary, W. T. de, ed., *Sources of the Chinese Tradition* (New York, 1960), vol. I

Bayly, C. A., *Indian Society and the Making of the British Empire* (Cambridge, 1988)

Beasley, W. G., 'Meiji Political Institutions', in *The Cambridge History of Japan*, ed. M. B. Jansen., vol. V

—, *The Meiji Restoration* (Stanford, CA, 1972)

—, *The Rise of Modern Japan* (New York, 1995)

Bendix, R., *Kings or People: Power and the Mandate to Rule* (Berkeley, CA, 1979)

Biggs-Davidson, J., *Africa: Hope Deferred* (London, 1972)

Bismarck, *The Memoirs*, trans. A. J. Butler, 2 vols (New York, 1966)

Black, A., *Political Thought in Europe, 1250–1450* (Cambridge, 1992)

Black, J., *Convergence or Divergence? Britain and the Continent* (New York, 1994)

—, *War and the World: Military Power and the Fate of Continents* (New Haven, CT, 1998)

—, *Why Wars Happen* (New York, 1998)

Bloch, M., *The Royal Touch*, trans. J. E. Anderson (London, 1973)

Bodin, J., *The Six Books of a Commonweal*, trans. R. Knolles (London, 1606), ed. K. D. McRae (Cambridge, MA, 1962)

Bogle, Emory C., *Islam: Origin and Belief* (Austin, TX, 1998)

Bohannan, P. and P. Curtin, *Africa and Africans* (Prospect Heights, IL, 1988)

Botman, S., 'The Liberal Age, 1923–1952', in *The Cambridge History of Egypt*, ed. M. W. Daly (Cambridge, 1998), vol. II

Braudel, F., *The Mediterranean World in the Age of Philip II* (New York, 1972), vol. II

Bridge, F. R., *The Hapsburg Monarchy among the Great Powers, 1815–1918* (Oxford, 1990)

Brook, T., *The Confusions of Pleasure: Commerce and Culture in Ming China* (Berkeley, CA, 1998)

Brown, A. L., *The Governance of Late Medieval England, 1272–1461* (Stanford, 1989)

Brown, L. C., *International Politics and the Middle East* (Princeton, 1984)

Burkholder, M. A. and L. L. Johnson, *Colonial Latin America*, 3rd edn (Oxford, 1998)

Burns, E. B., *A History of Brazil*, 3rd edn (New York, 1993)

Burns, J. H., *The Cambridge History of Medieval Political Thought* (Cambridge, 1988)

Bushnell, D. and N. Macaulay, *The Emergence of Latin America in the Nineteenth Century* (New York, 1988)

Cannadine, D. and S. Price, eds, *Rituals of Royalty: Power and Ceremonial in Traditional Societies* (Cambridge, 1987)

Cappon, L. J., ed., *The Adams-Jefferson Letters* (Chapel Hill, NC, 1959), vol. II

Chan, A., *The Glory and Fall of the Ming Dynasty* (Norman, OK, 1982)

Cleveland, W. L., *A History of the Modern Middle East* (Boulder, CO, 1994)

Cockcroft, L., *Africa's Way: A Journey from the Past* (London, 1990)

Cohen, B. J., *The Question of Imperialism* (New York, 1973)

Coles, P., *The Ottoman Impact on Europe* (New York, 1968)

Collins, R. O., *African History* (New York, 1971)

Collins, Roger, *Charlemagne* (Toronto, 1998)

Cortes, H., *Letters from Mexico*, trans. and ed. A. Pagden (New Haven, CT, 1986)

Costin, W. C., *Great Britain and China, 1833–1860* (Oxford, 1968)

Craig, G., *Germany: 1866–1945* (Oxford, 1978)

Crone, P., *God's Caliph: Religious Authority in the First Centuries of Islam* (Cambridge, 1986)

Crosby, A. W., *Germs, Seeds and Animals* (Armonk, NY, 1994)

Crow, J. A., *The Epic of Latin America*, 3rd edn (Berkeley, CA, 1980)

Curtin, P., S. Feierman, L. Thompson and J. Vansina, *African History* (Boston, 1978)

Dante, *Monarchia*, ed. and trans. P. Shaw (Cambridge, 1995)

Davidson, B., *The Africans: An Entry to Cultural History* (London, 1969)

Davies, N., *The Aztec Empire: The Toltec Resurgence* (Norman, OK, 1987)

Davies, O., *God Within: the Mystical Tradition of Northern Europe* (New York, 1988)

Davis, R. H. C., *A History of Medieval Europe* (London, 1991)

Deanesly, M., *A History of the Medieval Church, 590–1500* (London, 1994)

Di Scala, S. M. and S. Mastellone, *European Political Thought, 1815–1989* (Boulder, CO, 1998)

Drea, E. J., *In the Service of the Emperor: Essays on the Imperial Japanese Army* (Lincoln, NB, 1998)

Dreyer, E. L., *Early Ming China: A Political History* (Stanford, CA, 1982)

Duffy, E. *Saints and Sinners: A History of the Popes* (New Haven, CT, 1997)

Dull, J. L., 'The Evolution of Government in China', in *Heritage of China: Contemporary Perspectives on Chinese Civilization*, ed. P. S. Ropp (Berkeley, CA, 1990)

Dunn, J., ed., *Democracy: The Unfinished Journey* (Oxford, 1992)

El Fasi, M. and I. Hrbek, 'Stages in the Development of Islam and its Dissemination in Africa', in *Unesco General History of Africa*, ed. M. El Fasi (Berkeley, CA, 1988), vol. III, pp. 67–91

Elliot, J. H., 'Spain and America in the Sixteenth and Seventeenth Centuries', in *The Cambridge History of Latin America* (Cambridge, 1984), vol. I

Elwell-Sutton, L. P., 'Reza Shah the Great', in *Iran Under the Pahlavis*, ed. G. Lenczowski (Stanford, CA, 1978)

Esposito, J. L., *Islam: The Straight Path* (New York, 1991)

Fage, J. D., *A History of Africa*, 3rd edn (New York, 1996)

Fairbank, J. K., *China: A New History* (Cambridge, MA, 1992)

Farquhar, D. M., 'Structure and Function in Yuan Imperial Government', in J. D. Langlois, Jr., *China Under Mongol Rule* (Princeton, 1981), pp. 25–55

Fawtier, R., *The Capetian Kings of France*, trans., L. Butler and R. J. Adam (New York, 1960)

Ferro, M., *Nicholas II: Last of the Tsars*, trans. B. Pearce (New York, 1993)

Fisher, S. N. and W. Ochsenwald, *The Middle East: A History* (New York, 1997), vol. II

Frank, A. G., *Reorient: Global Economy in the Asian Age* (Berkeley, 1998)

Freund, B., *The Making of Contemporary Africa* (Boulder, CO, 1998)

Fukui, H., 'Postwar Politics, 1945–1973', in *The Cambridge History of Japan*, ed. P. Duus, vol. VI

Gailey, H. A., Jr., *History of Africa from Earliest Times to 1800* (New York, 1970), vol. I

Gallagher, L. J., trans., *China in the Sixteenth Century: The Journals of Matteo Ricci, 1583–1610* (New York, 1943)

Gibb, H. A. R., ed. and trans., *Ibn Battuta: Travels in Asia and Africa, 1325–1354* (New York, 1969)

Gilbert, F., *The End of the European Era, 1890 to the Present* (New York, 1970)

Gillespie, S., *The Aztec Kings: The Construction of Rulership in Mexica History* (Tucson, AZ, 1989)

Goldschmidt, A., Jr., *Modern Egypt: the Formation of a Nation-State* (Boulder, CO, 1988)

Gollwitzer, H., *Europe in the Age of Imperialism, 1880–1914* (New York, 1969)

Grasso, J. and M. Kort, *Modernization and Revolution in China* (New York, 1991)

Gray, J., *Rebellions and Revolutions: China from the 1800s to the 1980s* (Oxford, 1990)

Greaves, R. *et al.*, *Civilizations of the World* (New York, 1997)

Guenee, B., *States and Rulers in Later Medieval Europe*, trans. J. Vale (Oxford, 1985)

Guerdan, R., *Byzantium* (New York, 1962)

Guillou, A., 'Functionaries', in *The Byzantines*, ed. G. Cavallo (Chicago, 1997)

Habib, I., 'India during the Mughal Period', in *Ananya: A Portrait of India*, ed. S. N. Sridhar (New York, 1997).

Haj, S., *The Making of Iraq, 1900–1963* (Albany, NY, 1997)

Hall, J. W., 'A Monarch for Modern Japan', in *Political Development in Modern Japan*, ed. R. E. Ward (Princeton, NJ, 1968)

Hallam, E. M., *Capetian France, 987–1328* (London, 1983)

Hallett, R., *Africa to 1875* (Ann Arbor, MI, 1970)

Hane, M., *Premodern Japan* (Boulder, CO, 1991)

Hanson, J. H., 'Islam and African Societies', in *Africa*, ed. P. M. Martin and P. O'Meara (Bloomington, IN, 1995), pp. 105–7

Harrison, J. A., *The Chinese Empire* (New York, 1972)

Head, C., *Imperial Twilight* (Chicago, 1977)

Hilgarth, J. N., *The Spanish Kingdoms, 1250–1516* (Oxford, 1978)

Hirobumi, I., 'Commentaries on Constitutional Provisions Relating to the Emperor's Position', in *Japan: A Documentary History*, ed. D. J. Lu (New York, 1997), vol. II

Hocart, A. M., *Kings and Councillors: An Essay in the Comparative Anatomy of Human Society* (Chicago, 1970), originally published 1936

Hodgson, M. G. S., *The Venture of Islam* (Chicago, 1974), vol. III

Holt, P. M., A. K. S. Lambton and B. Lewis, eds, *The Cambridge History of Islam* (Cambridge, 1970), vol. IA.

Howard, M., 'Europe on the Eve of the First World War', in *The Coming of the First World War*, ed. R. J. W. Evans and H. P. von Strandmann (Oxford, 1990), pp. 1–18

Hsu, I. C. Y., *The Rise of Modern China* 4th edn (New York, 1990)

Huang, R., *China: A Macrohistory* (Armonk, NY, 1988)

Hucker, C. O., *The Censorial System of Ming China* (Stanford, CA, 1966)

—, *China's Imperial Past* (Stanford, 1975)

—, *China to 1850: A Short History* (Stanford, 1978)

—, *A Dictionary of Official Titles in Imperial China* (Stanford, 1985)

—, 'Ming Government', in *The Cambridge History of China* (Cambridge, 1986), vol. VIII

Ikram, S. M., *Muslim Civilization in India* (New York, 1964)

Iliffe, J., *Africans: The History of a Continent* (Cambridge, 1995)

Inalcik, H., *The Ottoman Empire: The Classical Age, 1300–1600* (New York, 1973)

James I, *The Trew Law of Free Monarchy*, in *The Political Works of James I*, ed. J. McIlwain (New York, 1965)

Jenner, W. J. F., *The Tyranny of History: The Roots of China's Crisis*

(Harmondsworth, 1992)

John of Paris, 'Potestate et Papali', in *The Middle Ages: Sources of Medieval History*, ed. B. Tierney (New York, 1999)

Joll, J., 'The Mood of 1914', in *The Outbreak of World War I*, ed. H. H. Herwig (Lexington, MA, 1991), pp. 13–18

Jones, P., *The 1848 Revolutions* (London, 1991)

Jones, W. C., 'The Capetians from the Death of Philip II to Philip IV', in *The New Cambridge Medieval History*, ed. D. Abulafia (Cambridge, 1999), vol. V, pp. 279–89

Josephy, A. M., Jr., *The Indian Heritage of America* (New York, 1973)

July, R. W., *A History of the African People* (Prospect Heights, IL, 1992)

Kamen, H., *Golden Age Spain* (Atlantic Highlands, NJ, 1988)

Karawan, I. A., *The Islamist Impasse* (Oxford, 1997)

Keay, J., *The Honourable Company: A History of the English East India Company* (New York, 1991)

Keen, M., *Medieval Europe* (New York, 1968)

—, *The Pelican History of Medieval Europe* (Harmondsworth, 1969)

Kennedy, P., *The Rise and Fall of the Great Powers* (New York, 1987)

Keohane, N., *Philosophy and the State in France: The Renaissance to the Enlightenment* (Princeton, NJ, 1980)

Kessler, L. D., *K'ang-Hsi and the Consolidation of Ch'ing Rule, 1661–1684* (Chicago, 1976)

Keylor, W. R., *The Twentieth-Century World: An International History*, 3rd edn (New York, 1996)

King, L., ed., *Memoirs of Babur*, 2 vols, trans. J. Leyden and W. Erskine (Oxford, 1921)

Kohut, T. A., *William II and the Germans* (New York, 1991)

Kracke, E. A. Jr., 'The Chinese and the Art of Government', in *The Legacy of China*, ed. R. Dawson (Boston, 1990)

Kulke, H. and D. Rothermund, *A History of India* (London, 1998)

Lafore, L., *The Long Fuse: An Interpretation of the Origins of World War I* (New York, 1971)

Landes, D., *The Wealth and Poverty of Nations* (New York, 1998)

Langlois, J. D., 'The Hung-wu Reign', in *The Cambridge History of China*, vol. VII, pp. 149–69

Lapidus, I. M., *A History of Islamic Societies* (Cambridge, 1988)

Lehmann, J-P., *The Roots of Modern Japan* (New York, 1982)

Leon-Portilla, M., 'Mesoamerica before 1519', in *The Cambridge History of Latin America*, ed. L. Bethell (Cambridge, 1984), vol. I

Levathes, L., *When China Ruled the Seas* (New York, 1994)

Levtzion, N., 'The Shara and the Sudan from the Arab Conquest of the Magrib to the Rise of the Almoravids', in *The Cambridge History of Africa*, ed. J. D. Fage (Cambridge, 1978), vol. II, pp. 637–84

—, 'The Western Maghrib and Sudan', in *Cambridge History of Africa*, vol. III

Lewis, B., *Istanbul and the Civilization of the Ottoman Empire* (Norman, OK, 1963)

—, *The Political Language of Islam* (Chicago, 1988)

—, *Islam in History* (Chicago, 1993)

Lippmann, W., *A Preface to Morals* (New York, 1935)

Locke, J., *Two Treatises of Government*, ed. P. Laslett (Cambridge, 1967), Book 1

Loewe, M., *Imperial China: The Historical Background to the Modern Age* (New York, 1966)

—, *Everyday Life in Early Imperial China* (New York, 1968)

—, *The Cambridge History of China* (Cambridge, 1986), vol. 1

—, *The Pride that was China* (New York, 1990)

Long, D. D., *The Kingdom of Saudi Arabia* (Gainesville, FL, 1997)

Lowe, J., *The Great Powers, Imperialism and the German Problem* (London, 1994)

Luscombe, D. E., 'The Formation of Political Thought in the West', in *The Cambridge History of Medieval Political Thought*, ed. J. H. Burns (Cambridge, 1988)

Lybyer, A. H., *The Government of the Ottoman Empire in the Time of Suleiman* (New York, 1966)

Macartney, Lord, *An Embassy to China*, ed. J. Cranmer-Byng (Hamden, CT, 1963)

McCormick, M., 'Emperors', in *The Byzantines*, ed. G. Cavallo (Chicago, 1997)

MacKay, A., *Spain in the Middle Ages* (London, 1977)

Mckay, J. et al., *A History of World Societies* (Boston, 1992), vol. 11

McLynn, N. B., *Ambrose of Milan* (Berkeley, 1994)

McNeill, W. H., *The Rise of the West* (Chicago, 1963)

—, *Plagues and Peoples* (New York, 1997)

—, *A History of the Human Community* (New York, 1997), vol. 11

—, *A World History* (Oxford, 1999)

Mancall, M., *China at the Center: 300 Years of Foreign Policy* (New York, 1984)

Mansfield, P., *A History of the Middle East* (Harmondsworth, 1991)

Marsilius of Padua, *Defensor Pacis*, trans. A. Gewirth (Toronto, 1986)

Mayer, A. J., *The Persistence of the Old Regime: Europe to the Great War* (London, 1981)

Mbiti, J., *African Religions and Philosophy* (New York, 1969)

Merrick, J. W., *The Desacralization of the French Monarchy in the Eighteenth Century* (Baton Rouge, LA, 1990)

Merrimoan, R. B., *Suleiman the Magnificent, 1520–1566* (New York, 1966)

Meyendorff, J., 'Byzantine Church', in *Dictionary of the Middle Ages*, ed. J. Strayer (New York, 1983), vol. 11

Meyers, H. A., *Medieval Kingship* (Chicago, 1982)

Mill, J. S., *On Liberty* (Harmondsworth, 1968)

Miller, D. A., *The Byzantine Tradition* (New York, 1966)

Minogue, K., *Politics: A Very Short Introduction* (Oxford, 1995)

Mommsen, W. J., *Imperial Germany, 1867–1918* (New York, 1990).

Moon, P., *The British Conquest and Dominion of India* (London, 1989)

Moorhouse, G., *India Britannica* (New York, 1983)

Moreland, W. H. and A. C. Chatterjee, *A Short History of India* (London, 1962)

Mornay, P. D., *Vindiciae contra tyrannos*, in *Constitutionalism and Resistance in the Sixteenth Century*, ed. J. H. Franklin (New York, 1960)

Morrall, J., *Political Thought in Medieval Times* (London, 1958)

Morris, C., *The Papal Monarchy* (Oxford, 1989)

Mortimer, R., *Angevin England, 1154–1258* (Oxford, 1994)

Naquin, S. and E. S. Rawski, *Chinese Society in the Eighteenth Century* (New Haven, 1987)

Nenner, H., *The Right to be King* (Chapel Hill, NC, 1995)

Nicholas, D., *The Evolution of the Medieval World* (London, 1992)

Nicholas II, *The Complete Wartime Correspondence of Tsar Nicholas II and the Empress Alexandra*, ed. J. T. Fuhrmann (Westport, CT, 1999)

Nicolson, H., *Kings, Courts and Monarchies* (New York, 1962)

Nicol, D. M., *Byzantium and Venice* (Cambridge, 1988)

Oliver, R., *The African Experience* (New York, 1996)

Oliver, R. and J. D. Fage, *A Short History of Africa* (Harmondsworth, 1985)

Omari, A., 'Mali in the Fourteenth Century', in *The African Past: Chronicles from Antiquity to Modern Times*, ed. B. Davidson (Boston, 1964)

Packard, J. M., *Sons of Heaven: A Portrait of the Japanese Monarchy* (New York, 1987)

Paine, T., *The Life and Works of Thomas Paine*, ed. W. M. Van der Weyde (New York, 1925), vol. 1

Parsons, J. B., *Peasant Rebellions of the Late Ming Dynasty* (Ann Arbor, MI, 1970)

Pennington, K., *Europe in the Seventeenth Century* (London, 1989)

Perez, L. G., *The History of Japan* (Westport, CT, 1998)

Peters, E., *Europe and the Middle Ages* (New York, 1997)

Polk, W. R., *The Arab World Today* (Cambridge, 1991)

Prestwich, M., *Edward I* (Berkeley, CA, 1988)

Pye, L. W., *China: An Introduction*, 4th edn (New York, 1991)

Ralph, P. L., *World Civilizations* (New York, 1991), vol. 1

Ranger, T., 'The Invention of Tradition in Colonial Africa', in *The Invention of Tradition*, ed. E. Hobsbawm and T. Ranger (Cambridge, 1984)

Rawski, E. S., *The Last Emperors: A Social History of Qing Imperial Institutions* (Berkeley, CA, 1998)

Reischauer, E. O., *Japan: The Story of a Nation* (New York, 1970)

Rejwan, N., *Arabs Face the Modern World: Religious, Cultural and Political Responses to the West* (Gainesville, FL, 1998)

Reynolds, S., *Kingdoms and Communities in Western Europe, 900–1300* (Oxford, 1984)

Rice, G. P. Jr., ed., *The Public Speaking of Queen Elizabeth* (New York, 1966)

Richards, J. F., *The Mughal Empire* (Cambridge, 1993)

Richardson, A., *History Sacred and Profane* (Philadelphia, 1964)

Riche, P., *The Carolingians*, trans. M. I. Allen (Philadelphia, 1993)

Rich, N., *The Age of Nationalism and Reform, 1850–1890* (New York, 1977)

Riley, P. F., ed., *The Global Experience: Readings in World History Since 1500* (Englewood Cliffs, NJ, 1992), vol. II.

Robbins, K., *The First World War* (Oxford, 1984)

Roberts, J. M., *Europe, 1880–1945* (New York, 1989)

—, *History of the World* (Oxford, 1993)

Rohl, J. C. G., *The Kaiser and His Court: Wilhelm II and the Government of Germany* (Cambridge, 1994)

Runciman, S., *Byzantine Civilization* (New York, 1965)

Salibi, K., *The Modern History of Jordan* (London, 1998)

Shaw, S., *History of the Ottoman Empire and Modern Turkey* (Cambridge, 1976), vol. I

Shih, V. Y. C., *The Taiping Ideology* (Seattle, WA, 1972)

Simon, R., *Iraq Between the Two World Wars* (New York, 1986)

Singhal, D. P., *India and World Civilization* (Lansing, MI, 1969), vol. II

Skidmore, T. E. and P. H. Smith, *Modern Latin America*, 4th edn (New York, 1997)

Smith, D. M., *Italy and its Monarchy* (New Haven, 1989)

Smith, M. E., *The Aztecs* (Cambridge, MA, 1996)

Smith, R. J., *China's Cultural Heritage: The Qing Dynasty, 1644–1912*, 2nd edn (Boulder, CO, 1994)

Southern, R. W., *Western Society and the Church in the Middle Ages* (Harmondsworth, 1986)

Spear, P., *A History of India: from the Sixteenth Century to the Twentieth Century* (London, 1990)

Spellman, W. M., *European Political Thought, 1600–1700* (London, 1998)

Spence, J., *Emperor of China: Self-Portrait of K'ang-hsi* (New York, 1974)

—, *The Search for Modern China* (New York, 1990)

Stadler, K. R., *Austria* (New York, 1971)

Stearns, P. N. *et al.*, *World Civilizations: The Global Experience* (New York, 1996), vol. I

Stein, B., *A History of India* (Oxford, 1998)

Stenton, F., *Anglo-Saxon England* (Oxford, 1992)

Stevenson, D., *The First World War and International Politics* (Oxford, 1988)

Stromberg, R. N., *European Intellectual History since 1789* (Englewood Cliffs, NJ, 1994)

Thomas Aquinas, *On Kingship* (Toronto, 1949)

Thomson, J. A. F., *The Western Church in the Middle Ages* (London, 1998)

Tierney, B., *Religion, Law and the Growth of Constitutional Thought, 1150–1650* (Cambridge, 1982)

—, ed., *The Crisis of Church and State, 1050–1300* (Englewood Cliffs, NJ, 1964)

Totman, C., *Japan Before Perry* (Berkeley, CA, 1981)

—, *Early Modern Japan* (Berkeley, CA, 1993)

Treadgold, W., *A History of the Byzantine State and Society* (Stanford, CA, 1997)

Treitschke, H. von, *Politics*, ed. and trans. H. Kohn (New York, 1963)

Tripathi, R. P., 'The Turko-Mongol Theory of Kingship', in *The Mughal State, 1526–1750*, ed. M. Alam and S. Subrahmanyam (Oxford, 1998), pp. 115–25

Tucker, S. C., *The Great War, 1914–18* (Bloomington, IN, 1998)

Ullmann, W., *The Growth of Papal Government in the Middle Ages* (London, 1965)

Upshur, J-H. *et al.*, *World History* (St Paul, MN, 1995)

Upton, A. F., 'Sweden', in *Absolutism in Seventeenth-Century Europe*, ed. J. Miller (London, 1990)

Vasiliev, A. A., *History of the Byzantine Empire* (Madison, WI, 1961), vol. II

Vohra, R., *The Making of India: A Historical Survey* (New York, 1997)

Voltaire, *Ancient and Modern History*, in *The Works of Voltaire* (New York, 1901)

Vucinich, W., *The Ottoman Empire: Its Record and Legacy* (Huntington, NY, 1979)

Wallbank, T. W., *A Short History of India and Pakistan* (New York, 1965)

Wang Gungwu, 'Early Ming Relations with Southeast Asia', in *The Chinese World Order: Traditional China's Foreign Relations*, ed. J. Fairbank (Cambridge, MA, 1968)

Warren, W. L., *Henry II* (Berkeley, CA, 1973)

Webb, S. S., *The Governors General* (Chapel Hill, 1979)

—, *1676: The End of American Independence* (New York, 1984)

Whittow, M., *The Making of Byzantium, 600–1025* (Berkeley, CA, 1996)

Williams, D. D., 'Deity, Monarchy, and Metaphysics: Whitehead's Critique of the Theological Tradition', in *The Relevance of Whitehead*, ed. I. LeClerc (London, 1961), pp. 353–72

Wilson, G. M., *Patriots and Redeemers in Japan* (Chicago, 1992)

Wilson, M. C., *King Abdullah, Britain and the Making of Jordon* (Cambridge, 1990)

Winn, P., *Americas: The Changing Face of Latin America and the Caribbean* (Berkeley, CA, 1995)

Wortman, R., 'Moscow and Petersburg: the Problem of Political Center in Tsarist Russia, 1881–1913', in *Rights of Power: Symbolism, Ritual and Politics since the Middle Ages*, ed. S. Wilentz (Philadelphia, 1985)

Zeldin, T., *France, 1848–1945* (Oxford, 1973), vol. 1

Zeman, Z. A. B., *The Break-up of the Hapsburg Empire, 1914–1918* (London, 1961)

Index